ALAN & IRENE BROGAN

Not Without You

HODDER &
STOUGHTON

Publisher's Note

Names and locations have been changed throughout in order to protect the identities of individuals.

First published in Great Britain in 2008 by Hodder & Stoughton
An Hachette UK company

1

Copyright © 2008 Alan and Irene Brogan

A CIP catalogue record for this title is available from the British Library

Hardback ISBN 978 0340 976388
Trade Paperback ISBN 978 0340976395

Typeset in Sabon by Hewer Text UK Ltd, Edinburgh
Printed and bound by CPI Mackays, Chatham ME5 8TD

Hodder & Stoughton policy is to use papers that are natural, renewable
and recyclable products and made from wood grown in sustainable forests.
The logging and manufacturing processes are expected to conform
to the environmental regulations of the country of origin.

Hodder & Stoughton Ltd
338 Euston Road
London NW1 3BH

www.hodder.co.uk

We would like to dedicate this book to the many hundreds of children who were in care during the 1950s and early 1960s, victims of a system in conflict. We hope that one day their stories may be heard too.

And to everyone else, remember, love will always find a way.

Acknowledgements

To Julie for inspiring us to tell our story when we never knew we had one, and the constant support and friendship of Tom, Sharon, John and Pauline.

For the love and understanding given over many years from Joanne and Dean, and the grandchildren Faye and Liam. To Yvonne and Keith who have become a little corner of light in our lives. And thanks to all our family members who have listened with patience.

Also a special thanks to Rowena Webb, whose insight made our book possible, and to the hard work and dedication of Judith Longman and Cecilia Moore and all of the team at Hodder.

Last but far from least, to Caro Handley, whose painstaking professionalism and sympathetic approach has transformed our long hidden and often forgotten experiences into a readable story.

Alan & Irene

November 1959

It was a cold, grey day. I sat in the playroom, on the wide window ledge, staring out at the empty street and the field in the distance.

I was seven years old, my mum had died and I didn't know where my dad or my brothers were, or if I would ever see them again. I was stuck in this place, where I had to follow endless rules and where nobody was kind or friendly.

Just then, a big black car came around the corner and drew up in front of the home. A man got out, and then a little girl. She was smaller than I was, with red hair cut short in the usual pudding-basin style, and wearing the same grey pinafore dress all the girls were given, with little black lace-up boots.

As she followed the man to the door, I watched her. And at that moment something deep inside me burned like hot fire. I knew her! I didn't know where from or how. We had never met, but I knew her. It was as if everything went bright and I felt I could run for miles and miles with her and never tire.

Suddenly I knew that I wasn't going to be alone any more. I jumped down from the window ledge and ran to open the front door …

I

Alan

Not long after the end of the Second World War, the old East End of Sunderland contained one of the worst slums in Europe. A maze of several hundred tumbledown one-up and one-down houses, it was a dark and appalling place where whole families lived in a single small room.

This network of rat-infested, damp terraces, owned by landlords who never paid a penny on repairs, was my first home. I was born there, in 1952, and our house, in Moorgate Street, was at the centre of the many cobbled alleyways and lanes that criss-crossed the slum.

My family lived in the upstairs room of one of the row of houses, while another family lived downstairs. There was Mum, Dad, my older brothers Michael, four, and George, two, me – and often a passing uncle or two as well, especially our Uncle Willie if his wife had beaten him up again. Dad came from a large family; he had three brothers and six sisters and often told us about the violent escapades of his own dad, who seemed to enjoy punishing them with his leather belt. We never met our grandfather, who I believe had died before I was born; we just heard the tales of the terrible punishments he gave out to his sons – and presumably daughters, too – if they got on the wrong side of him.

We had a single bed, where my mum, Eileen, slept, and a double bed, where all the men slept, adults at the top and boys at the bottom. I was in with Mum, until my younger brother Brian was born when I was two, when I moved over to join the others in the double bed.

The only other furniture we had was a square table with two wooden chairs. The table stood in front of the coal range that, on the days when we could afford coal, heated the room and cooked our food. Apart from that, all we owned was a couple of tin pails and a tin bath. The walls and floor were bare and there were lines strung across the room for hanging out washing. At mealtimes we'd all stand round the table while our mum doled out whatever there was to eat – and usually it wasn't a lot.

It must have been tough for Mum, who no doubt went hungry herself many times, but we boys were too young to worry. We would gobble down whatever there was and run out to play again. Those grubby streets were home, and as long as we had Mum, Dad and one another, not much else mattered. Despite the hardships ours was a close family, and we felt loved. At the end of the day Mum would give each of us a cuddle when she put us to bed, while Dad would ruffle our hair or pat us on the back with a 'G'night, son', and we'd be asleep in seconds.

We were always as black as coal from playing on the bomb-sites that were scattered through the slum. The older boys climbed in among the rubble, squeezing into buried rooms and digging under old fireplaces. There were bits of wall that still had wallpaper on and were covered in coloured patterns or flowers, some of them two floors up, left there when the rest of the building had collapsed. These patterns were fascinating to us because we didn't have any paper on the walls in our home.

It was never an easy job getting us clean, because there was no bathroom or running water. The houses were serviced by communal washhouses – one to every four or five houses, which meant they were shared by up to ten families. Each washhouse was a kind of brick shelter with wooden barn doors that were always broken. Inside was a cold water tap fixed to the wall at one end, and at the other a toilet with a 'courtesy screen' someone had made out of old sheets hanging on a string line. Squares of newspaper hung next to it on the brick wall, to be used as toilet paper. In the middle of the washhouse was a row of poss-pots, tin barrels used for washing clothes – and any children the hard-pressed mothers could catch. Beside the poss-pots stood a mangle, for wringing the water out of the clothes.

On washdays, Mum, like all the other women in the street, had to go downstairs to the washhouse, collect a pail of water and carry it upstairs to heat on the coal range. Then she would carry it back down the stairs again to fill the poss-pot to do the washing. This would be repeated several times, first for the washing and again for rinsing. Occasionally a few pails got tipped into the tin bath by the fire so she could have a private bath when no one was around. Then it had to be carried downstairs, a pail at a time, and emptied.

Our slum was like a dirty island set at the very end of town. To the north, only a few hundred yards away, there were three shipyards, built on the bank of the river, with several more across the other side. In those days Sunderland was the biggest ship-building town in the world with shipyards along the length and breadth of the river. To the east were the main dock gates, the warehouses and the fuel storage tanks. To the south of us were the great rail-shunting yards, leading to the coal-staiths where, for twenty-four hours a day, coal was tipped from the steam train wagons down the chutes and into the coastal colliers, which set off for London and other major ports. To the west were the old garths: blocks of flats four storeys high with open verandas running around them, full to the brim with the families of dockers, fishermen and miners.

The muck generated by these huge industries blew across us and coated everything. Many of the slum houses had broken windows with cardboard or newspaper taped over the holes, so the dirt blew straight in and lay thick on the sparse furniture. It coated our skin, hair and clothes and, when it was windy, the freshly washed sheets hanging out in the lane.

As well as the dirt, there was the noise. We lived with the never-ending din of the shipyards. Day and night there was the constant rat-tat-tat of the riveters' guns as they fixed the steel plates of the hulls together, the banging of steel on steel and the shouts of the workers. Then there was the clack-clack-clack on the cobbles from steel wheels of the hand barrows which were used to transport anything and everything. And when a new ship was being launched, as often happened, there was the vast roar of the crowds and the greeting wail of a host of ships' horns as the vessel slipped into the water, pushing a wave of water before it, accompanied by the loud grating noise of the huge chains which were used as a brake on the slipway.

We children were so used to all the noise that we barely noticed it. Besides, our streets were full of their own noise. There were children swinging on old ropes tied to the top of the iron lamp-posts, and the girls singing rhyming songs as they played two-ball against the walls or skipped – up to ten of them jumping over a rope at once. The smaller kids sat in big prams, wailing, while the boys made machine-gun noises or played Cowboys and Indians, chasing each other across the rubble of the bomb-sites which were dotted through the slum.

The women stood in the doorways, wearing coloured headscarves or curlers in their hair and spotty pinnies over their clothes, crossed over at the back and tied at the front. They chatted away, while in the background Rediffusion radios – one of the few luxuries most families could afford – blared out the big band music and jazz sounds that were all the rage.

Every now and then came the clip-clop sound of hooves along the cobbles as the tatters – rag and bone men who collected anything and everything that could be salvaged or sold – came along, shouting, 'Lumbaaaay!' or 'Rags and woollens!'

Then there was the old fishwife, Mrs Bulmer, who brought fish in a cloth-lined basket from the nearby fish quay and shouted, 'Fresh fiiiish!' in a high-pitched wailing voice. There were barely ever any cars along our lanes, but sometimes we heard the ding-a-ling of a fire-engine, ambulance or police car ringing out, and all the kids would pile out to see which one it was.

Even at night the noise from the surrounding yards carried on, the hooters blaring out to mark the shift changes that went on around the clock. We lay in bed and listened to the whoop-whoop of the tugboats that towed great cargo ships up and down the river from the sea and the whistles of the steam-driven coal trains heading for the docks on the other side of the high coal-yard wall. And in the darkened streets, lit only by the dim street lamps, there were the sounds of drunks singing their way home after closing time. Frequent fights broke out, with women screaming at the men to pack it in, accompanied by the sounds of a bottle or two rolling on the ground, glass breaking and all the neighbourhood dogs barking.

Not far from us stood the Welcome Arms, the last pub in Sunderland before the sea, with its back gate open to the steep steps which led down to the inner road inside the perimeter wall around the docks. This was the only chink in the docks' tight security, the only hole in a wall that stretched for a couple of miles. I can't imagine that the authorities didn't know about it, but perhaps they felt it wise to turn a blind eye, or perhaps money changed hands with the security guards who regularly patrolled the wall.

This chink in the wall was a highway for smuggled goods, brought up under cover of darkness from the many foreign cargo ships and the bonded warehouses where all kinds of things often vanished, despite the sharp eyes of the customs men.

Going in the other direction, into the docks, were the 'working girls' heading for a night's activity along the quaysides. If they were lucky they might be smuggled on board visiting ships, where the drinks would flow and the only language spoken was of love of a kind and money.

In the early mornings, we children would spot a queue of people staggering out from behind the 'closed' pub. Bleary-eyed customers who'd spent the night in the dark so as to avoid the passing polass, as the police were known. Girls with ruffled hair and smeared make-up, barefoot, with shoes in their hands, still reeling from their nights of excess. We thought they must be tired from having to climb the precariously steep steps in the dark. It was quite a hike down to the docks.

In those days all the men wore suit jackets and trousers every day, with flat caps and mufflers round their necks. It was like a uniform, and my dad was no different. Early every morning he would put on his cap and muffler and go to the shipyard gates in the hope of finding a day's work. This meant getting a token from a foreman who wanted extra hands that day. After a full shift, if the foreman said you had done all right, you could take the token to the pay office and get cash in hand. This earned a man enough money to buy a decent meal for the family or to put a little in the gas meter, if you had one, with a bit of cash to spare.

The value of a token was such that occasional scraps would break out among the would-be labourers waiting at the gates. Sometimes an unscrupulous foreman would throw a couple of tokens on the ground and watch the ensuing fight. Dad had apparently turned to fisticuffs on several occasions and usually emerged triumphant, with a token and a couple of black eyes.

If there was no work he headed for the beach along with the other desperates to pick up the miniscule bits of copper and brass washed up from the yards. Picking for a whole day could produce a few ounces of metal, if you were very lucky. It was risky work, because it was illegal and the police would chase and arrest men caught on dock property.

At the end of the day any pickings were hurriedly taken along to the scrap yard for a 'weigh-in', and cash was paid on the spot. It was a long hard day's work for no more than a few shillings, but enough for bread and milk or fish and chips, which was the cheapest meal available then.

I don't know why my father didn't have a full-time job, because there seemed to be plenty of work, even for unskilled labourers, in the industries that surrounded us. The wages weren't high, but they would have been regular. Instead, my dad, along with a handful of other men from our neighbourhood, preferred to take his chances day by day.

Plenty of men in our neck of the woods loved a drink, and many wives were left complaining that the little money they had was squandered in the pub. My dad wasn't one of these, as he preferred the horses and the pools. His dreams of riches led him to the bookie's on many occasions, so more often than not our dinner was a pile of chips and the odd bit of fish, lying on old newspaper, in the middle of the table.

Mum never showed us her feelings as we boys downed our portion in seconds, but it must have been tough for her. I had rickets, through lack of nutrition, which meant the bones in my legs were too soft and my legs bent outwards with the weight of my body. The kids in the street would tease me and say I was born on a horse, or call me 'Bandy legs', the term used for all the kids with rickets – and there were plenty of us, though none of my brothers had it.

Rationing, introduced during the war, was still going on. Items such as sugar, sweets and tea were only just becoming available again between 1952 and 1953, and meat and bacon not until 1954. Not that it made a lot of difference to us, because we never had the money for these luxury items. We lived mostly on bread and chips. Fresh fruit and vegetables were almost unheard of.

One day when I was only three or four I was sent to the shops for a loaf of bread. Usually one of the older boys went, but for some reason they weren't around, so I wandered up the cobbled street, heading for the corner shop, when what looked like an ice-cream van appeared at the end of the street and headed down towards me. Its big headlights looked like eyes and I thought they were looking at me. The van came closer and closer and I got a little frightened, so I crossed over to the other side to avoid it. It still seemed to be coming for me, so I ran back across the street, but I was convinced it was still after me.

I raced up the street, reached the shop and ran in. There were three or four women wearing long coats and headscarves, waiting at the counter for bread. Still terrified after my ordeal with the van, I panicked. I was afraid it would come to get me again and wanted to run home, so I went to the other end of the counter where there wasn't anyone waiting. It just happened to be the sweet counter. I left the shop with a bar of chocolate, one of those Fry's bars with all the little kids' faces on the wrapping.

Well, the van didn't get me, but Mum wasn't too pleased and I was never sent to the shops again. As for my scary encounter with the van, apparently malnutrition was causing me to have hallucinations.

How my parents ended up living in such dire poverty is hard to say. My mother had certainly come from a very different background. It was said that her parents were very well off and owned a number of properties around the city as well as some apple orchards in Kent. They had two daughters, my mother and her sister Margaret, who married a ship's captain. When my mother fell for my father, who was from the wrong side of town, her parents were outraged. Dad was a good-looking Jack-the-lad from a big family with a bad reputation. Mum's parents threatened to cut her off if she married him, and they stuck to their word. As far as I know, she never heard from them again. It must have been very hard for her, but she loved Dad very much and was devoted to us boys, and if she had any regrets she buried them deep inside.

Soon after Brian was born, Mum became ill. She had to stay in bed a lot, and was very tired. We used to come in after playing out all day and jump on her bed and she'd laugh and tickle us. We didn't know what was wrong; we just thought she'd get better and get up again. But Mum didn't get better. She had cervical cancer. She was only twenty-eight years old, but it hadn't been discovered until it was very advanced, and there was little available then in the way of treatment. So she suffered in silence, knowing that she would not recover, and no doubt worrying about what would happen to her children.

We boys, ignorant of what was going on around us, were happy as skylarks. We were adventurous, playful and full of life. Day after day I ran around in my dirty shorts and vest, barefoot, pot-bellied and bowlegged, with a big grin on my face.

One evening we came home after playing out all day and we knew something was different. Dad wouldn't let us jump on Mum's bed and a couple of aunties had turned up and were fussing around the room. Mum had tears in her eyes and she was saying something to us but I don't remember what. I was four years old and had no idea what was going on.

Mum left us soon after that, and all went quiet. It's as if time froze and my memories froze with it. I don't remember a funeral or a family gathering to say goodbye. I was probably considered too young to attend. No one ever talked about that time again. Not Dad, or my older brothers, who must have remembered it more clearly, and not the aunties and uncles who came in and out. It was as if a dark cloud came over and hid the past from view, never to be spoken of again.

Dad managed as best he could. We boys played in the street while he went to look for work each day, and neighbours kept an eye on us. But one day, a few weeks later, everything changed.

It was one of those days when the dampness in the air made the cobbles look a shiny grey-blue. The street was full of the usual noises of children playing: the girls with their skipping songs and we boys playing 'footy' with an old tennis ball. Dad was at the shipyard gates, looking for a day's work again, and Dad's brother, Uncle Willie, who'd moved in with us, was down at the beach collecting scrap metal. Little Brian, who was still only two, was with a neighbour.

Suddenly an old black car with big headlights turned into the street. No one around our way had a car or for the most part even knew of someone who had a car, so this ranked as one of the great sights to be seen and we kids all stopped playing and stared. A car like that generally meant either bailiffs or police.

It trundled slowly up the street and we ran over to investigate. A middle-aged lady wearing a tweed suit and hard brown shoes stepped out of the car and began talking to the children, asking their names. She took a particular interest in my brothers and me and asked if we would like to have a ride in her car. We couldn't believe our luck and jumped up and down, yelling, 'Yes!' For us it was like going into space for the first time. The other kids were shouting for a ride, but she said it could only take three. So Michael, George and I climbed into the back, wild with excitement.

We set off up the street at a slow pace. We were waving and shouting at our friends, who were running alongside, dead jealous of us. Then the car speeded up and left them behind. We left our maze of cobbled streets and travelled into a different world. We boys stared out of the window in amazement as we passed large houses and gardens, buses, cars, shops and well-dressed people with clean children.

We went up a long tree-lined hill with very large houses on either side until we reached the junction at the very top. Across the road stood the largest house of all, with a couple of towers rising up from the roof. It was surrounded by tall trees and a high wall with a large set of wooden gates at the entrance. We drove up to them and the lady honked the car-horn. An old man appeared and opened the gates and in we drove, as the gates were closed behind us.

By this time the three of us were beginning to get a little worried. What was this place? Our ride was supposed to end back at home. We sat in a row on the back seat, staring at the lady, as she turned and looked at us.

'Come on, boys,' she said. 'Out you get. The ride is over.'

2

Irene

My first home was in Deptford, a small area of Sunderland filled with neat streets of terraced houses, tucked in between a huge glassworks factory and the dockyards. When I was born, in October 1950, my parents already had three daughters – Joan, who was thirteen, Greta, who was ten, and three-year-old Pat. My father, Jimmy, was a crane driver for a local company that made mobile cranes. It was a skilled job and he made a reasonable wage, so we weren't among the poorest families. But in those days, after so many houses had been bombed in the war and so few new ones had been built, there was a desperate shortage of housing, so even slightly better-off families like ours were only able to afford to rent one floor of a house.

We lived on the first floor of a large, mid-terrace house and reached our door via an entrance in the back lane and up a set of green wooden steps. The family who lived downstairs used the front door and we all shared an outside toilet in the back yard. We had a big kitchen, where we ate our meals and washed at the sink, a living room and two bedrooms, one for Mum and Dad and one for us girls.

Dad and Mum – who was also named Greta – had met when she was fifteen and he was three years older and in the army. Mum became pregnant and a hasty wedding was organised in June 1937, when my parents were sixteen and nineteen years old. It may have been a shotgun wedding, but my parents loved one another deeply. They settled down together and never looked back; theirs was a good, stable marriage.

Joan was born a few months after they married. It can't have been easy for them, becoming parents so young, but Dad had work and they were able to rent the house in Deptford. Three years later Greta arrived, but by that time the war had begun and Dad had to enlist. He went away to fight, and Mum, still only nineteen, was left to manage with a toddler and a baby.

When Dad came home Pat was born, and three years later I arrived. I remember very little of those early days, but I know, from my sisters, that we were a normal, noisy, happy family. Mum stayed at home and looked after us girls, while Dad went out to work and came home in time for tea every evening.

I was just two when tragedy struck. My mother, still only thirty-one, was diagnosed with tuberculosis, or TB. This terrible disease of the lungs was very common then, and it was often a killer. Mum was taken to the TB wing of Ryhope Hospital, on the outskirts of town, where she stayed for many months. It must have been heartbreaking for her, isolated with the other TB patients, unable to be with her family, and becoming gradually weaker and sicker.

Dad was left to manage the family. Joan and Greta, then fifteen and twelve, were old enough to stay at home. They came in from school and did their homework, kept the house clean and cooked tea for Dad. But he couldn't look after me and Pat. His sister, Aunt Jenny – who everyone called Aunt Jen – and her husband, Uncle Charlie, offered to take Pat but they couldn't manage two of us, so I was put into care.

It must have been hard for Dad to send me away, but he had little choice. And I imagine both he and Mum hoped against hope that she would get better and the family would come back together.

I was sent to a children's home named Burdon Hall, on the outskirts of Sunderland. I was too young to remember how I got there, but the bewilderment of finding that my family had disappeared and I was in a strange place, with people and children I didn't know, stayed with me for a long time. It was a scary and sad time.

Burdon Hall happened to be close to the hospital where Mum was. Just a few fields separated us. It was only many years later that I learned from Aunt Jen that on more than one occasion Mum had got up from her sickbed and trudged across those fields through the snow to see me. I don't remember her visits, but it means a lot to me to know that she went to such lengths to be with me. Aunt Jen told me that after Mum's visits I used to spend hours sitting in one of the bay windows of the home, staring in the direction Mum had come from; and one of my earliest memories is of a footprint in the snow.

Little over a year after becoming ill, Mum died. It was March 1954, two weeks before her thirty-third birthday. I didn't know anything about it. But one day Dad came to collect me and said he was taking me home. I was so happy to see him and thought I was going back to the home I knew, and to Mum. But the house he took me to was a different one. While I had been away the family had moved into a brand new three-bedroom house on an estate called Pennywell. A huge building programme was underway, and all over the city families were being moved out of dilapidated, rundown homes into new housing with wonderful mod cons like inside toilets.

We were among the lucky ones, though to me, aged three and a half, the new house was a shock. Mum was gone, and so was Pat, who stayed with Aunt Jen and Uncle Charlie. Instead, Dad's brother, Uncle Bob, had moved in. He was a tiny man with a big smile and bow legs that were a legacy of childhood rickets.

Dad never really got over Mum's death. He was distraught and he never married again. Instead, he began drinking too much, burying his grief in the bottom of a bottle. So it was Uncle Bob who became our surrogate dad, taking over most of the parental duties and doing his best to look after us, while Dad struggled to cope with his grief.

I don't remember much about that house, other than snuggling between my big sisters in the bedroom we all shared. I wasn't there for more than a few weeks, because it soon became clear that Dad and Bob couldn't keep me at home. They both had to go out to work, and so did Joan. Greta was still at school, so there was no one to look after me during the day.

Dad wanted us all to stay together, but he was in a state of grief and not really able to cope. Perhaps if he'd felt stronger he could have found someone to have me during the day, and brought Pat home too. But caring for small girls was beyond him, and much as Uncle Bob did his best to help, he couldn't manage a small girl either, so when their sister Meg offered to take me, Dad reluctantly accepted.

Once again my things were packed and I was moved. I cried when I realised I was being taken from my sisters. I clung to Joan and begged to stay. I couldn't understand it – why did I have to go to another place again? No explanation was offered. Dad simply picked up my bag, took my hand and off we went, with him pulling me, sobbing, along the street.

Aunt Meg and her daughter Kathleen, who had just turned sixteen, lived about a mile and a half from Pennywell, in a small corner house. As with so many homes in those days, the front door was in the back lane. The house was quite large, with three bedrooms upstairs and a very large room downstairs that served as living room, dining room and kitchen all in one. This room was very dark, lit only by a gas mantle in the centre of the ceiling, which gave out very little light. The only other sources of light were a small window that looked out into the back yard, and the fire.

The room had a large cast-iron coal range with a mantelpiece that took up the entire wall opposite the front door. There was usually a roaring fire blazing away, with an old, blackened kettle sitting on the coals. I used to watch, fascinated, as the steam gushed up the chimney when it boiled.

It couldn't have been more different from the new house I had just left. But Meg and Kathleen were kind to me, and once I got used to the strangeness of yet another home, I settled down with them.

Meg was a hard-working, jolly woman who had a smile for everyone and would roll up her sleeves and get stuck into any job that needed doing, no matter how hard or dirty it was. She was small and plump, but her crowning glory was her lovely long black hair. Apparently it ran in the family; all her sisters had it, and so did Kathleen who, like her mum, was always jolly and fun to be with. Meg had a son and three daughters, of whom Kathleen was the youngest and the only one still living at home. I never did find out what had happened to Meg's husband; it wasn't something she ever talked about.

Meg was a wonderful cook and the smell of freshly baked bread often filled the house. I loved seeing her open the iron door of the oven with tea towels on her hands and slide out the bread tins. She would knock the bread, all brown and crusty on top, on to the large wooden table in the middle of the room and leave it to cool. Sometimes she would slice off a piece while it was still warm, and coat it with best butter before giving it to me. It tasted like heaven.

Even better was Meg's mince and dumplings – a wonderful meal for a hungry little girl, with thick mince and dumplings the size of houses, all bubbling away in the pot. Meg would open the oven door to see if the tops of the dumplings were crispy as I hopped up and down, impatiently waiting for dinnertime.

Every few days or so, Meg would get out the big old pram she kept in the brick outhouse in the back yard, lift me into it and set off down to the coal yard which stood alongside the old railway line nearby. She would find the coalman in among the stacks of coal and coke, and he would shovel coal into a large scooped bucket on a weighing machine. Then Meg would lift me out and push the pram under the scoop. The coalman would tip the coal in, sending up a small cloud of black dust that left me with a sooty face if I stood too close. Once the coalman was paid we set off, sweating and panting as we pushed the now laden pram back up the hill to home, where the coal would be tipped into a bucket next to the fire.

Each week the tin bath was brought out and placed on the rug in front of the fireplace in the bedroom. The fire was lit, and the old metal kettle was filled with water and brought up from downstairs to be heated and then tipped into the bath. Meg and Kathleen would go up and down the stairs, refilling the kettle from the tap out in the back yard. It took an age but eventually the bath was filled. Kathleen would be first in, and then I would have my bath after her.

I shared Kathleen's bedroom and slept in the cosy double bed with her. Snuggled up at night, we would watch the changing shapes and shadows on the ceiling from the flickering fire and Kathleen would tell me stories about princesses and fairies and wishes coming true. I loved those stories and wished I could be a princess whose wishes would be granted. I knew just what I would wish for – to be with my sisters and my dad and mum, all of us happy together.

But outside our bedroom, demons were lurking. Our window looked out across the main road, into the grounds of the dreaded Cottage Homes. There, Meg warned me, lived the naughty children who had little to eat and were beaten if they didn't do as they were told. All the local mothers used to warn their children that if they didn't behave they'd be sent there, so every child regarded the place with dread.

The grounds of the Homes were separated from the road by a long iron fence with spikes on the top. At the main entrance was a huge set of metal gates. I could hear them creaking every time they were opened, and the sound always filled me with fear. I used to sit at the bedroom window and look out at the spiked fence and the buildings beyond, determined to be good so that I wouldn't be sent there.

One day, after I had been at Meg's for a few months, there was a pounding on the front door. It scared me so much that I ran to hide. Then I heard my dad's voice, talking to Meg. She answered him, and suddenly Dad's voice became loud and angry. Meg spoke angrily too, and soon they were having a raging row. I could hear Dad demanding to take me home, while Meg told him he couldn't look after me and I was best off staying with her. Dad tried to push his way in and Meg tried to bar his way. The two of them began to lash out at each other, while I cowered behind the table, terrified of the raised, angry voices. Pushing his way past Meg, Dad grabbed me by the arm and dragged me, sobbing with fright, out of the house and all the way back to Pennywell.

I didn't understand why he was taking me, and why he was so angry. I hadn't been able to say goodbye to Meg and Kathleen, or even get my things.

And so I found myself once again back at home. It seemed Dad had come to get me because Joan had agreed to give up her job to look after me during the day. I was happy to be with her and together we shopped, cleaned and cooked for the family. But Dad paid very little attention to me – or to any of us. He was drinking heavily and was almost always out of the house, at work and then in the pub. Uncle Bob would often argue with him about his neglect of us girls, and me in particular, but it never did any good.

One day Aunt Meg came to the door. I heard her asking Dad to let her take me back. But Dad was furious. There was another fight and Dad jammed Meg's arm in the door and kept it there while she screamed and screamed. The sound was awful and I began crying and begged Joan to stop him, but she couldn't do anything. Eventually he let Meg go. She left, and that was the last time I saw her for many years. I was very sad, because although I was happy to be at home with my sisters, Meg had been very kind to me.

In many ways it's a pity Dad didn't let Meg take me, because I felt safe and loved there. I imagine that, after their row, it was just stubborn pride that stopped him. As it was, when Joan had to return to work a few weeks later, Dad sent me to live with another of his brothers, Uncle Tom, and his wife Aunt Jane. Still just four, I arrived in my fifth home in two years: a two-roomed ground-floor flat in the Springwell area of town. Confused and unhappy, I nonetheless accepted the changes without complaint. What else could I do? Every time I came close to feeling settled, I was wrenched away and sent somewhere else. But I was never told when or why I was moving, and if I cried or showed how upset I was my feelings were ignored. So I learned to keep them hidden, and to be silent.

Uncle Tom and Aunt Jane's son Ned, who was nineteen, had recently left home to get married, so it was just the two of them and me in their small home. They had no other children apart from a daughter who had died at birth.

The flat was small and gloomy. The main room was used as the sitting room, kitchen and dining room all in one. It had only one little window looking out into the back garden, so it was always rather dark. There was a gas cooker, a sink where I was given my weekly bath, a table with four wooden chairs, and two comfy chairs, one by the coal fire, where Tom would sit, the other nearby for Aunt Jane. I had to sit on one of the wooden chairs.

The second room was the bedroom. I was given a musty-smelling old bed-settee made of horsehair to sleep on, across the room from their bed. It was lumpy and uncomfortable and it smelled bad.

There was no warmth or cuddles from Uncle Tom and Aunt Jane. Both of them were stiff and distant and not given to demonstrations of affection. I was expected to do as I was told and keep out of the way as much as possible. They were often cross with me and made it plain that I was a burden.

I didn't like it there. Always anxious to please, I tried hard to be good and to keep as quiet as possible, so as not to annoy them, but it seemed as if nothing I did was right. I used to lie in my horsehair bed and long to be in Meg's motherly arms, or back home with my sisters.

Soon afterwards Uncle Tom told me that Dad had gone away, to London. I didn't know where London was, or why Dad had left. First Mum had gone, and now Dad. And I couldn't understand why Dad had taken me away from Meg, and then gone away so that I had to live with miserable Aunt Jane and Uncle Tom. No doubt Dad was finding it hard to cope without Mum, and perhaps he hoped to make some kind of new start. But he left his daughters high and dry. Joan was seventeen and she decided to marry her young man, Alan Smith, and Greta moved in with other relatives, while Pat stayed on with Aunt Jen and Uncle Charlie. But I was stuck where I was, with no hope of rescue.

Mealtimes were often an ordeal. While the food at Aunt Meg's had been mouth-watering, the opposite was true at Aunt Jane's. I dreaded Mondays most of all, because that's when we had tripe for tea, with bread and butter. Tripe – the lining of a cow's stomach – was the most revolting thing I had ever eaten. It was slithery and cold, and even the mug of hot tea I had with it didn't help me to wash it down. I wasn't a rebellious child, but eating that tripe was almost more than I could bear. I spent hours sitting at the table, struggling to swallow it, while Uncle Tom and Aunt Jane frowned and muttered about how ungrateful I was. By the time I'd finished I would be crying and feeling sick, and they would send me to the bedroom in disgrace.

Aunt Jane was only in her late thirties but, like many women then, she looked far older. She had a dumpy figure and straight grey hair pinned back with grips, and like most of the women round about she always wore a pinnie over her clothes. She was deaf and she carried a hearing aid with large batteries that she kept in the pocket of her pinnie, with a wire leading up to the bit plugged into her ear. She had a terrible problem with the controls and could never get them right even though she fiddled with them constantly. There was always a loud whistling noise coming from the earpiece, so she would often turn it off. But even when she had the hearing aid on, most of the time she couldn't hear what anyone said and would often give answers that were completely unrelated to the questions she was asked, which caused some amusement. At night when she went to bed I could still hear the whistling, and Uncle Tom would wake up and shout, 'Turn it off!'

She also had a condition that caused her to have seizures, which I found absolutely terrifying. With no warning she would begin to shake violently. She would fall on the floor and foam at the mouth, and her eyes would roll upwards in her head and stare at the ceiling. When this happened I would run and hide until the 'normal' Jane came back.

Luckily, most of the time these seizures happened at home, where Uncle Tom or a neighbour was on hand to help. But one day Aunt Jane had an attack as we were crossing a busy main road. To my horror she fell to the ground, shaking, in front of all the traffic. I had no idea what to do. Paralysed, I stood, horrified, watching her and praying for her to stop jerking and get up again.

Sadly, no one came to help her. Perhaps they thought she was drunk, but for whatever reason the traffic just stood still until she was able to move again. Poor Jane had been injured when she fell, and as she tried to get up there was blood pouring from her nose and her hand. This frightened me even more and I began sobbing; I had no idea what to do and kept looking around for someone to help. But eventually

Aunt Jane crawled on to the grass verge, with me still crying and trying to help her up.

We were only about a hundred yards from the flat, but it took us a long time to get there. It was a neighbour who took Aunt Jane to the hospital, where they found she had broken her nose and her finger. She came home with her hand bandaged, and her face was black and blue for several weeks.

This incident shocked and frightened me so badly that afterwards I dreaded going anywhere with Aunt Jane, in case it happened again. It didn't seem to deter her from carrying on as normal – or perhaps there was simply no choice – but whenever we went out I trailed along beside her, terrified that at any moment she would fall down again.

A few weeks after this I turned five and started at the local infant school. This meant fewer outings with Aunt Jane, which was a relief, but school brought with it a whole new set of problems.

Aunt Jane took me the first day, and after that I was expected to find my own way there and back. It wasn't too hard to find the school; we could see it from our front door, and although I had to go through a few side streets to reach it, I soon learned the route. But unfortunately I hated school, from the first moment I got there. Nothing terrible happened – and the free lunch was a lot better than Aunt Jane's food. But even the prospect of a hot meal each day wasn't enough to make me like it. I found it overwhelming and scary, and as most of the changes in my life so far had been bad, I decided school was bad too.

I began telling Aunt Jane I felt sick. She would put me to bed and leave me all day, which was boring but still better than going to school. When Jane tired of my excuses and insisted I go to school, I began hiding in shop doorways. Whenever I saw a policeman coming I slipped out of sight, terrified I'd be caught and taken to the Cottage Homes.

Inevitably, after a few weeks of this my teachers and Aunt Jane caught on and made me go to school. And eventually I did settle there, helped by one of the teachers, who befriended me. She was kind and thoughtful and encouraged me to study, knowing that for a child like me it was a way out of all the hardship. I was always very poorly dressed, and now and then she would bring in a bag of second-hand clothes and give it to me at the end of the day to take home.

Eventually I got used to school, but life in my new home remained bleak. I was a small child living with two middle-aged people who didn't really want me. I felt unloved and in the way. There were no other children to play with – our neighbours didn't have children, and I couldn't ask any other children home from school to the tiny flat. So I spent most of my time alone, wishing that Dad would come and get me again and take me back home.

The happiest times were my visits to my sisters. Joan had married and had a baby daughter, and sometimes she would call for me and take me to the little flat she and her family shared. Greta had also got married, to a lad called Ken who worked on the trains, and most Saturdays Uncle Tom would walk me the three or four miles to see her.

I loved these visits. Greta and Ken lived with his mother, Mrs Skinner, who always wore the same rusty-coloured cardigan when I visited. Their house was a lovely two-bedroom cottage, with a small sitting room at the front, which was rarely used, and a large kitchen and dining area at the back. The fire was always burning because it heated the water, and it always felt warm and cosy there. Mrs Skinner liked to bake, so the house always smelled of freshly baked bread. When I arrived she would clear the table and sit me down for a slice or two of her hot bread and best butter. Then later Greta would walk me to the Maws pie shop on Hylton Road and we would have hot pie and peas for dinner.

Uncle Bob came to see me too, and he'd take me out for the afternoon, usually on the train to Seaham Harbour to see my sister Pat. Bob was cheery and warm and we'd have a lovely time looking out of the train window, trying to spot cows and sheep. Then when we arrived at Aunt Jen's she would hug me warmly and there would be cakes for tea. Those days were special.

I was so glad to see any of my family and longed for them to come more often. I missed Dad, and when Joan told me he had come back from London I hoped every day that he would come and get me. But when eventually he did come it was only for a visit. He seemed subdued, and there was no cuddle. He led me down the street and we spent the afternoon in the local pub, where he sat drinking pints while I sat beside him, wishing he wouldn't take me back to Aunt Jane's but not brave enough to say so.

After that Dad came to see me a handful of times. But his visits were rare, and there was never any suggestion that he would take me home, so I tried to resign myself to having to stay with Aunt Jane and Uncle Tom. I did my best to be good and obedient, largely because I was still afraid of ending up in the Cottage Homes, where Aunt Jane warned me I'd be heading if I misbehaved.

I knew that, unhappy as I was, things had to be far worse in the Cottage Homes. I heard tales of the goings-on there which made me quake. All the children there were beaten and starved, so the whispers went, and recently a terrible fire had broken out there, and a nurse from the nearby nurses' home had died in the inferno. Another time, it was said, a bull had escaped from the abattoir and managed to get on to the field in front of the Homes, trapping a little boy at the top of the swing frame while it frothed and foamed at the mouth below. When I imagined being cornered by a rampaging bull, I felt relieved I only had to face Aunt Jane's pursed lips and frowning brow. I was certain that, unloved and unwanted as I felt, my life couldn't be as bad as those of the children stuck in that awful place.

3

Alan

My brothers and I were taken into the big house and up a grand flight of stairs, before they were led off in one direction and I was told to wait. Scared and bewildered, I stood where I was, until the lady from the car came back and led me through a door into a large room.

Sitting by the bay window were three women and a man. I didn't like the look of any of them. All four had very severe faces and they looked at me as if I was something the cat had brought in. I was told to go and stand in front of them and take all my clothes off. I took off my shorts and shirt, but refused to take off my vest and pants. I didn't like these people staring at me, and I wanted to go home.

I got my first lesson in obedience with a swift slap across my ear, after which my clothes were yanked off. They made me stand there for a long time while they made loud comments about my bent legs, my pot belly and then my private parts, saying, 'What's that there?' and pointing. They spoke to each other and kept laughing, while I stood naked and cold, trying not to cry and wanting to go home.

After they had finished with me I was led out, washed and put into clean clothes. I was given a pair of black shoes to put on, but because I had never worn shoes before they felt hard and heavy on my feet. I hated them. I was shown to a room with lots of beds and told this was where I would be sleeping, and then sent outside to play with the other children. There I found my brothers, both of them as confused and frightened as I was. We knew Dad would come home and find us gone, but we couldn't escape over the high wall, and if we did we had no idea where home was.

There were a dozen or so other children there, boys and girls, and they told us we were in Ashbrooke Towers, a home for children. In fact, as I would learn much later, Ashbrooke was an assessment centre. All the children brought into care by the council were taken there before being sent on to other long-term homes.

My brothers and I had been legally kidnapped and taken into care. It was assumed by the authorities at that time that a man could not properly look after children. It was the culture; women stayed at home and looked after kids and men were the breadwinners. So kids who lost their mums were often placed into care. And if there were additional elements to support their case, then children could be snatched off the streets, as we were. No doubt we were classed as neglected, but that wasn't how we saw it. We loved our home and felt safe in the streets we had always known, with neighbours around who kept an eye on us and Dad there at the end of the day. Now, all of a sudden, we were in this strange new world with no explanation and no kind or reassuring words. They behaved as though we were grubby little animals – objects to be dealt with, not children with feelings.

At the end of the afternoon we were called in for tea. We sat in rows in the dining room, eating in silence, while a man with a grim face watched over us, ready to pounce on anyone who misbehaved. Even though I was hungry, I struggled to eat. And that night, my new bed felt strange and cold and lonely. I was used to cuddling up in the double bed with my brothers and my dad. Where was Dad? I wanted him to come and get us. I cried into my pillow, quietly so that the others in the beds nearby wouldn't hear. I hated this hard, cold, disinfected house where no one smiled or had a kind word to say.

Over the following days we learned about life in care. Rules governed every minute of our day, dictating when we got up, ate, played, washed and went to bed. Whatever we did, there was a rule telling us how and when to do it. Until we were taken into care the only rule we had was to come home for tea when Mum said we had to. So it was a shock to find ourselves in this harsh world, where there were dozens of rules to be followed and any small transgression could result in a hiding.

Ashbrooke Towers was run by carers, known to the children as aunties and uncles. As in every other care home at that time, these 'carers' could be anyone and sometimes were, which made this dangerous territory for us kids. Promotion was based on length of service, not qualification. Anyone who asked for a job was given one, and it wasn't unusual for a cleaner to take over as a carer.

In among this assortment of carers there were some angels, dedicated to the children and always trying to improve the system. But they were few and far between. Most simply saw it as a job to be done, and had little sympathy for the children. And then there were the monsters. They were a small minority but always on the prowl. We quickly learned who they were – word spread among the children that a certain adult was to be avoided like the plague. But sometimes, when you were a little kid with a certain look or way about you, there was no escape from the dark where the monsters took you. Only if an angel reached you quickly would you be saved.

There was a particular carer at Ashbrooke Towers who was one of the monsters. Uncle Walter had a stern, cold face and eyes in the back of his head. He never smiled, and we all learned to avoid him if we possibly could. All but the poor little kids he ordered to go into his room with him and who later crawled into bed and cried all night. Thankfully I wasn't one of them; I was wild and trouble so he never dared try anything with me. That didn't stop him beating me, though. We got beaten all the time, with a slipper or a belt. Very few managed to avoid Uncle Walter's wrath; he seemed to delight in picking his victims each day.

Every morning we had to line up in the dormitory for inspection. This meant having your bed made, the area round your bed tidy, and being dressed and clean, with polished shoes and neat hair. Whichever carer was on duty would walk up and down the room, looking for anything out of place. For me, just four years old and completely unused to this kind of routine, it was torture. I was always getting something wrong – my hair would be sticking up, or my bed not neat enough, and each time I was given a beating.

Breakfast came next, and like all the mealtimes, it was preceded by prayers – and followed by another beating if you didn't eat all the food put on your plate, even if it made you sick. After breakfast the older kids went to school while we younger ones were sent outside to play. We were kept outside in all weathers and we used to stand with our cold noses pressed against the steamy windows of the kitchen, smelling the food being cooked and watching the fire burning.

I tried hard to remember all the rules, but there was one thing I just couldn't stand, and that was the shoes. I kept refusing to wear them. I usually hid them in the sandpit but they would find them and I'd be punished and then forced to put them on again.

One day I flung the hated shoes over the wall. A few minutes later, I was playing in the sandpit when I heard a voice calling, 'Sons, sons, come here.' I looked up and there was our dad, looking over the wall!

It turned out that he had been searching for us ever since he came home from work to be told by a crowd of neighbours that we'd been taken into care. He'd been chasing Social Services for weeks, trying to find out where we were, without much luck. Then someone had told him that kids taken into care usually went to Ashbrooke Towers. He'd come up to take a look and was walking around the wall when – by amazing coincidence – my shoes came flying over it. He knew then that there were kids on the other side, so up he climbed on his bike and there we were.

All three of us ran over to the wall, shouting, 'Dad, Dad!'

'Quick now, climb over,' he said – and we did, shoving one another up while Dad grabbed our hands and yanked us over. Once we were over we all climbed on to his old bike. Michael was on the seat having a 'backer', George was on the handlebars and – having put my discarded shoes back on – I was standing on the nuts jutting out from the front wheel.

With Dad pedalling like mad we headed for home. But it wasn't the home we knew – Dad had moved in with his brother, Uncle Willie, who had a house in Cannon Cotton Street. It was a little bigger but otherwise in much the same state as our old house.

It turned out that our youngest brother Brian had been taken into care too, and no one knew where he was. So there were just the three of us, and Uncle Willie was given the task of hiding us each day while Dad went to work. He got us to practise climbing inside an old rolled-up mattress and keeping very, very quiet. We thought it was a great game.

Willie was only five feet two or so and the softest little man you ever met. It was us kids looking after him, rather than the other way around. He actually looked like a monkey; his features matched those of a chimpanzee, spot on. And all the neighbourhood kids recognised him from the Tarzan films at the pictures (those who couldn't afford the tanner entrance fee sneaked in) and loved him.

The day came when there was a loud banging on the door. Willie looked out and it was the police! We were sent to hide in the mattress and told to keep quiet. We heard Willie open the door, then loud shouts and Willie protesting. Heavy footsteps came up the stairs and into the room and started moving around. By now we were laughing: it had to be Willie playing games as he always did, trying to frighten us.

Our muffled giggles blew our cover. 'Hello, boys,' said a very tall policeman, leaning over and looking into the mattress. Meanwhile a scuffle had broken out at the bottom of the stairs. Dad had come home from work to find the police there and Willie wringing his hands. A social worker, who had come with the police, told Dad they were taking us back into care. Dad's reply was to knock him out and then try to fight off the policemen arresting him.

Eventually Dad was carted away in a Black Maria – the old black police vans they used in those days – escorted by a few heavily bruised policemen. We were bundled into the black car with big headlights and returned to Ashbrooke Towers, and Uncle Willie was left standing on the doorstep, his little face heartbroken as he waved us goodbye.

Once again we were thrust back into Ashbrooke's harsh regime with its endless rules and beatings. The only good thing – though I didn't appreciate it until later – was that I was given callipers, to help straighten my bent legs, and fed extra doses of tinned national milk powder in order build me up. The leg-irons were heavy and I could only take them off at night. I didn't like them, but I got used to them and I didn't let them stop me playing. In fact they came in rather handy, especially when it came to scoring goals at football. My steel legs were lethal to anyone who got in my way!

The boys would often play a game we called 'kingy'. We would all line up against the wall, apart from one boy who had an old tennis ball. He would throw it at us as hard as he could until he hit one of us. The boy who was hit took the ball and did the same and so on. The last one left was the king for that day.

One day the girls joined in and one of them won. This caused a real problem with the older boys, so the ball was replaced with a chunk of brick. It did the trick: there were no girls in the next game, and a couple of the lads dropped out too. They thought we were stupid, and of course they were right, but we didn't think so. One by one out the remaining lads went, bruised but fortunately not really hurt, though one lad had a cut ear. I made it to the last three before I was hit. The brick hit my callipers so it didn't hurt me at all. Only my brothers were left, so we declared them both kings that day.

One of the inner walls by the gardens had a small gate in it. It was under six feet high with an arched top, while the wall on either side of it was about seven feet high. This gate was hardly ever used, but for some reason one particular day we were let through it. On the other side there was a grassy bank that stretched right down to the outer wall.

The lads were playing 'kingy' again, with a ball this time, and I stood next to the wall, watching them. Suddenly everything went blank for a moment. When I opened my eyes I was on the grass with a lump on my head and a boulder lying beside me. It had been thrown over the wall and hit me. I got to my feet and walked further along the wall, rubbing my head like mad. The others were waving at me; they'd seen it and were gesturing for me to come to them. But before I could – bang! Another boulder landed on my head and I hit the ground again. Now my head was really hurting.

I looked down to the others and they were on the ground too, rolling about with laughter. It must have looked so funny and so unbelievable as first one boulder, then another, flew over the wall and hit me.

I got up, feeling pretty dizzy, and started walking towards them, when – bang! A third, even bigger, boulder hit me and down I went, completely unconscious. This time the laughter stopped and the lads came running and shouting as loudly as they could. The gate opened and the gardener came through to see what the fuss was all about. When he saw me he was shocked. He had been clearing a small area and threw the boulders over the wall to save getting the barrow. As that gate was hardly ever used, he thought no one would be there.

I woke in hospital sometime later. When I returned, my head was wrapped in bandages, which were kept on for weeks. The lads made me king, but only because it was the best laugh they'd had in ages.

I had been in Ashbrooke Towers for a few months when one day the gates opened and an old black car with large headlights drove in, and a middle-aged lady in tweed got out. I was over by the sandpit and a shiver went down my spine when I saw her, because it reminded me of how we had been taken from home – twice. That day I was put in the car again, with no time to say goodbye to my brothers and friends and no idea where I was going. After what seemed to be a very long time we arrived at a row of large houses at the end of a long field. This, I was to discover, was a children's home known as the Cottage Homes. There was a row of about ten large houses, with about twelve or thirteen children living in each one. Out in front of them was a large field and in one corner was a small set of swings and a slide for the children to play on. I had never heard of the Cottage Homes. But I soon learned that the place was known all over town, because children who misbehaved were told they would be sent there. In fact the children there weren't bad, they were sad. Most had lost parents or had been abused or battered.

The regime at the Cottage Homes was just like the one at Ashbrooke, except that now I was alone. I was five years old and I had lost everyone I loved. I missed our mum and dad, my brothers and Uncle Willie. It was a long time before I saw any of them again.

We children were allowed to play out on the field in front. On one side was a spiked metal fence, next to the main Hylton Road leading to town, and on the other was a row of army-style huts that formed the local hospital. One of the huts was used as nurses' quarters.

We often used to get under the old huts and make dens, little places to hide from the world for a while until we were ordered inside. But we stopped playing there after a kid lit a candle and accidentally knocked it over, causing a terrible fire which destroyed the hut above and killed a sleeping nurse.

Across the main road there was an abattoir, and one day, not long after I got there, a bull got loose. It charged up and down the street and then got through the gates at the top of the field. Down it came towards us kids, mad as hell. The kids scattered into the houses, but I was stuck by the little set of swings near the fence because the bull had cut me off before I could get away. I climbed up the pole, slipping a bit but making it to the top, where I sat on the cross-bar with the bull banging its head on the pole below me.

There were crowds of people watching from the road, safe behind the fence, of course. It must have been funny, seeing this small boy stuck at the top of the swing with a large angry bull hanging about. After about an hour I was getting fed up and really wanted to come down, so I started to sing to the bull to amuse myself. Amazingly, the bull calmed right down and eventually wandered off. So I shot down the pole and into the house.

As soon as I got in I was beaten for being outside when there was a bull about and sent upstairs to bed. As I lay under the covers, my backside aching, I decided the bull and I had something in common: being where we weren't wanted. A short while later I watched from the window as a small group of policemen came into the field. One was carrying a rifle, and he shot the bull. Then a tractor came and hauled it away. I felt very sad.

A few days later, I was standing by the fence, watching the people and the traffic passing, when I saw Dad. He was on the same old bike and I ran along, wild with excitement, shouting to him. He stopped and came over, but he seemed almost reluctant and kept looking over his shoulder. He said hello and gave me some sweets, then mumbled something, said he had to go and pedalled off.

I stared after him, wondering why he didn't seem happy to see me. Did Dad not love me any more? Did he not want me to come home? There was no one to tell me and I felt miserable. I moped around for the next few weeks, wondering if I would see him again, and hoping he would come back, now that he knew where I was, and talk to me through the railings. But he never came.

It wasn't until years later that I was told that he had been sent to Durham Jail for six months for taking us from Ashbrooke Towers and then hitting the social worker. It was the only time I ever heard this story and, like some of the others from the same period, it may not have been true. But I believed it when I was told because it explained why he seemed so afraid to talk to me, worried that he would get into trouble again. He'd been punished for trying to be with his children, and after that he didn't dare come near us. It was to be years before I saw him again, and for all of that time I was left wondering why he hadn't seemed happy to see me that day and why he didn't try to get me back again.

It was while I was at the Cottage Homes that I first went to school. It was called Diamond Hall and all the kids from the home went there, along with the local kids. From the start I was a little tearaway; something inside was making me wild and I couldn't stay still, so I wasn't very popular with the teachers.

The children from the home walked to school together, with no adult to keep an eye on us, so it was easy to get up to mischief. And I certainly did. The old town buses used to have a number-plate on the back, with a cavity above it which housed a light. I used to grip the edge of the cavity with my hands and put my feet up on the bumper when the bus left the stop and get a free ride down the lane to the next stop. By the time it got there I was losing my grip and I'd let go and jump off.

This was great, until the time when the bus didn't pause at the next stop along, but went straight out on to the main road. Cars were beeping their horns and pedestrians were shouting as they spotted me clinging to the back. My grip was slipping and I knew I couldn't hold on much longer, when fortunately the bus stopped. I leaped off and was away, with what felt like half the planet in hot pursuit. Inevitably, when I got back to the home I was beaten again.

It was easy to spot us kids from care, because our clothes were old and never fitted. That was because none of us had our own clothes: we all shared. The staff used to bring a big bag of clothes from the laundry somewhere in town. It was tipped out and you grabbed what you could. We had baggy short trousers hanging below the knee, an itchy shirt and a stripy tank top, with long grey socks, darned of course, which were usually around our ankles.

We all had the same haircut too. For us boys that meant a short back and sides. I remember my lugs – the local word for ears – were always cold. It was worse for the girls, who were given identical pudding-basin haircuts, because they cared more about their appearance.

I remained at the Cottage Homes for a couple of years and often wondered where my dad and brothers were and if I would ever see funny old Uncle Willie again. No adult showed me any kindness or tenderness. To them I was a problem to be solved, a child who had to be put in his place.

The one real blessing during this time was that when the callipers finally came off – after many months – my legs were straight. I was very glad of that, because I didn't want to grow up with bow legs and a funny walk like some of the men I'd seen. I'd got so used to the callipers that it felt strange without them for the first few days, and I kept staring down at my legs, amazed by how straight they were.

Birthdays and Christmases just made me sadder and lonelier. Only one Christmas from that time stands out. It was Christmas Eve and I was looking out of my bedroom window when I saw gently swaying lights moving down the field from the nurses' huts. As they got closer I could see there was a long line of nurses, wearing their dark blue cloaks and carrying lanterns with candles in them. They were singing carols, and when they drew closer I could see the odd flash of red from the inner lining of their cloaks, and the white crosses on the front of their uniforms. The whole scene held a kind of magic. Their singing sounded like angels and I watched, spellbound.

One day, not long before my seventh birthday, all of us children were told to pack our things. The whole house was on the move, including the staff. The Cottage Homes were to be closed down and we were all going to other children's homes. The bags and boxes were put into a large van and driven off, and some of us children followed in a bus that took us across the river to a brand new housing estate.

Eventually we arrived in front of a double-fronted house, newly built and surrounded by other houses that weren't even finished yet. This, we were told, was Rennie Road Children's Home. We traipsed inside and were shown to our rooms by a lady called Auntie Doris, who was to be one of our new carers. We spent that afternoon unpacking and sorting out our rooms. Girls in one, boys in another. We had to make beds and get the house sorted before we were allowed to eat.

Rennie Road was all very clean and new, but that didn't really interest me. It was just another home, and not much better than the last one. The only thing I liked was that it was close to the top of a big hill, and we children could play out on the hilltop and run down its sloping sides with the wind in our hair. That part was good, but the rest was the same. We were sent to a new school, and on school nights we weren't allowed out to play as we had jobs to do. Mine was cleaning shoes – twelve pairs every evening before cocoa and bed. It took me over an hour to polish and brush all the shoes, and by the end I was often covered in polish myself. But I didn't mind. I preferred sitting and cleaning the shoes to doing the washing up, or sweeping.

Although there were just twelve of us, there was room for thirteen children, so we all wondered who the new kid would be. New kids in a home always got the third degree – what homes have you been in, what games do you know, did you get any bother (you know the type I mean) from that uncle or auntie? But time passed and the last kid still didn't arrive, so I began to think they never would.

4

Irene

I had been with Aunt Jane and Uncle Tom for about three
years when Uncle Tom suffered a stroke that left him
paralysed down one side and blind in one eye. Still only in
his late thirties, he was unable to go back to work in the
shipyards. He loved his job, and stuck at home he became
very depressed. He would often shake with frustration at
his inability to do even the simplest things for himself, such
as getting dressed and moving around the flat. He had to
rely on Aunt Jane for everything, and was never able to go
out. He had been a man who loved to walk, often for miles
every day, so being unable to move around must have felt
like torture.

As Uncle Tom's depression worsened and Aunt Jane fretted
over him, I crept around the flat, doing my best to help.

Six months after Tom's stroke I was sitting in class when
a neighbour came to the school to say I had to return home
as Tom had taken a bad turn. When I arrived home the flat
was full of neighbours, all shaking their heads and muttering
quietly.

I was taken to the bedroom, where Aunt Jane and a few
other people I didn't know were gathered around the bed.
Uncle Tom was sitting up in the bed with his eyes bulging,
frothing at the mouth and making frantic moaning sounds.
He looked so frightening I wanted to run from the room, but

when he saw me he lunged forward and grabbed me with his good hand, dragging me close. His bulging eyes were staring at me and he was frothing and gurgling and trying to say something, but all that came out were moaning noises. I was so terrified that I stood, rooted to the spot, staring at him with my mouth wide open in a kind of frozen scream.

After a few moments someone in the room yanked me from his grip and took me into the other room, where I sat, horrified by the memory of his bulging eyes and foaming mouth. No doubt the people with him had meant well, but for a small girl of just seven, the sight of a man in such a dreadful state was a terrible experience.

Uncle Tom died later that night. After he had gone I couldn't get the memories of that last encounter out of my mind. I felt haunted by it, and terrified that he would somehow come back from the grave to claim me. It wasn't until years later that I learned he had taken an overdose of aspirins, preferring death to a life imprisoned in that tiny, grim flat.

After the funeral, Aunt Jane decided that she needed to get away, so she took me to her sister Kate's farm for a short break. It took us only an hour on the bus to get to the farm, and I wondered why we had never been there before.

The contrast between the cramped and gloomy flat and the wide open spaces of the farm couldn't have been more marked. From the moment we arrived, I loved it. I felt as if a heavy weight had been lifted from me and I could just float away. Kate was exactly how I imagined a farmer's wife to be; large and jolly with apple-red cheeks. Warm and cheery, she hugged me as if I was her own child, and I wished that I was.

Kate's husband and daughter were both just as jolly, with the same cheeks. They lived in their wellies and I rarely saw them – apart from early morning and evening – as they were out working the farm most of the time. They also had a son who was in the RAF, and whenever aeroplanes flew over the farmyard from the nearby base where he was stationed, Kate would say, 'That's my boy!'

The farmhouse was a long, one-storey building with a large yard. Inside, it had a corridor that ran almost the length of the building, with windows looking out into the yard on one side and a row of doors, leading into various rooms, on the other. I shared a room, and a double bed, with Aunt Jane.

The days were warm and sunny and I spent as much time as I could helping to feed the animals and watching the chickens in the yard and the pigs running around the barns. I made friends with the two little girls whose parents ran the country pub a few hundred yards away. They had a brick playhouse in their back garden where the three of us played for hours.

In the evenings we sat around the large log fire in the living room and I would watch the sparks from the burning logs jump and spit their way up the chimney. When bedtime came I slept deeply and well, exhausted by all the fresh air.

Even Aunt Jane seemed more cheerful. She and I took long walks across the fields, and on one occasion realised we were passing a bull which was taking a bit too much interest in us. We ran for the gate, laughing and, referring to my red dress, Aunt Jane said, 'That's what happens when you wear red!' Those were happy days and my spirits soared. I wandered the fields looking at the brightness of the sky above and dreaming that it might always be like this, and that somehow I could stay on this lovely farm for ever.

Sadly, after a wonderful week away, Aunt Jane and I had to catch the bus back to the city. The flat seemed so much worse after the brightness and warmth of the farm. It felt like being locked back into a dark box, and I went over and over my memories of our week away, desperate to hang on to a reminder of something good in a world that seemed otherwise very bleak.

I was now sharing the double bed with Aunt Jane instead of the lumpy horsehair settee on which I had slept for the past four years. It was more comfortable in the bed, but while I hadn't minded sharing with her at the farm, back at the flat I didn't find it easy to settle beside her because of the dreaded whistling of her hearing aid. I didn't dare wake her – I was too afraid it might remind her of Uncle Tom.

I was haunted by nightmares. I couldn't get the pictures of Uncle Tom's staring eyes and foaming mouth out of my head. Between the nightmares and Aunt Jane's hearing aid, I was often kept awake well into the night.

One night, well after midnight, I lay trying to get to sleep when I suddenly became aware of what appeared to be the outline of Uncle Tom, reflected on the wall in the light from the street lamp. He was wearing his cloth cap and leaning forward, as if he were looking through the window. I felt as if his icy hand had hold of me again and I pulled the blankets over my head to hide from him. Unable to sleep for the rest of the night, I lay in a sweat, terrified that he was coming to get me.

That image of Tom stayed with me. It was as if it was some kind of omen, and from that night on I felt afraid that something bad was going to happen. Then one evening, a few weeks later, I was sitting quietly in the living room with Aunt Jane when suddenly she jumped out of her seat and began screaming at me.

I was astonished – Aunt Jane was often very disapproving, but she never shouted or hit me. Now suddenly she was red-faced and hysterical. Terrified, I ran behind the chair to hide. Aunt Jane strode over, grabbed my arm and dragged me out. She began to slap me, screaming, 'It's all your fault that Tom's dead!' The blows stung, but what she said was worse. My fault? How could it be my fault?

Finally she stopped and let go of me. I ran, sobbing and trembling, to hide back behind the chair, until a few minutes later she told me to get to bed.

I went into the bedroom, got into my nightdress and crawled between the covers, where I lay crying into the pillow. Why had Aunt Jane blamed me for Tom's death? Was she right, I wondered anxiously. Had I done something to kill him? I felt I must be a terrible, wicked child, to cause Uncle Tom to die and Aunt Jane to be so angry.

After that I was quieter than ever. Afraid that I had done something dreadful without knowing it, I crept around the flat, miserable and frightened. Aunt Jane, her face set in a permanent frown, barely spoke to me, which only heightened my sense of guilt.

A couple of weeks later, as I was washing up after tea, there was a knock at the door. We hardly ever had visitors, so I wondered who it could be. Aunt Jane told me to answer it, and to my great surprise and delight it was my sister Joan. She beckoned me outside and bent close to tell me that Aunt Jane couldn't look after me any more and I was coming to live with her. My face lit up – could it be true? Was I really going home with Joan?

Joan turned towards Aunt Jane, who was standing in the doorway. 'Shall I fetch her things?' she asked.

'No need,' Aunt Jane replied. 'I have them here,' and she handed over a small bag containing all my clothes, as well as a golly and a black doll Uncle Bob had given me. I was startled – I hadn't noticed her packing my things that day.

She nodded briefly at us, turned and, without another word, closed the door firmly behind her.

Confused, all I could think to say to Joan was 'We've left my scooter.' Apart from the golly and the doll my most prized possession was a little scooter which Aunt Jane and Uncle Tom had bought me. They'd propped it up against my horsehair bed on Christmas morning and I'd walked straight past it – they'd had to lead me back into the room before I spotted it. I loved that scooter; I used to buzz up and down the pavement outside the flat on it. But Joan thought it best not to knock on Aunt Jane's door again, so I had to leave it behind.

I was upset about the scooter, but so very glad to be away from Aunt Jane. I trotted up the street next to Joan, looking anxiously over my shoulder in case Aunt Jane changed her mind. After four years in that sad little flat, it was hard to believe I was leaving. And to live with Joan! The best possible news. I wanted to sing and skip and shout with happiness. But I was sure that wouldn't be the right thing to do. Joan looked very serious, so I said nothing. But inside, I felt happy. No more sad, angry Aunt Jane. No more whining hearing aid. No more tripe.

Joan and her family had moved to a new house. It was a bus-ride and a good walk from Aunt Jane's, on a new council estate in the Redhouse area where all the streets and roads began with 'R'. Their small two-up, two-down house was in Revenna Road. At the top of their road was Bunny Hill with its views across the fields. Most of the surrounding streets were filled with building sites, as new houses were still being built.

The next street to Joan's was called Rennie Road. On one side the houses were ready, but on the other there were simply stacks of bricks and timber sitting among concrete foundations. All the local children used to play in among the builders' materials and use them as dens.

In the new house I shared the second bedroom with Joan's little girl, Elaine, who was a toddler. Joan was expecting another baby, and I couldn't wait to see if I had a niece or a nephew. I was so happy to be with my sister, I was determined to help her and make her and her husband glad they had taken me. But one night I heard Alan arguing with Joan, and telling her that they couldn't afford to feed and clothe me. My stomach twisted into a tight knot and I lay, wide awake, feeling very scared. Once again I felt like a cuckoo in the nest. Would I have to leave? Where would I go? I couldn't think of any other relatives who might have me. Why was it that nobody seemed to want me?

For the next few weeks I tried as hard as I could to make them want me. I helped Joan and looked after Elaine and tried not to be in the way when Alan was home. But several more times I heard him telling Joan they couldn't afford to have me. Joan argued with him, but I knew he would win; he always did when they argued.

I became so fearful that I couldn't think about anything else. What would become of me? Would there be another aunt somewhere who would take me?

When the day finally came that Joan called me in and told me that they couldn't keep me any more, it was almost a relief. At least now I would find out where I would be going. Joan was upset, so I tried very hard not to cry. She told me they needed my bed for the new baby, but that I was going to live in a big house with lots of children, where I would be well looked after.

What big house could she be talking about? I had no idea. All I knew was that I didn't want to go. I wanted to sob and beg her to keep me. But I didn't. I sat, white-faced, my lip trembling, telling myself over and over not to cry. I wasn't going to be a baby and make Joan even sadder.

Joan packed my clothes, but said I wouldn't be allowed to take my doll or my golly so they had to be left behind. I kissed them and asked Elaine to look after them for me, then I kissed Elaine goodbye and, swallowing back my tears, followed Joan to the bus stop.

As we sat on the bus, with my small bag at my feet, Joan did her best to reassure me that everything would be all right and said she would come and see me whenever she could.

I tried to smile, but inside I felt despair. No one wanted me, and now I was being sent to a place where I didn't know anyone, and I couldn't even have my precious doll and golly. By the time we got off the bus I was trembling with the effort of trying to be brave.

We were in a wide leafy lane full of very grand houses where I was sure very rich people must live. What sort of place was I going to, I wondered. We walked to the front of the biggest house of all. The name Ashbrooke Towers was written on a plate in the wall next to the huge iron gates. I thought it looked very dark and gloomy. We walked up the drive to the front door and I could see a grassy area with a sand-pit.

The door was opened and a man ushered us inside. There was something about him that made me very scared. I kept my head down and didn't dare look up at him. Without a word of welcome he told me to go up the stairs and wait at the top. Joan kissed and hugged me, promising to visit, then turned and left.

I dragged my feet slowly up the stairs. A moment later the man followed me. Coldly he told me his name was Uncle Walter and that from now on I was to do exactly as I was told. He showed me into a dormitory with a row of beds, and the locker room where my things would be kept, then told me to go outside and play with the other children until dinnertime.

I made my way nervously back down the stairs and outside, to where ten or twelve other children were playing in the grounds. I wandered around, then went and sat under a tree, looking up at the high brick wall surrounding the house. This was where the children no one wanted were taken, I thought. Children like me. I didn't talk to any of the other children. I felt too sad and frightened. I didn't want to be there, I wanted to be back with Joan.

I wandered desolately around the grounds of the house until we were called in for tea, where we sat in long rows at the dining tables and prayers were said before the food was served. I barely noticed what was put in front of me, and only ate it because the little girl next to me whispered that I'd get a beating if I didn't.

Before bed I was given my new school uniform and told I'd be going to a new school with the others in the morning. I was shocked. A new school? Wasn't I going back to my school any more? After lights out I sobbed silently under the covers. The thought of having to change schools was terrible. It had taken me so long to get used to the school I was in. Now I would never see the teachers and my friends again. I would have to go into a school where I didn't know anyone, and had no idea how things were done. I felt so frightened by the idea that I wondered if I could run away in the night. But I knew there would be no way out of the big house. I was a prisoner.

Without my doll and golly I had nothing to cuddle. I missed them so much. And I missed Joan. Even going back to Aunt Jane's would have been better than this. But she didn't want me. No one wanted me. I had been rejected by everyone and now I was alone in this awful place.

I finally fell into an exhausted sleep, only to wake a few hours later, tired and with tear-stung eyes. I put on my new uniform, went down to breakfast and then followed the other children to school without uttering a word. I felt empty and sad and abandoned. I didn't believe that anything good would ever happen to me again.

The only possession I'd been allowed to take with me to Ashbrooke Towers was the brown leather satchel Uncle Bob had given me. I clutched it to me as I walked up the street in my stiff school dress and heavy black shoes, too lost and lonely to speak to the other children walking with me.

In the new school I was led to my classroom. The teacher was pleasant, but I felt out of my depth and couldn't concentrate. I hung about the edge of the playground on my own at break time, and in class I spent most of my time staring out of the window.

The days that followed dragged painfully slowly. I obeyed the many rules at Ashbrooke, and mostly I avoided getting into trouble, but I was a sad little girl, grieving for my family. I didn't really care what happened to me.

I was in Ashbrooke for several months, and I never got used to it. It was summer, yet it always felt cold, and there was nowhere we children could go to get warm. Every day, come rain or shine, we were locked out in the yard. In bad weather we huddled in the doorways to shelter and try to get warm.

The big basement kitchen had a large sash window which opened into the yard, and when it got hot inside the cook would open it to let the cool air in. The smells of food would waft around the yard and our eyes would be glued to the window, watching the food being prepared on the big wooden table. The cook was a lovely lady who often took pity on the frozen children in the yard. She let us huddle around the window to get warm, though she didn't dare open the door for fear of getting sacked. When it was bitter cold I would put my hands through the window and she would lean over the workbench and hold my hands to warm them.

We made our own entertainment, hanging a sheet over the doorway of the locker room so that with the light on behind it we could make silhouettes. We spent hours acting out stories or making shadow-puppets.

The only clothes that were ours were our school uniforms. At weekends a bag of clothes would be brought into the dormitory and laid out. These were our weekend clothes and we used to get really excited about wearing something different. Except that most of the time none of us could find anything in the bag to fit us. We'd go through the pile, trying different things on and swapping them with one another, but we'd still end up in something too big or too small.

We had to wear ugly black lace-up shoes, which we all hated. So we saved the little bit of pocket money we got each week and spent it on plimsolls. Every day when we got outside the gates we would take off our hated shoes and hide them in a bag which we'd throw back over the wall at the bottom of the garden, where it wouldn't be noticed among the bushes. We'd put on the plimsolls to go to school, and then at the end of the day we'd meet up with the lads, who walked back separately, and they would scramble over the wall and throw the bag of shoes over for us. We'd change back and then hide the plimsolls in the bushes for the next day.

I was allowed visits from family members, so now and then Joan or Greta would come and take me out for a day. We'd go on the bus to Seaham Harbour to visit Pat, who was still living there with Aunt Jen and Uncle Charlie. I used to play with Pat's dolls and wish I could stay there with her and not go back to Ashbrooke Towers.

Uncle Bob came too and, more rarely, Dad. They were still sharing the house in Pennywell and I wanted Dad to take me to live there, but I didn't ask. I knew he would say no because there was no one to look after me.

One day, about six months after arriving at Ashbrooke and just after my ninth birthday, Uncle Walter told me not to go to school with the others but to wait in the hall by the front door. I did as I was told, wondering what was happening. I saw a big black car come through the gates and drive up to the front door. The driver got out and came in. 'Irene?' he said. When I said yes, he told me to get into the car. One of the aunties handed me a small bag with my things in it, and only then did I realise that I was being moved.

This was the heartless way in which things were done then, with no explanations and no goodbyes. Like so many children before me, I was told nothing and not allowed to say goodbye to my friends. I'd have loved to have thanked the cook for all her kindness and her warm hands. But I was spirited away, and the other children would return from school to find me gone.

It was November 1959 and very cold. I sat in the back of the car, shivering, with my bag on my knees. We swept out of the gates and down roads I had never seen before. I didn't dare ask where I was going, and the man never spoke; he just looked ahead and kept driving. We crossed the Alexander Bridge over the river and I saw the ships and a multitude of smaller boats down on the water, and even in the car I could hear the sounds from the shipyards.

On we went, to a newer part of town, driving along streets of red-brick houses, when suddenly I realised we were going through the estate where Joan lived. We stopped in the next street to hers, Rennie Road – the one that had been half-built when I'd been living with her. Was this really where I was going to live? Now the street had been finished, and where there had been nothing but concrete foundations and piles of bricks there were new houses.

The house we stopped outside looked like the others in the street, except it seemed a little longer and it had a small porch and steps up to the front door. It was much smaller than Ashbrooke Towers and looked more like a family home than a children's home. The driver told me to get out of the car, and I waited as he got my bag out.

The front door was opened by a plump, friendly-looking lady who said, 'You must be Irene.' Beside her stood a boy with piercing blue eyes and blonde hair. He was wearing the usual short trousers to just below his knees, with a tank-top and the same short back and sides haircut all the boys in care had. He was smiling at me, and looking at him I felt warm inside. I was sure I recognised him, but I couldn't think where from. It was as if I knew him, but I couldn't, surely? Somehow I knew this smiling boy would be my friend. Perhaps it wasn't going to be so bad here. I smiled back at him and stepped inside.

5

Alan

It was a cold, grey day. I sat in the playroom, on the wide window ledge, staring out at the empty street, and the field in the distance.

Just then, a big black car came around the corner and drew up outside. A man got out, and then a little girl. She was smaller than I was, with red hair cut short in the usual pudding-basin style, and wearing the same grey pinafore dress all the girls were given, with little black lace-up boots.

As she followed the man to the door, I watched her. And at that moment something deep inside me burned like hot fire. I knew her! I didn't know where from or how. We had never met, but I knew her. It was as if everything went bright and I felt I could run for miles and miles with her and never tire.

Suddenly I knew that I wasn't going to be alone any more. I jumped down from the window ledge and ran to open the front door. I stood in the hall and watched as Auntie Doris took her upstairs to put her things away. I knew she'd be down in a few minutes for tea and I couldn't wait to see her again, so I hung around at the bottom of the stairs and when she came down we smiled at one another again and swapped names. She told me she was called Irene. I showed her around until Auntie Doris told us it was time for tea.

In the dining room there was one large wooden table around which the thirteen of us would sit for meals. The boys sat on one side and the girls on the other. Sometimes there were more girls than boys or the other way around, depending on who had left and who had just arrived. But even if one side of the table was a bit crowded and the other had plenty of room, boys and girls were not allowed to sit next to one another. In those days girls and boys weren't allowed to sit together or play together, unless it was in a big group of children. Even then it wasn't encouraged and girls and boys who got too friendly – even very young ones – were punished. So Irene took her place on one side of the table, while I went to the other, smiling shyly at her whenever Auntie Doris's back was turned.

After tea we all had to do our jobs. I got busy with the shoe-cleaning; other children cleared the table, cleaned the floors or did the washing, ironing and mending. Irene and I didn't get another chance to talk that night, but I smiled at her as we went up to bed, and she smiled back. And that night I lay in bed thinking, 'I've got a friend, a real friend.' I still had the powerful feeling that somehow I knew her.

Over the next few days I looked for chances to talk to Irene. The children nicknamed her Rusty, because of her red hair, and the name stuck – it suited her. Despite the strict rules we managed to steal time to play together. We had to be careful, so we only talked when the aunties weren't about.

We took to sitting behind the curtain in the playroom. The window ledge was wide enough to sit on, so we could be completely hidden, and in that cosy space we talked whenever we got the chance. We had a lot in common – Irene was one of four girls, I was one of four boys, and both of us had been taken into care because our mums had died when we were small. I had never talked about losing my mum to anyone else, but somehow I could talk to Irene about it, and even tell her how I felt. I told her how much I missed Dad and my brothers. And she said she missed her dad and her sisters too. It was good to know that someone else understood what it felt like to lose your mum and then the rest of your family, and be sent away.

Cosy as the windowsill was, our best times were when we were outside. The top of Bunny Hill was a few yards away, at the end of the street. All of us children were allowed to go and play there at weekends, and that's when Irene and I often managed to sneak away from the others and have adventures together. We used to sit on the side of the hill, where we could see for miles, and look down on Hylton Castle below us, which was over four hundred years old. Behind it the woods stretched to the river and across to Penshaw Monument in the distance. This was a large folly, based on an ancient Greek temple, sitting proudly on a hilltop some miles away.

We would watch the planes from the aerodrome in the distance. It had been an RAF station during the war and was now used to train parachutists. Sometimes they would be blown fairly close to where we sat, and we watched the billowing white parachutes and the tiny figures dangling below them and waved madly, imagining that they could see us.

When we got the chance, we would go down the hill and cross the road. This was strictly forbidden, but adventure called and we followed. We climbed over the stone wall and headed through the castle grounds until we reached the far woods. It was wonderful, walking through the trees. We were used to bricks and walls, so kicking our way through the leaves felt great. These were bluebell woods: the sweetly scented, delicate blue blooms carpeted the ground in spring and Irene picked bunches of them, even though she couldn't take them back without giving us away.

This became our special place. The peace and solitude and the brilliant colour of the bluebells felt magical, and we used to pretend that it was our home.

On the other side of the woods we reached the river, and we walked along its bank until we came to the little old church which stood disused and overgrown. A tiny place, the size of a room, its old doors were always open and we used to shelter from the rain, and from the outside world. We sat on an old pew, talking in whispers because it was a church, our voices quietly echoing around the stone walls.

We loved to watch the beams of coloured light shining through the stained glass windows, and the way the light beams on the floor brightened then dimmed as the clouds raced by, blocking the sun. We often wondered about the stories the windows depicted, and whether things had been better in those times. Sometimes we would lose track of time in this mystical place, and when we realised we were late we'd run all the way back, panting up the hillside.

We made sure never to return to the house together, so one of us would wait, or try to come back with some of the other children. If we were late we got punished. In my case that meant a crack around the ear, additional chores, then bed, for ever! At least that's how it felt then. Irene was older, so even more punishments were applied – she got triple chores and early bed for a week. So we ran like the wind to avoid trouble.

I was always adventurous, and one day when I was out playing with Irene and the other kids I set out to prove to her that I was the bravest of them all. On the slopes of the hill where we played there was the old air-raid shelter built into the hillside. We didn't know where the door was, only the narrow concrete slits that those inside had been able to use to look out during the war.

59

Because of the narrowness of the slits most of the kids couldn't get into it. But two or three of us smaller boys could. We would squeeze through the slits into the cavernous interior, then peer out at the others on the hill. It was pitch black inside, so no one had ever ventured further in, even though there was the entrance to a tunnel at the back.

On this particular day I plucked up the courage to explore the tunnel. I went in slowly, feeling my way along the walls because it was too dark to see a thing. All of the stories I'd been told, of holes in the ground too deep to get out of and monsters waiting in the dark, came to mind, but I pressed on, knowing that Irene was outside, waiting for me with the others. The tunnel went into the hillside for about fifty feet. On the way it curved slightly, and as I went around the bend I lost sight of the light coming through the slits in the distance behind me. I grew more and more scared. But as I stood in the inky darkness I became even more determined to find out what was at the end of the tunnel. It was like a test, and I wasn't going to give up.

Eventually, after what seemed like an age of feeling my way along the rough wall, I saw a chink of light and headed towards it. When I got to the end there was a slope going up to a hole. It was a little tricky to get up to the hole, but it was much bigger than the slits. I was excited – this meant all of the kids could get in. I emerged into a thick patch of nettles. No wonder we hadn't found the entrance before: it was completely hidden by the nettle patch. My bare legs and arms got badly stung. But when I ran back to the other kids I was a hero – at least for a day. They were delighted that they could all get in, and as they piled in Irene smiled at me and whispered, 'Well done.' After that we all played in the shelter, and the bigger lads used it when they wanted a secret ciggie.

I learned a great lesson that day that was to see me through many trials ahead. Making my way through that tunnel taught me that when you are at the darkest point, light is just around the next corner. All you need is persistence and a little faith to reach it, and you only have to overcome your fears for a moment to win through.

Until I met Irene I'd been considered a naughty, troublesome child. I could never concentrate for long and my imagination would carry me off to different worlds when I was supposed to be paying attention, particularly at school. I was always in trouble, mainly because I forgot the time and became lost for a while in some game. There were so many rules it was almost impossible not to break one. And if I did I was punished, time after time. But with Irene around I began to calm down. Knowing I had a real friend helped me to become more content with things. I started to improve at school and to behave better, and became – almost – a model little boy. I felt my feet more firmly on the ground and was better able to focus on what I was doing. I was also learning to hide my wilder side so as to avoid drawing attention to myself, as it was harder to be with Irene if I was being watched.

Though Irene and I did our best to hide our closeness, all the kids knew, and some of the older boys got jealous. Because she was nine and I was seven they thought she should be paying attention to them, not me, so they started picking on her. On one occasion five of them had started on her, pushing her and calling her names. I wasn't having that; I flew at them in fury. I was never going to win against so many, and I ended up with a bloody nose, but I managed to hurt a couple of them so much that they never picked on her again.

Most of the time the boys in the house got on well together. We used to meet some of the local lads each weekend and gather on Bunny Hill, calling ourselves the Redhousers because the home was on the Redhouse estate. At the bottom of the hill, not far from Hylton Castle, another new estate was under construction. The whole place was like a building site, which was great for us. We used to play among the pallets of bricks and timber. The kids from this estate were called the Castlers and were our sworn enemies. Both gangs believed the hill belonged to them, and each was determined to punish trespassers from the rival gang.

The two gangs would regularly meet and have a battle. For the most part that meant throwing stones or a bit of wrestling, kicking and punching, which left a few black eyes on either side. We usually won as we had the bigger gang – there were about twenty lads in all. Sometimes the girls joined in too. Irene was quite a tomboy: she could clobber a lad with a crack to his lug in half a second, and she kicked like a mule. The boys avoided her little black shoes; they were as hard as they were quick.

One day we kids from Rennie Road were playing on the hill when I wandered into a rival group of Castler boys from below the hill. I thought they were our lot, and by the time I realised my mistake it was too late and I was grabbed. I was put on trial as a spy and ordered to confess. Full of bravado, I refused, and was found guilty and sentenced to hang.

I wasn't too worried by this, until I saw that there was a tree there, and they had a box and a rope. At this point I began to feel a bit nervous, as I was made to stand on the box with a noose round my neck, tied to the tree above me. But I still didn't think they'd really do anything to me – until the box was kicked away. The shock was enormous. Suddenly I was dangling from the end of a rope that was tightening around my throat. I couldn't speak or shout; I was choking and trying to grab at the rope. But the more I fought and twisted around, the tighter the rope got.

When the Castlers realised what they'd done, panic set in, and instead of getting help, they all ran away. Terrified, I watched as the whole gang of them fled up the hill. Gasping for air, I knew I was in real trouble. If the rope tightened much more, I would black out, and that would be it.

I didn't want to die! I had to find a way to get free.

Trying not to panic, I managed to grab the rope above me and pull myself up, so that with one hand I could grab the branch it was tied to. I was a strong, wiry kid, and luckily I didn't weigh too much, so I was able to pull myself up on to the branch, and then loosen the rope, untie myself and jump to the ground.

I lay there panting for a few minutes. Air had never tasted so sweet. I put my hands up to my neck. I could feel the raw skin and I winced. I had a painful rope burn, and my throat hurt – inside and out.

Slowly I got to my feet and started the trek back to Rennie Road. I knew I was late, but at least I'd be able to tell them what had happened. As I rounded the corner I saw Auntie Nan standing on the front step. When she spotted me, she grabbed me and frogmarched me into the house.

'I don't know what you've been up to, my boy, but you're in deep trouble,' she snapped. 'You're extremely late and we've all been out looking for you.'

'I can explain,' I started, and launched into my story about being caught by the Castlers.

'Rubbish,' sniffed Auntie Nan. 'I don't know how you've done this to yourself, but making up some story about other children holding you hostage and trying to hang you is ridiculous. You will be beaten, and will remain indoors for a week.'

I tried to protest, but Nan wasn't interested. 'Another word out of you, and the punishment will be worse,' she hissed, hauling me by one ear towards the office.

The beating she gave me hurt, but the injustice hurt more. I lay in bed that night angry and tearful, hating Nan and wishing that I could tell Irene what had happened. I knew she would believe me.

For the next week I had to stay indoors when all the others went out to play. That was really hard. I hated being cooped up and longed to be running around in the open. And I felt deeply wounded at not being believed. How could I ever trust adults, when they wouldn't listen to the truth?

I didn't get much chance to talk to Irene that week, but she shot me sympathetic glances at mealtimes and whenever we passed, and I knew she felt sorry for me.

At the end of the week it was good to get out again, and not long after that the boys in our gang had our revenge on the Castlers. We captured three of them and held them prisoner. They were found guilty of spying and taken to the sandstone quarry on the other side of the hill. It was always flooded, four or five feet deep, which wasn't a lot if you could swim, but many of the kids couldn't.

The prisoners were taken to the edge and made to kneel, looking down at the water, which was about twenty feet below them. They were asked to become spies for us or be thrown off in revenge for my hanging. They were very brave and refused. But I could hardly believe it when one of our lads, a boy known as Rubberneck, ran up behind them and quick as a flash, pushed them all off. Down they went, and each one hit the water with a big splash and went under. The water was freezing and they shot back up to the surface splashing about and shouting. Luckily they all managed to get to the edge, and once out of reach on the other side, shouted their curses and promises of revenge.

Rubberneck, whose real name was Ray, was a tall, skinny kid of eight or nine who got his nickname because if he fell over or got hit he just seemed to bounce back up and never get hurt. He wasn't the brightest star in the firmament by a vast distance, but he could be extremely crafty at times. So when we boys needed someone to go on a secret mission, we all picked Rubberneck.

This mission was a real test of manhood, a secret never to be told, a fight against the odds: he had to get sweets for us all, at dead of night.

We did get a little pocket money each week, enough for a comic or a few sweets. But other than that we never got treats, and we'd heard that there was a whole factory full of them across town.

As a punishment, one of the younger lads had been chosen to go with him. We called him Snotty because he was, always. He sniffed and dribbled and wiped his nose on his sleeve. And he wore a pair of black, thick-rimmed glasses that always had a piece of sticking plaster around the front rim. His instructions were to go with Rubberneck, help out if he got into trouble and run back to warn everyone if he got caught. It was well known that Rubberneck would do just about anything if you dared him, so he often needed a rescuer.

Out the two of them went, through the bedroom window at about midnight, heading for the sweet factory near the Roker Park football ground across town. They crept down back lanes, avoiding street lights and wandering bobbies on the beat. There was little in the way of traffic in those days, particularly at night, apart from the odd Black Maria picking up drunks. If there was any sign of headlights the two boys rushed to hide until they passed.

After a couple of hours of hunting they found the factory. They crept round to the back wall of the building and climbed up a drainpipe and on to the sloping roof. It was covered in corrugated asbestos sheets, the brittle ones that break easily. Rubberneck started to walk across it and promptly fell through, with a loud crash. He landed on the factory floor about twenty feet below, and bounced without harm. As his eyes became accustomed to the dim light, he began to look around. He was in heaven, surrounded by shelf upon shelf of every kind of sweet and chocolate bar! And row upon row of shelves! He could hardly move for excitement.

Fortunately his assistant had been given a pillowcase in anticipation of the impossible. He threw it down and Rubberneck proceeded to fill the sack with goodies, while stuffing his face with chocolate bars in the semi-darkness of the factory. Eventually he climbed back up to the corner and through the broken roof. His assistant was fed on the spot, and because Snotty had a little more sense, he replaced bits of the roof to try to cover their tracks.

They returned through the bedroom window at around four in the morning. We were stunned and wildly excited as Ray clung to the bulging bag and the tale was told, supported by his chocolate-smeared partner. They duly received our adulation and praise, before we began whispering, as loudly as we dared, 'The bag, the bag!'

Rubberneck untied the bag with us in a circle around him, and tipped it on to the floor. Out came loads of – chewing gum! Not a sweet in sight, just boxes and boxes of chewy. We nearly killed him. But we had discovered a permanent supply of sweets, and every month after that a couple of brave lads were chosen to complete the mission.

I always shared mine with Irene, stuffing them into my pockets until we could sneak away for an hour or two and lie on our backs in the woods, our cheeks bulging with goodies as we watched the clouds passing above us. We used to try to imagine where they were going and what it would be like to be there. We would talk of escaping and going to live in the bluebell woods, just the two of us, free and happy.

We did a lot of dreaming together. All our dreams were based on the kinds of children's books that had a large jolly lady baking pies and bread, and feeding lots of happy children in a thatched cottage surrounded with bright flowers, where it was always warm. We knew the beds there would be deep and soft, with large pillows and patchwork quilts, and the sun always shining through the little windows.

Sometimes, walking back to Rennie Road, we'd look through the windows of the houses in the street and see warm fires, and birthday cards on the mantelpiece, and children playing. We saw mothers giving them hugs and kisses and all of them laughing, and wondered, 'Why not us?' Why couldn't we live in a home like that, with someone to love us?

Still, we had each other. One day, sitting on the hill watching the parachutists, I told Irene that when we were grown up I was going to marry her. She thought about it for a moment and then said that she would marry me too, and we shook on it to seal our pact. Then we stole a kiss. A fleeting brush of the lips, a moment of pure joy that lingered with me for all of the years to come.

6

Irene

Until I got to Rennie Road and met Alan, I had gone through life just following the orders of the adults around me. It was as if I wore blinkers, shutting out most of the world and holding back emotions and feelings that were too painful. I did as I was told, and learned not to expect anything good to happen because there had been so much loss in my life. But when the door of Rennie Road opened and Alan was waiting there to say hello, everything changed.

I had never been greeted in a friendly way like that before. I went upstairs with Auntie Doris that first day, wishing the nice boy would be there when I came down again. And he was. That was when I knew I had a real friend.

It was Alan who showed me round and made me feel welcomed. After that we played together, or sat and talked, whenever we could. And something inside me, that had been empty, was filled. I knew that I could rely on Alan, and trust him. He would be there for me, and that meant everything.

Rennie Road was more like a real home although, as I soon discovered, the rules were just as strict as those at Ashbrooke Towers. The house had a large sitting area and a playroom, the two rooms separated by a folding wooden partition. I was very impressed that there was a television in the sitting area, as I'd never seen one before. There was a dining room and kitchen, and outside a paved back yard for the children to play in and to hang out the washing.

Upstairs there were several bedrooms. The two aunties each had their own, which were kept permanently locked. There was a large bedroom that slept six and two smaller bedrooms that slept the other seven. I was put into the smallest room, sharing with two sisters, one older and the other younger than me. I tried to be friends with them, but they talked to one another and ignored me until I gave up trying. Later I discovered that no one stayed in the same room for very long. It all depended on how many girls or boys were in the home at any given time, and you could be moved from one room to another when a child arrived or left. This was really unsettling, because you never had a space of your own for very long.

Though the sisters didn't seem to want to know me, some of the other children seemed friendly. They nicknamed me Rusty, which I didn't mind because almost everyone had a nickname. A few of the children seemed very troubled. There was a little brother and sister who'd come not long before me, around five or six years old and both very thin, with pale dry skin around their eyes as if they had been constantly crying. They looked undernourished and always seemed to be frightened and clinging to one another. I often wondered what had hurt them so much, I was haunted by their gaunt little faces. And despite the fact that they seemed to need one another so much, house rules had to be followed, so they weren't allowed to sleep in the same bedroom.

There were three members of staff – Auntie Doris, Auntie Nan and Margaret the cleaner. Auntie Doris was plump and pleasant, with short mousy permed hair. She was a stickler for the rules but she had a kind heart, and if she caught you misbehaving or breaking a rule she didn't punish you too harshly, unless it was very serious. She never showed much open affection to us children, though there were times when I felt she wanted to. Perhaps she was afraid of becoming too involved, because, as I soon learned, the children could – and did – vanish overnight, whisked off to another home by the authorities.

Auntie Nan was thin, with short auburn hair, also permed. Cold and distant, she was quick to scold and punish for the slightest misdemeanour. You knew if she caught you misbehaving that you would be punished without question. We children went about silently when she was on duty.

Margaret the cleaner was thin with long dark hair. The aunties did the cooking and Margaret would often help with serving and cleaning up, but her main job was supervising the children's cleaning and washing-up duties. She wasn't unkind, but she didn't say much and it was clear that her work with us was just a job. She lived with her elderly mother and, like the two aunties, she was unmarried and had no children of her own.

Each of the children was given chores. My job was washing and drying the dishes, three times a day – after breakfast, tea and evening cocoa – on schooldays and four times at weekends, when I had to do lunch too. I did them for two or three adults and thirteen children, and it was a dull job which took the best part of an hour each time. I hated the endless repetition, and I longed to be allowed to do something else. But I never was – the aunties insisted that was my job and I had to keep to it.

I also had to clean the locker area and the floors near the back door every evening. By the time all these chores were done there was very little time left before bed. And on top of our household jobs, every night we had to hand-wash our socks and underwear. There were two bathrooms, one for the boys and one for the girls. Each morning and evening we all had to queue outside, waiting for our turn to get washed. In the mornings it wasn't too bad: a quick face-wash and teeth-clean. But in the evening we had to wash ourselves and our socks, pants and vests too.

The auntie on duty would inspect them, and if one spot or mark was found, the child responsible had to do them again. If they still failed the 'spotless' test, the child was given a whole week of early bedtime. This meant that we each spent ages in the bathroom scrubbing away at our socks, while the others waited outside, impatient for their turn.

We all failed the 'spotless' test from time to time – it wasn't easy to get our socks perfectly clean, especially for the little ones. Sometimes they'd be in tears, after trying to get their washing clean and failing. We always felt sorry for one another and wanted to help, but we didn't dare. You just had to watch as Auntie Nan's eagle eye scanned the offending item of clothing and she barked at the quaking child to do it again. It happened to me a few times in those early days and I hated it. I learned to do my washing very carefully, so that I didn't get singled out.

All of the children, no matter what their ages, had to be in bed by 8.30 at the latest each night, seven nights a week. This, of course, was very tough on the older children of thirteen and fourteen, who had to go to bed with the five- and six-year-olds and then lie awake for hours. But the house rules were rigid, and no questioning was allowed.

I didn't mind the bedtime when I first arrived – at Ashbrooke Towers we'd had to go to bed even earlier, so 8.30 was fine for me. I was tired by that time, especially after an evening of washing up and cleaning.

Weekdays were always the same: school, followed in the evening by homework and chores. There was never time for us to go outside and play. I would hear the other children in the street playing games and sometimes I'd watch them through the windows. But only at weekends were we allowed outside to run free. That's when I would try to sneak away from the other children to be with Alan.

I had been a cautious little girl until then, always anxious about getting into trouble, but with Alan I became more adventurous. I loved going out to Bunny Hill with him, and escaping. We would tickle each other or hold each other tightly and roll down the hill until we couldn't hold on any longer and fell apart, yelling with laughter.

We both knew children were sent away for anything that broke the rules. And a boy and girl playing together definitely did that. So we were careful. We used to leave for school separately and then meet round the corner and walk the rest of the way together. We couldn't play together at school, where we were in separate classes, but we'd walk most of the way back together and then part round the corner. The other children knew we liked one another, but we managed to hide our school walks from them most of the time, because there were different routes to school and children left at different times.

One day, sitting on the hill looking up at the blue sky and fluffy white clouds, Alan took my hand, squeezed it and, looking at me with his clear blue eyes, said, 'When I'm grown up I'm going to marry you. So will you marry me?' I said, 'Yes I will, but you'll have to wait till we're grown up.' We shook hands on it and then, after checking to see that no one was looking, Alan kissed me. A quick, soft, innocent kiss, to seal the pact. My face went all hot and I felt suddenly shy.

72

From that moment on I felt somehow safe and secure. Knowing that someone cared for me, and was looking out for me, gave me confidence. I had been so insecure after all the changes in my life, but with Alan around I began to find a new confidence.

We used to sneak off on adventures. We'd run into the grounds of Hylton Castle and wander through the trees. It felt very magical and frightening, because we'd heard that the castle was haunted by the Cauld Lad of Hylton, a young stable boy who had been murdered by his master, Baron Hylton, three hundred and fifty years earlier. Beyond the castle we came to a stone bridge across a stream, which led into the bluebell woods. We felt so free in those woods, running about and laughing, picking flowers or lying on a bed of leaves, looking up at the branches. I used to think that the gentle rustling of the breeze in the leaves of the trees was the sound of fairies whispering. We dreamed of living in a little house among the trees and the bluebells. Safe and warm, and far away from aunties and chores.

Best of all was the tiny old church. It smelled musty and damp, but it was our secret place and we sat there for hours, watching the coloured light streaming through the stained glass windows.

In later years I would look back and think that, if I could have, I would have married Alan there and then in that little derelict church, hidden away in those magical woods.

We could never stay for as long as we wanted. We had no watches, so we had to guess what time it was and run back. The longer we stayed the faster we had to run. Sometimes when we got back the other children would ask where we had been, but we were always careful to arrive at different times to avoid suspicion and I would just say I had been playing on the hillside. At teatime Alan and I would look at one another, eyes shining, knowing that where we had been was our secret.

Some of the other children suspected, and at times they would pick on me, trying to find out about me and Alan. But I never told them. Neither of us talked to anyone about our adventures, knowing that if we did we would be in serious trouble.

One day Alan went out to play with the other boys and disappeared. No one realised he was missing till they came in for tea. Auntie Doris came and asked me if I knew where Alan was and this made me anxious – it meant that she knew he and I were close. I knew we would have to be more careful in the future, but at that moment all I could think about was that he was missing.

I went and sat on the windowsill in the playroom, behind the curtain, and looked out along the road, worrying that something had happened to him. It was getting dark, and the aunties stood outside the house, waiting, and sent two of the older children to the top of the road to see if he was there. When someone mentioned calling the police I began to feel frightened.

Sometime later there was a commotion in the living room. I ran in to see what was happening and there was Alan, looking as if he had been dragged through a hedge, he was in such a mess. Both the aunties had hold of him, trying to find out what had happened. He told them he had been captured on the hill by the Castlers. But the aunties were having none of it and took him upstairs for a beating, and I felt so sorry for him that I wanted to run and give him a hug, but I couldn't. He was banned from going out to play for a week, so I had to wait until we got a few moments on the windowsill behind the curtain before I could ask him to tell me the whole story. When I finally heard what had happened, I told him how brave I thought he was to escape.

After that some of the older boys declared war between the gangs. I joined in with them as it was the only way I could express what I really felt without anyone getting suspicious. On several occasions I fought the Castlers alongside the rest of the boys, and I gave my fair share of black eyes. As a result everyone decided I was a real tomboy and the other girls began to have less to do with me. I didn't mind this at the time, because I enjoyed playing with the boys, especially as Alan was there with them. But it was to have repercussions later, when I wanted to be friends with the girls and they rejected me.

Every now and then kids simply disappeared from Rennie Road. We knew they'd been sent to other homes, but it always happened so fast that they never even got the chance to say goodbye. Someone new would appear in their place, and life would go on, without a thing being said by the adults. But although on the surface there was barely a ripple as one child left and another came, underneath we all found it deeply upsetting. A child we had lived with for many months and played with every day would one afternoon just not be there any more. It was a threat we all lived with; any one of us could be taken away, goodness knows where to. We children were the nearest any of us got to having a family and we stuck together. It was shocking when one of us just vanished. For days afterwards the atmosphere would be muted.

Many times I grieved silently for lost friends. Along with the other children I would stare at the newly empty place at the table, willing the child to reappear while knowing they never would. We weren't allowed to ask the aunties where a child had gone – any question of that kind would be met with a fiercely disapproving look and a reprimand. All we could do was try to get used to the loss and hope the child who had left had gone somewhere nice. Sometimes I used to imagine that they went to good homes, with loving parents. The thought comforted me, though I knew it probably wasn't where they'd gone at all.

I coped with life in care by being a good girl. I was always anxious to keep things running smoothly, so I tried not to get into trouble and hated it when anyone else did. I was so desperate to keep the peace, and keep the aunties happy, that on one occasion I even confessed to a crime I hadn't committed. It happened one night when, after we were all asleep in bed, the lights were suddenly turned on and everyone was made to get up. All thirteen of us, still half-asleep and with no idea what on earth was going on, were lined up by a furious Auntie Doris.

'There is a thief in this house,' she shouted at the top of her voice. 'Someone has been into my room and stolen something.' She went to each child in turn, demanding to know if they were the culprit. In her hand was a slipper, and every child knew what that was for.

As child after child denied the crime, Auntie Doris began shouting about getting in the police. I was terrified; I knew the police would arrest you and throw you into the Cottage Homes. None of us knew then that the Cottage Homes had been closed, and kids all over town were still threatened with going there for many years afterwards. I imagined all of us, including Alan, locked away for ever. The idea was too much for me; I burst into tears and confessed to the crime.

'It was me, Auntie,' I sobbed. Alan stared at me, his mouth open in disbelief. Auntie came over to me and in a quiet voice loaded with menace, said, 'Well, what did you steal, Irene?' I stared at her, comprehension dawning, and was forced to whisper, 'I don't know.'

Auntie turned back to the others and glared at each one in turn. When she got to Snotty his cheeks burned red. He couldn't contain his guilt any longer and he confessed to taking jewellery and cash. He had got into her room after the cleaner had inadvertently left the door unlocked, and had hidden under the bed until she had gone.

He handed over his contraband, but it wasn't enough to save him. Soon the whack of a slipper and his wails were heard coming from Auntie's office. We all felt for him,

The next day Snotty appeared for breakfast looking downcast. That was the last time any of us saw him. By the time we all got in from school he had gone. At tea I looked at his empty place. Snotty was our friend, part of the gang. Surely he couldn't have just gone. Surely everyone was allowed a mistake – even a bad one like stealing – without their world being turned inside out. But the care world was harsh and extreme.

We all missed Snotty, but we weren't allowed to ask what had happened to him, or even to mention him again. We didn't talk about him much, even among ourselves. Somehow it seemed to hurt even more to talk about the person who had gone. Or perhaps it was just that we didn't dare, because we knew what the aunties would do if they found out.

The shockwaves from his disappearance took a few weeks to settle. But things brightened up a little as the summer holidays approached. The prospect of six weeks of freedom to go out and play every day cheered us all up. And once the holidays came the aunties were a little less vigilant – after our chores were done we were free to play until lunchtime, and again in the afternoon until tea. It was blissful, and Alan and I spent long, happy hours on Bunny Hill and managed to escape to the bluebell woods several times.

Towards the end of the holidays it was announced that we would be going to Whitby for a week. This caused huge excitement. A real holiday, travelling on a coach and then staying by the sea, sounded brilliant. We couldn't wait.

When the day came we piled on to a coach, along with children from the other local care homes. We passed the journey chatting excitedly and singing songs that were well known at the time, such as 'The Corporation Stores' and 'The Driver's Got a Lovely Pair of Legs'.

The camp where we stayed was situated just outside Staithes, a tiny fishing village just north of Whitby on the north Yorkshire coast. It was set at the top of a very steep hill, leading down to the village and the harbour, and consisted of a row of ex-army wooden huts that were used as dormitories: half for the girls, the other half for the boys, with one set aside for the aunties.

We had a wonderful time. Heady with the sea air and the joy of being free, we would climb the cliffs and play on the beach for hours on end. All the aunties seemed more relaxed and less inclined to bark orders, and apart from mealtimes and bedtime, we were mostly free.

We girls would all crowd into the tiny café, called the Igloo, where we would have fizzy drinks and listen to the juke box playing all the latest records. We felt really grown up, and it was exciting because back at Rennie Road we could never listen to records. But the time I enjoyed most was when I met up with Alan on the beach. Because we were allowed to play unsupervised, we were able to spend hours together. We would scamper around the fishing boats or walk along the beach, looking for crabs in the rock pools at low tide.

Sometimes we would find a pool that had been warmed by the sun and sit with our feet in it, watching families having picnics. Their children always seemed to be happy and laughing. We'd watch them run to the water and paddle, and when they ran back their mums would be waiting to rub them down with big towels and then feed them sandwiches. I always felt a little sad when I saw them. I couldn't help wishing that I could be wrapped in one of those big towels.

The only part of the holiday that I didn't like was the organised outings with the aunties. They would line all thirteen of us up and then march us along, one auntie at the front, the other at the back, so that everyone could see we were from the 'homes'. We had to stay in line and I'd see people watching us. It felt humiliating and I wanted to curl up in a ball. I'd stare straight ahead, cheeks burning, refusing to look at anyone.

Several times we were taken to Whitby and then allowed to roam the sea front. I loved everything about Whitby – the beaches, piers, boats, shops and arcades. All of us would rush in and spend our pocket money on rides, candy-floss and treats. If we saved our money for a couple of days we could afford fish and chips, which was the biggest treat of all.

Beyond the seafront lay the town's cobbled streets and little shops, and up on a hill at the top of a flight of 199 steps stood St Mary's Church, as if looking out to sea to watch for long-lost sailors.

Behind the church stood a ruined abbey. Alan and I would look up in awe at the great arches, which were still standing. We used to run through the graveyard looking for the pirate's grave we had been told about. We did find it, but the lettering was faded and hard to see so it was easy to lose, which only added to its mystery.

Back in the harbour we'd watch the fishing boats coming in, followed by screaming gulls. The fishermen would haul their catch out of the boats in crates, winching them up and on to the quayside. We'd gaze at the crates of fish and crabs, astonished because we'd never seen so many before. Alan was always very curious. He would talk to the fishermen and they would show him their nets and boats and tell him about life on the sea. Sometimes he was allowed to sit in their boats, and, face shining with pleasure, he would sit and ask them question after question.

Further along the quay there were large rowing boats for hire. People used to pack into them like sardines and off they went towards the piers, all of them excited and laughing.

Over the swing bridge and through the tiny cobbled streets we would find our way to a little beach beneath the fishermen's cottages. Once on this small beach we felt safe and, out of sight of the aunties and the other children, it became our special place, where we could disappear for hours. We'd spend the time playing in the sand or collecting shells along the shoreline. I used to think that one day Alan and I would come back to that beach, with no aunties to watch out for and no need to hide.

The old fisherman who sat by the quayside told us tales of vampires which Bram Stoker, author of *Dracula*, had written on that very beach. The old man warned us that on dark nights, when the moon was full, the vampires emerged from their graves to look for victims and drink their blood. We loved the stories and would squeal with pretend horror and then laugh. It was only when it grew dark that suddenly they seemed horribly real, and once or twice I lay in bed trying not to think about sharpened fangs sinking into my neck.

One day, on the beach at Staithes, we children were all crammed into a fishing boat and taken out to sea for a short trip. I wasn't sure about going in a boat, but I decided it was safe because we were all huddled together and there was a fisherman steering. But as we bobbed along what felt like a mile out to sea, someone suddenly shouted, 'There's water in the boat!'

Water was rapidly rising around our feet, and I began to panic. Most of the others did too – very few of us could swim and we thought we were all going to drown. I looked at Alan, who was white-faced but calm amid the chaos. I wished I could be with him, but he was on the other side of the boat.

The fisherman steered the boat to shore as fast as he could, which can't have been easy with a boat full of screaming children. It seemed to take a lifetime to get back, and by the time we did the water was past my ankles. Children were falling over each other as we all made a dash to get out. People had run down the beach, hearing all the cries, and were lifting wet children out of the boat. Most of us were in tears, soaking wet and shaking. After that day I developed a fear of deep water, and sadly it meant that I never learned to swim. And I wasn't alone – most of the children stayed clear of the boats from then on.

All too soon it was the last day of our holiday. The next day it would be back to Rennie Road, chores and school, so we were determined to make the most of our last few hours. Perhaps that's why Alan and I forgot how important it was to keep apart, in front of the aunties.

The two of us had been larking about on the beach and we were still laughing and teasing one another as we reached the entrance to the camp. Until then we'd always come back separately. But as we reached the first hut, Alan began to tickle me and I tickled him back. It became a tickle fight and we ended up rolling on the ground laughing, with me screaming.

If we hadn't been seen it would have been one more little childish incident. But our timing was tragic, because at that moment Auntie Nan came out of the door of the adults' hut. She spotted us on the ground and screamed at us to get up.

The second I looked up at her livid face I knew we'd made a terrible mistake. In that moment I would have given anything to undo the last few minutes. But it was too late. Auntie Nan grabbed me and clipped me hard across the face, shouting that it wasn't ladylike to be on the ground with a boy. Then she pulled me away and into the hut.

I was shocked. She had never slapped me before. Sitting on my bed, holding my face in my hands, I heard her shouting at Alan and worried that he would get a severe beating. 'We were only playing,' I whispered.

Surely Auntie Nan wouldn't do anything too mean to Alan. We were on holiday, and it was just a game that went a bit too far. Surely she would understand that. I prayed he would get away with a few whacks of the slipper or some extra chores when we got back.

But as I lay in bed that night, my face still smarting, even in my worst imaginings I couldn't have known that what would happen would tear our world apart.

7

Alan

Our holiday was like seven days of non-stop happiness, when almost all the usual rules were suspended.

On our first full day there I had a surprise – my two older brothers were there too. All the children's homes in the area sent their children to the camp, so those kids with brothers and sisters in care were reunited. I was very glad to see Michael and George. Inevitably, perhaps, we'd all got used to being apart, so there was no great reunion: I just remember the odd occasion when we got together to play on the beach and it was good to be with them.

Most of the time, I was with Irene. We used to wander, hand in hand, down the tiny backstreets of Staithes and watch the old sailors carving out sea urchins to sell to visitors. I was fascinated by the urchins' hard, sharp outer shells which had the same colourings as starfish. We would walk down a very narrow alley that ran behind the sailors' cottages to where an old man sat on a little stool in a tiny back garden behind his cottage. All around him lay seashells, bits of rope, lobster pots and netting. He made small model sailing ships out of wood and bits of canvas, and put them inside bottles. The ships sat all around his garden and on his windowsills, waiting to go into the bottles, where they sat on stormy seas.

He would never show us the trick of getting a full-masted ship, with all its sails unfurled, into a tiny bottle. I found that out years later, but back then, when I was seven and stood watching the old man work, I thought it was a kind of magic.

Irene and I would sit and watch the creek filling with water as the tide came in. When it was deep enough, the fishermen would take their boats out for a day's catch. Sometimes they let us hold the nets or the lobster pots while they were repaired by an old salt with a white beard. And all the while he would be telling us yarns about the sea, tales of Davy Jones's locker and pirate treasure.

For several years, I'd had a recurring dream in which I was being chased by faceless shadows down a dark tunnel. I found that if I imagined it hard enough a secret door would open in the tunnel wall and I could slip through to the other side. There the sky was pure blue and white clouds were tinged with gold from the sun's rays and the grass was greener than any I'd ever seen. The door would close behind me and the shadows chasing me would disappear. The feeling I had in that magical place was pure joy – I felt warm and safe from the outside world. And that's how I felt when I was on holiday that week with Irene.

In Whitby we'd hang around the amusement arcades, or walk over the swing bridge and along the narrow cobbled streets until we reached 'our beach' on the south side of the harbour. Here it was quiet and there were few people, so we would play in the sand and pick up shells along the shoreline, revelling in being far from the watchful gaze of the aunties.

One afternoon Irene decided to go to the tiny Igloo café in Staithes with some of the girls, to listen to the latest music being played on the juke box, while I went off on a jaunt with my brothers. Hoping for a bit of fun on the quayside, the three of us headed down the very steep bank that led to the harbour. On our way down we met some of the other boys. One of them shouted that he had seen a girl up on the north cliff, about a hundred feet above us. Another boy said it was Irene and she was going to jump! I couldn't believe what I was hearing. I looked up to the cliff and I could see the girl near the edge. She was too far away for us to see who she was.

Michael started running, followed by George and then me, heading up to the little bridge that crossed the creek and up the road leading to the cliffs. My heart was pounding as we made our way to the cliff top. It was a long way, so it took some time. We had to go across fields and allotments, getting chased on the way by a farmer who was shouting and shaking his fist at us as we ran through his vegetable patch. But all I could think of was Irene. 'It can't be,' I was thinking over and over. 'It just can't be.'

Eventually, exhausted, we reached the top and ran to the edge, where the girl was still standing. And I thanked God when I realised it wasn't my Irene. It was a girl from another children's home, a girl of about nine years old. We knew her little brother, as he was in Rennie Road with us. They had both been through a hard time before they came into care, but we couldn't imagine what terrible trauma had hurt her so badly that she wanted to leave this world.

Michael reached her first. When she saw him, she threw herself towards the edge. But Michael dived forward and, with a kind of rugby tackle, grabbed her legs. They both slid over the edge, down a short incline, towards the sheer drop no more than three feet away, when George hurled himself at them and grabbed Michael's legs. That stopped them both from sliding any further, and I got there next and grabbed George's feet. We all hung on for dear life as the girl started kicking and screaming for us to let her go. There was no way we were going to do that, but we weren't strong enough to pull her back up the incline and on to the cliff top and away from danger. As we hung on, I tried not to look over the edge to the terrifying sight of the jagged rocks and the sea below.

A minute later the breathless old farmer got there and, seeing what was happening, slid down on his backside and grabbed one of Irene's flailing arms. Then a policeman arrived, probably alerted by allotment holders thinking we were vandals. He took off his helmet, slid down and got hold of Irene's other arm and between all of us we got her back. She calmed down as she was led back across the fields by the policeman, while we boys got our breath back and patted one another on the backs for a job well done.

Sadly, we knew it was likely that the girl would try to do away with herself again. We had all heard that she had made several suicide attempts at the home where she lived, and it seemed that, despite being so young, she was utterly determined to leave this world. When we got back down to the harbour we met her brother, who was only five or six years old, and told him what had happened. He burst into tears and ran away, and we never saw him or his sister again for the rest of the holiday.

I was proud of my brothers that day and saw them as brave heroes. They hadn't hesitated to help, despite the danger to themselves.

By the time the last day of the holiday came we'd had a wonderful time and felt sad at the idea of going back. Irene and I managed a last visit to the beach, and were just arriving back at the huts when we started our tickle fight. It was so innocent, just two kids fooling around and having a good time. But when Auntie Nan caught us, all hell broke loose.

We'd forgotten the rules, and now we would pay for it. We were sent off to our respective dormitories, and a little later Auntie Nan told me in no uncertain manner that I was forbidden to go near any of the girls, especially Irene. This was reinforced with the usual clout around the lug.

There was only a day left before we returned to Rennie Road, and I wasn't able to get close enough to talk to Irene during that time.

I went off to play on the beach with some of the boys, but I didn't know then that some of the other kids were being interrogated, by the aunties, about just how close Irene and I really were.

On the coach home, all the children were singing 'Show Me the Way to Go Home' but I didn't feel like joining in. I stared out of the window, feeling sad and a little frightened. Would this mean that I couldn't play with Irene again? Would the aunties make us keep apart? I prayed it would all be forgotten soon and that Irene and I would be able to slip off to the woods again, for another adventure.

When we got back we were all kept busy unpacking and preparing to go back to school. Under the aunties' watchful eyes Irene and I could only exchange the occasional sympathetic glance with one another.

Monday morning came, and as we all got ready for school I felt more cheerful. With any luck I would be seeing Irene on the way, as usual. Once we were out of the aunties' sight we could meet up and walk together. But just before it was time to leave, Auntie Nan took me aside and told me to go and wait in the playroom. 'Stay there until I come for you,' she ordered.

In the playroom I sat, looking out of the window as the other children left for school, wondering what was going to happen. Were they still angry about me playing with Irene? Was I in for a beating? But why keep me off school for that?

I saw Irene wave at me as she headed down the road. How I wished I could be with her, chatting and swinging my school bag instead of stuck here in the playroom all alone. I'd never been put in a room and kept there like this before. I waited and waited, but no one came in to check on me. I put my ear to the door and I could hear the cleaner getting on with her tasks and the aunties chatting in the background, though I couldn't make out what they were saying.

After what felt like an age but was probably an hour or two, I saw an old black car with big headlights drive slowly up the street and stop outside the front door. Suddenly, in a moment of shock, it dawned on me what was about to happen. We all knew what it meant when a black car turned up. Someone was going to be taken away. And this time it was me.

I felt scared and desperate. They couldn't – surely they couldn't – take me away from Irene. I didn't mind if they beat me or put me to bed or gave me extra chores for a year, if only they didn't send me away.

A grey-haired lady, smartly dressed in a tweed suit, stepped out of the car and walked the few steps to the front door. She came into the house and I heard her talking to the aunties. I sat, frozen to the spot, waiting, desperate for it not to be true.

I jumped when the door was suddenly opened. Auntie Nan came in and said, 'Come along.' She led me from the house, opened the back door of the car and nodded to me to get in. I wanted to cry and shout and beg her to keep me, but one look at her stern face told me it would be hopeless. Numbly I climbed into the car, while Auntie Nan went back in and came out with a couple of paper bags, which she put in the boot. Then, without saying a word or even looking at me, she turned on her heels and walked back into the house, pausing only for a moment to say something to the grey-haired lady, before closing the door behind her.

The lady got in and drove off, and as we went around the corner I turned and saw the house disappear, and with it my whole world. All I could think about was Irene. She wouldn't know where I was. How was I going to tell her where I was?

The lady was chatting pleasantly. She told me to call her Matron and asked if I knew where I was going. I told her that I didn't and she said, 'You're coming to live with me.' Even though I had guessed that I was leaving, her words stunned me. I didn't want to go and live with her; I already lived at Rennie Road.

My insides were knotted into a tight ball and I felt panicky. I wanted to bang on the car window and beg her to take me back. But I had learned to hide my feelings from the adults in charge, as it only ever led to more punishments. I wasn't going to show them how much it hurt. So I sat quite still, staring out of the window, not hearing anything the lady said as she chatted on.

My mind was racing. I had to remember where we were going, so that I could find my way back to Irene. We crossed the river heading south and went through the town centre. But after that there were so many windings and crossings that, hard as I tried, I couldn't memorise the route. I didn't know the places we were passing, and we were going such a long way. I could feel a terrible pain rising in me but I kept pushing it back down, determined not to let anyone see.

I felt as if I was falling into a black hole. My safe and secret world with Irene was slipping away with every mile and I began to feel vulnerable and raw. The child who left Rennie Road that day was gone by the time we reached our destination. I fell into being someone else, a darker version of myself, full of anger and bitterness towards the aunties and uncles who always brought pain in their wake, and I determined to get them back in some way.

Eventually we arrived outside a large house with steps leading up to a big front door. The grey-haired lady led me in. 'This house is called The Esplanade,' she said. 'This is where you'll be living from now on. We've several other boys – you'll meet them when they come in from school.' She was nice enough, but I didn't care. I didn't want to be in this place, such a long way from Irene and everything that was familiar in Rennie Road. Why did I have to be taken away? Was it just for the tickle fight with Irene? How I wished I could turn back time and undo that.

Matron showed me around the house. It was a four-storey Victorian terraced house that was rather grand; the type of house that's often used today as a doctor's or dentist's surgery or has been converted into flats.

On the first floor was a room for the new boys, and this was where I was to sleep, with two other recent arrivals. The very top floor was for the older boys, the middle floor for the younger ones. So as you got older you would move from the new boys' room to the second and then the third floor. On the ground floor there were offices and a large room with a full-size billiard table in the centre which, I was to discover, was never ever used. And down in the basement there was a large kitchen and a dining room, with five or six small round tables and a hatch through to the kitchen.

I was told to put my things away and go and wait in the back garden. It was a warm day, and I sat under a tree and tried to think about what Irene would be doing in school. How I wished I was with her.

Over tea, I was introduced to the other boys. There were about twelve of them; the youngest seemed about my age, the oldest fourteen or fifteen. They were friendly, but I didn't want new friends. I was silent and withdrawn and went through the motions of eating without really noticing my surroundings. I was still in a state of shock about being in this strange place.

That night I lay in my new bed and thought about Irene. I would find her again. I had to. She wouldn't know where I had gone and she'd worry. I needed to tell her that I hadn't wanted to go or run away, but they had taken me from her.

That's when the pain came. It felt as if something inside me was broken, and there was an ache that went deep down, a pain so bad that I didn't know how to hold it in. I sobbed into my pillow for a long time, but the pain didn't feel any better. I had found a special person in the world, a friend like no other, and they had taken me from her. Nothing would ever be the same.

I didn't know it then, but that indescribable pain of loss burned a furrow in me that it would take a lifetime to fill. A physical wound might have healed, in time, but this was a wound to my spirit that was to affect me deeply for many years to come.

Eventually I fell into a restless sleep, full of frightening dreams. The next morning I woke and for a few seconds, before I opened my eyes, I forgot where I was and believed I would get up and see Irene at breakfast, then walk with her to school as usual.

The reality of this new bed, in a new room, in a new home, hit me like a thump in the stomach. Like a little robot I got dressed and was taken to my new school in the town centre with some of the other boys. Yet another school, with new teachers and kids, and a new routine to get used to. I hadn't minded the last school, because Irene was there, but I hated this school.

I stared vacantly out of the window for most of the day, hearing very little of what the teacher said. At break time I wandered around the edge of the playground, alone. I didn't care about making friends or being good any more. I didn't care about anything except getting back to Irene.

Over the next few days I gradually got used to the new routines and people in my life. Matron was a warm woman and all the children loved her. Most of them looked upon her as someone you could always talk to, and she genuinely loved them. Her husband, Uncle Kennedy, also worked in The Esplanade. The two of them were senior carers in the system, who supervised other homes as well as ours, but they were about as different from one another as you could imagine. Uncle Kennedy was a very strict disciplinarian who laid down the law, which in his book was based on antiquated Victorian proverbs such as 'Little boys should be seen and not heard', 'Speak when you are spoken to' and 'Spare the rod and spoil the child'.

He certainly didn't spare the rod. Any transgression was met with a beating, though his weapon of choice varied and might be his hand or a slipper, followed by the cane, depending upon his mood and the nature of the offence. I disliked him, as did most of the other kids.

It was a strange system Matron and Uncle Kennedy had between them. He would beat you for some minor offence and then order you to your room, and Matron would then slip you some food and a comforting word. And I soon had plenty of experience of both.

Something in me had snapped when they took me away from Irene, and it affected everything I did from then on. I stopped caring what happened to me, and I became disruptive and determined not to co-operate. I had been doing well in school but now I began to fail, and in the home I refused to eat all my food, do all my chores or do as I was told.

A couple of weeks after I had arrived at The Esplanade I decided I couldn't wait any longer. That night I lay quietly in bed until I hoped everyone was asleep, before quietly getting dressed and climbing out through the bathroom window. I had no idea how I would do it, but somehow I was going to find my way back to Irene.

8

Irene

On the first morning back at school after our holiday, I got into my uniform and ran down to breakfast, happy because I knew Alan and I could meet on the way to school and walk together. I hadn't been able to speak to him since we'd left Whitby and it seemed like an age.

After breakfast, as I was going into the kitchen to wash up, I heard Auntie Nan tell Alan to wait in the playroom. I wondered what was up, but I couldn't ask. I did the dishes, got ready for school and left with the others.

As I walked away from the house I turned and saw Alan sitting by the window in the playroom. Somehow he looked different; his face seemed pale and sad. I waved to him, and he waved back. He must have to go to the doctor or something like that, I thought. Sometimes the kids did have to stay off school for an appointment. I would see him later.

The morning passed, and at lunchtime I headed back to the house with the other children. We sat down to eat, but Alan wasn't there. I was a little uneasy but not too worried. He would be there at teatime.

But when teatime came there was still no sign of him. Alan's chair was empty, and the other children glanced towards it before looking quickly away, as if something would happen to them if they looked for too long. I was feeling cold and empty and found it hard to eat my tea. I felt a kind of panic setting in. Was he gone? Had he been whisked away, with no goodbyes, like Snotty and the others before him? He couldn't have just gone. Not Alan. Surely not just for the tickle fight?

I wanted to ask Auntie Doris, who was in charge that evening. But I knew I could get both myself and Alan into trouble if I did, so I waited, hoping that he would reappear. As soon as we'd finished tea and I'd washed up, I went into the playroom, sat on our windowsill and pulled the curtain around me. Was Alan ill? Perhaps he'd had to go to hospital. If only Auntie Doris would say, but she behaved as though everything was perfectly normal and Alan had never existed.

I waited all evening, but there was no Alan. That night I lay in bed, praying that he wasn't gone for ever, waiting for the morning, hoping he would come back in the night. But the next morning his chair was empty again at breakfast.

By the time I got back from school that day, with still no sign of Alan, I knew I had to ask. I didn't care about getting into trouble any more. I missed him so much. I had to know where he was. So I asked Auntie Doris. She looked a little surprised, and then said, rather curtly, 'He has been adopted in Whitby and he won't be coming back.' And with that she turned and walked briskly away, to show me that the matter was closed and I must not ask anything more.

I felt hot and cold and sick, all at the same time. Alan had gone. For ever. My friend, my special friend, the one who made me laugh and feel brave and happy, had been taken away. And to Whitby. I knew I could never get that far. I would never see him again. I felt as if a part of me had been ripped out.

I wanted to run after Auntie Doris and cry in her arms. But she would have pushed me away. She wasn't an unkind person, but she never touched the children. So I turned and ran into the playroom, past the other children, over to the windowsill where Alan and I had sat together so many times, and pulled the curtains around me. Hugging my knees, I sat and cried, struggling to keep quiet so that no one would hear. I knew that if they realised how upset I was, the aunties would dismiss my feelings and tell me it was nonsense, and the other children would tease me.

I told myself that if he had been adopted that meant a family had wanted him. And he loved Whitby: he would be happy there, around the fishing boats and the beach. I wondered if it was someone we'd met on our holiday who had asked to take him.

I pictured Alan playing on the boats and staring out to sea with those clear blue eyes. I thought about all those good times we'd had together. And I told myself that, come what may, one day I would go to Whitby and see him again.

I tried to be happy for him. But from the moment he went, the days seemed dark and bleak. Each passing day was just like the last, as I struggled through school and my chores. A few times I went to the top of the hill, but I could never bring myself to go down it. I would watch the other kids run down the hill and play, and I could see the castle below, with the bluebell woods beyond. But it had all lost its magic with Alan no longer there.

I didn't want to play with anyone else. It felt as if my world had ended and nothing would make it better. For weeks after he left I waited for the time when my chores were done each day and I could creep on to the windowsill, rest my chin on my knees and think about Alan. I hoped that somehow he might suddenly reappear. Perhaps he wouldn't like being adopted, and they'd let him come back. I missed him so badly. But as the days dragged into weeks I began to realise that he really wasn't coming back. He had gone.

The other children, especially the boys, would taunt me, chanting, 'Alan's gone, Alan's gone, he's not coming ba-ack.' Furious and trying to hold back tears, I hit out at some of them. The taunting eventually stopped, but most of them stayed away from me after that. The girls had already lost interest, because of my tomboy ways and the amount of time I had spent with Alan, and they made no effort to play with me after he had gone so I spent most of my time on my own.

It was a bleak and desperate time for me. Try as I might to be happy that Alan had a new family, I felt so abandoned, as if I was the one nobody wanted.

My misery was made worse by a trip to the dentist a couple of weeks after Alan left. The dentist was a large man and very bad tempered. He sat me in the chair and forced my head painfully back with one hand, while using the other to pull the bright light on a stand close to my face. I panicked and jumped up, knocking into the big light, which toppled over on to the floor and broke. Furious, he slapped me hard across the face. I ran from the room in tears, with my face stinging, only to get another sharp slap from Auntie Doris for being disruptive. After that my phobia about going to the dentist never really went away.

My fear extended to our annual medical check-up, which was to happen soon after. This was a grim business, which all of us children hated. We were driven across town to a large Victorian house called The Esplanade, where the girls were led into one room and the boys into another. We were made to strip to our knickers and, with no gowns to cover us, form a line outside the door of another room, where the doctor was conducting the examinations. It was cold and embarrassing waiting in line, our bare feet freezing on the institutional brown lino. We stood, clasping our arms over our chests, waiting for our names to be called out.

Once inside the examination room I was asked to stand in the middle of the floor as the doctor poked a cold metal instrument into my ears, looked at my eyes, felt under my arms and listened to my chest and back with his freezing stethoscope. It made me feel like a specimen in a jar – something to be poked and prodded. I hated it, and I felt sorry for the older girls who, with all the self-consciousness of puberty, found it humiliating.

I had no idea that there were two Esplanade buildings, the first where we were being examined and the second, across the road, a children's home, where Alan had been taken. If only I could have known how close he was, I could have found a way to leave him a note, or hide and try to see him. But of course I didn't know and so, after a couple of hours, we were piled back into the mini-bus and driven back to Rennie Road.

I didn't dare tell anyone how empty and lonely and miserable I felt without Alan. I thought about him a hundred times a day, wishing every time that he would come back. I tried to imagine him with a family that really loved him, in our favourite place, Whitby. And I thought how no one could want to be with him more than I did.

I promised myself that the following summer, if we were taken back there on holiday, I would find him. That idea took root and was the only thing that kept me going. I would find Alan, and together we would run on the beach and feel the sun on our faces and laugh and be happy again.

9

Alan

Once I'd got out of The Esplanade I set off in the direction of town, trying to retrace the route we had taken from Rennie Road. I walked all through the night, avoiding policemen and main roads and often ending up down back lanes or in gardens. I spent the next day wandering about looking for landmarks I'd seen from the car. But I ended up completely lost. By the end of that day I had walked several miles and I wandered into a small village just outside town and close to the river.

I was tired and cold but still determined to carry on. That night I lay under a tree and watched the stars until I fell asleep. Early the next day I set off again, following the river. I hadn't eaten for thirty-six hours and I was terribly hungry. I began to imagine eating big hot pies followed by cream-filled cakes.

Suddenly, crossing some fields, I spotted in the distance the tower of the castle at the bottom of Bunny Hill. I was so excited. But I was on the wrong side of the river and had no idea how to get across.

I kept walking, hoping to find a bridge, and towards the end of the day I came to the little hamlet of Coxgreen and saw a footbridge across the river. As it was getting dark I crawled into some bushes and hid for the night, though I barely slept because I was so cold and hungry.

99

In the early hours of the morning, before dawn had broken, it began to rain heavily. Soaked through and bitterly cold I walked across the bridge to another small village. Although it was still dark I could hear people in the houses I passed, preparing for the day ahead.

Suddenly a car pulled up beside me. I hadn't heard it because of the rain. It was one of the little Minis used by the police in those days. A policeman got out and said, 'What's a small boy doing out at a time like this, and in this weather? Would you like a lift?'

I couldn't say no. He was a policeman, and you had to do what they said. He'd no doubt guessed I must be the missing boy, so I was bundled into the back of the car and taken off to the police station, where they dried me out and sat me behind the desk and fed me their spare sandwiches and hot tea. I was asked lots and lots of questions. Where have you been? Why did you run away? Did anybody talk to you? Where did you stay? On and on it went, but I said nothing, just crammed the sandwiches into my mouth and gulped at the tea.

After a while I was put in the Mini again and driven back to The Esplanade. When we arrived, Uncle Kennedy was waiting on the steps for me. He took me by the ear and led me straight to his office, where he gave me a vicious beating and then sent me to bed. After a while Matron came in with a hot meal and tea. She spent some time talking to me, trying to find out why I'd run away. But how could I tell her? She did seem to care, but I was trying to get back to Irene and this was forbidden. I knew I would be in even more trouble if I talked. So I just said, 'I don't know.' I think Matron was very sad that I wouldn't tell her what was really happening, but in the end she gave up and left me to sleep.

It wasn't long before I set off again, and this time I was ready. It was a cold day in December, but I had gone to school wearing a jumper and a mac to keep me dry and warm. I'd saved some pocket money instead of buying sweets, and I had some bread I'd sneaked on to my lap at tea the day before and wrapped in a piece of old paper. I'd got everything I needed. So after school, instead of going back with the other boys to The Esplanade, I slipped away.

I made my way along the same route I'd taken the first time, but this time I was much quicker because I knew where I was going. I spent my first night out across the river from the village of Coxgreen. It was bitter cold but at least it didn't rain. I was dry and I had my bread.

On the second day I was much more cautious. I made my way through the village, but this time sticking to backstreets. I ended up in the countryside again, and crossed several fields, heading in the direction of Hylton Castle but keeping out of sight behind hedges and trees. By evening I was very hungry and very cold. My bread was long gone, and although I had a little money I was nowhere near any shops. I decided to walk on through the night, and at about two in the morning I reached the Castle. Just beyond it, vast in the moonlight, lay Bunny Hill.

I was exhausted, but so happy. I'd made it! I climbed the hill in the dark, and after fumbling around a bit I found the slits leading into the air-raid shelter. I didn't look for the big end, because I wasn't sure I could find it in the dark, and I didn't want to get stung by the nettles again. My plan was to slip in there and wait until morning, then head down to the road and catch Irene on her way to school. The thought of seeing her was so wonderful. I could finally explain what had happened. She would know I hadn't wanted to go.

I squeezed into the shelter through the slits as I had done so many times before. But this time I almost got stuck. I'd grown since the last time I was here. Once in, I curled up on the concrete floor in a dark corner away from the draught by the slits, trying to keep warm, because by this time it was snowing. I nodded off once or twice but hunger and cold woke me. Slowly, as it got lighter, I could hear the odd early bus on the main road. Then I heard the distant noise of the newsagent's at the bottom of the hill opening. My hunger and the bitter cold got the better of me so I decided to go down to the shop and spend my money on something to eat while I waited the last few hours to catch Irene at the bus stop.

I squeezed out through the slits again and headed down the hill, stiff with cold, my teeth chattering. I walked into the shop and began looking around. The shopkeeper had his eye on me, so I decided to hurry. I grabbed a packet with 'strawberry' written on it. I wasn't sure what it was, but it looked yummy.

Once I'd paid for it I walked around the back of the shop, to get out of sight, and opened my strawberry sweet. I took a bite, but it tasted rubbery and not very nice. I was so hungry that I kept chomping and got it all down; it was only much later that I realised I'd bought uncooked strawberry jelly.

When I'd finished I decided to walk to the bus stop and wait for Irene. But as I rounded the corner of the shop, two policemen were coming towards me. The shopkeeper must have called them. Distraught, I looked around, hoping to escape, but they grabbed hold of me. As they hauled me towards their waiting car and shoved me inside, I fought and screamed and shouted with frustration.

In the car, with all hope of escape gone, I sat on the back seat in a small, crumpled, grubby heap, my hands over my face, and sobbed. Irene would be coming soon. She would walk past this spot. And I would miss her. She wouldn't know that I had got here and waited for her. She wouldn't know where I was, or that I had wanted to see her so badly. My heart broke.

I was driven to the police station, where, once again, I was given hot tea and sandwiches, though I couldn't eat them.

'What were you up to, lad?' one of the policemen asked me. But I wouldn't say. No one was going to tear my secret from me. I sat, silent and tear-stained, until they took me out to the car and drove me back to The Esplanade.

Uncle Kennedy looked triumphant when he saw me. As soon as the policeman who took me to the door had gone, he hauled me by my collar into his study and began lashing me with a slipper. He didn't stop until he'd tired himself out, and I hurt so much that I could barely crawl up the stairs to bed.

A little while later Matron came in with a hot drink. I had pulled the covers over my head, hoping to find oblivion in the darkness. She sat on the side of my bed and asked me, in a gentle voice, why I had run away. 'Were you going back to your old home?' she said. 'Why would you want to go there? Aren't you happy with us?'

I wasn't telling. Matron tried again, but after a while, with no response from me, she gave up and left me. I lay, aching, bruised and heart-sore, thinking of Irene. 'I'll find her,' I whispered to myself. 'I won't give up.'

I never stopped trying, and would make many more attempts, but they knew now where I was heading so I was always caught long before I got there. I spent many nights sleeping in fields, or garden sheds when it was too cold or wet to sleep out in the open. And every time I was brought back Uncle was waiting for me with his slipper.

Around this time my older brother Michael arrived at The Esplanade.

We hadn't seen one another since the holiday in Whitby, over a year and a half earlier. It was good to see him, but he was four years older than me and his interests and friends were very different from mine, so we never got close. In any case I was always in trouble with Uncle Kennedy and anyone close to me tended to get trouble from him too. But one day Michael did something I never forgot. He was coming down the stairs just as Uncle was giving me yet another beating, and Michael lost his temper and shouted for Uncle to leave me alone. 'You're always picking on him,' he yelled. They ended up swapping blows, until Matron intervened and pulled Michael away. I was left open-mouthed at his courage and my admiration for him grew. I knew he would get a beating for it later. But after that he declared that I had got him into trouble and told me to stay away from him. I didn't blame him for that.

One day, not long after Michael stood up for me, I was playing with friends after school when I realised I'd be late back to the home again. We boys from The Esplanade were supposed to go straight back after school; we weren't allowed to stay and play or go to friends' houses. But when all the other kids started playing, I wanted to join in. I'd plan to stay for just a few minutes and then leg it back. The trouble was, I often lost track of time.

Occasionally, when I realised I was late again, rather than face another beating I'd follow my friends home and sleep in their garden sheds and they would smuggle bits of food out of the house to feed me.

This time I decided to run back in the hope that if I was fast enough I might get let off. I went full speed ahead, and when I came to one of the busy roads in town I flew across it. Bang! The bumper of a very large van hit me right between the eyes. I was dragged beneath it and bumping along the road. Then the rear wheel hit my head and out I popped at the other end.

Apparently the driver never saw me. The bumpers on those old vans were head-height to a young boy, and the traffic was busy and noisy on that corner on that day, so he didn't even realise he had hit me.

Perhaps it was the shock, but I didn't feel a thing. I stood up and looked around, in a daze. A group of women were standing outside a shop calling to me to come over. I lurched over to them and they sat me down in the shop, while one asked my name and another offered me sweets. My head felt wet and clammy as I sat sucking on a sweet and I heard bells in the distance – the familiar ding-a-ling, ding-a-ling sound the ambulances and police cars used to use.

I must have passed out, because I woke up in hospital some time later. My head had been split open from top to nose. It had to be stitched up and wrapped in a big white bandage and I had a ferocious headache for several weeks.

I don't remember how long I was in hospital, or if anyone visited me, but when I got back to The Esplanade I was kept off school for several weeks. I spent most of my time playing, and watching Uncle Kennedy's friend Jack make musical boxes out of mahogany in the little shed at the bottom of the garden. He used to carve elaborate patterns in the wood, fit the hinges and insert the little musical mechanism in one corner, so that when you lifted the lid it would start playing.

Sometimes I would help the cook, picking fresh mint from the big bush outside the kitchen door or peeling potatoes for her. I also made friends with a boy who lived next door.

When he was there he would shout over the fence and I would squeeze through the bushes and spend an hour playing with him and his collection of toy guns. His mum or dad would bring us soft drinks as a treat. One day he offered to lend me a large realistic-looking machine-gun he had. His mum was there and she nodded approval so, overjoyed, I squeezed back through the hedge with it. It wasn't too long before Uncle Kennedy grabbed me by the ear and led me into his office, where he accused me of stealing the toy and gave me a sound beating with the slipper.

It was Matron who made him stop; she was concerned as I still had my head bandaged. So Uncle grabbed me by the ear again and, taking the toy gun, led me next door to return it to its owner.

When the boy's mum answered, Uncle handed it to her and said, 'This lad stole the gun. He's come to apologise.'

'He didn't steal it,' she replied. 'We lent it to him. Didn't he tell you that?'

Uncle looked startled. 'Well, erm, he did say something, but these kids are all liars,' he muttered.

'Well, he's not,' she said. 'He was telling the truth, and you should have believed him.'

Furious and red-faced, Uncle dragged me back to the home and forbade me to go next door ever again. But from that day on the mum next door was my heroine, and I wished I could move in with her. Although I couldn't go over any more, sometimes she would peep over the hedge and smile at me, and it lit up my day.

When they eventually took the bandages off, I could see the shape of my head had changed and it was pointy at the top. Fortunately, because I was still young enough to be a little soft-boned, it had squashed a bit during the accident rather than cracked. But the result left me looking a bit like a pixie.

One Saturday a few weeks after I went back to school, there was a knock at the door. A ginger-haired lady came in and stood talking to Matron for quite some time. Then I was sent for. I wondered if I was in trouble, because I usually was. I couldn't think why – I didn't know the lady.

Matron told me she was my 'new mother' and she was taking me out for the day. I was cross – I only had one mother, so how could this woman be my new mother? But my upset was quickly forgotten when she told me that my dad was waiting to see me at home. This was amazing news and I became very excited. Was I really going to see him again? I hadn't seen him since he'd passed the Cottage Homes on his bike a few years earlier. I'd wondered so many times where he was, and why he didn't come for me. Now here was this lady I didn't know, saying she'd take me to him.

I pulled on my coat and headed for the door, anxious to get out before anyone could change their mind. The lady, who said her name was Anita, was short and rounded, with a pale face and ginger hair down past her shoulders. It turned out that Matron had recognised her, as she had been in care too. Matron smiled a lot while they talked, so I had the impression she liked her.

We walked for about half an hour, during which Anita spoke very little. We went down to an old part of town and a row of ramshackle houses and Dad appeared at the door of one of them. I was overjoyed to see him and I wanted to run into his arms, but I was shy and hung back. Dad looked just the same as when I'd last seen him: he grinned at me and said, 'Aye aye, son,' and took me inside.

In the front room there was a little girl, running about shouting, and a baby girl in a cot in the corner. Dad said they were called Sonia and Yvonne and they were my half-sisters. This was a big surprise. While my brothers and I had been gone, Dad had got another family. But the little girls were sweet, and it felt nice, if a little strange, to have sisters.

This Saturday outing became a regular event for many weeks. Anita would come and collect me and take me to the house, where Dad would be waiting. Sonia was always shouting, and Yvonne used to hang on to the bars of her playpen and smile at me. Most times I just played outside with marbles or a football. But it was a lot better than being at the home, and I was glad to see Dad.

Once or twice Michael and George came on these visits too. It was great for us all to be together but inevitably, given how much time we'd spent apart, there was a distance between us now. George had been fostered by a German woman, though it was many years later that he told me about the severe beatings she used to give him. Only Brian was missing. We had no word about where he was, and if Dad knew anything about his whereabouts he never said.

At Dad's, George and Michael would stick together and spend most of their time playing football in the street, while I stayed in the back yard, feeling that I was somehow in the way. Dad never seemed to be very enthusiastic about me coming over and it put a strain on Anita. Dad was unemployed again, and having to feed us, even just for one day, was hard. And sometimes it seemed as if there was a tug-of-war going on between Dad and Anita over whether he gave attention to her and the girls or us boys.

Once or twice I got to meet Anita's brother John, who was a miner and a motorbike enthusiast. I loved watching as he stripped down his bike in the back yard, then reassembled it, leaving oil everywhere. He'd rev the engine to test that all was well, and it set the girls off screaming every time. Anita would start shouting at him to stop the noise and clean up the mess, but he never did.

Much later Anita told me that she and John had lived in London before the war. Their parents had been killed and they'd been evacuated to Sunderland and put into care.

I looked forward to my Saturday visits all week. I had my dad and my brothers back again at last and I stopped running away, because I didn't want to give Uncle Kennedy an excuse to stop me going.

One day Dad came in with a fishing rod and asked if I'd like to go fishing. Would I! So off we went with Uncle John to fish under the town bridge.

It was a noisy place, with the sounds of the traffic rumbling over the bridge eighty feet above us and the clacking of the riveters' guns from the shipyards around us. But Dad told me it was the best place to fish when it was raining, as we had shelter and the fish would shelter under the bridge too! He showed me how to bait my hook and to use the hand line, and I sat on the edge with my feet dangling, line in hand, for hours.

After that we went fishing most Saturdays. These were great days out for me, going on an adventure with my dad. What I didn't realise then was that, far from just having fun, we were actually fishing through necessity, for food. Dad was out of work again and the dole money was so little in those days that he had to find other ways to get by.

Dad told me that the home must not find out we'd been fishing, which was fine by me, but he didn't tell me that this was because there were strict orders that I was to stay in the house or in the street, supervised, and never to go anywhere else. I wish he had explained, because then I'd have known that it wasn't just the fishing I shouldn't mention.

One sunny day my line got snagged on a passing half-submerged log. The tide was racing out so the log was moving quickly and it pulled me along with it. The line was wrapped around my hand, so I struggled to undo it as I was pulled along the little quay under the bridge. Just as I loosened the line I reached the narrow spot at the end of the quay. There was a patch of slimy, green moss there and I slipped and plunged headfirst into the river. Thankfully I could swim, and when I got to the surface I swam like mad to the side and held on tight as the racing tide lifted my feet to the surface.

Uncle John stood, pipe in mouth, rod in hand, and shouted to Dad, 'He's in!' Nothing more – just that! Dad, further along the quay and barely hearing him, shouted, 'What?' John shouted, 'He's in!' followed by a kind of laugh, 'Hea, hea', as he continued fishing. Finally Dad clicked. 'He's in?' he shouted, and he dropped his rod and ran to the narrow bit. At that moment Dad ran on to the same bit of green slimy moss and skyward he went, shouting 'Whoa!' as he travelled towards me at great speed. I remember, in slow motion, counting the studs on his boots as they got closer and closer, then the crunch as they hit me, and I was under again. I managed to grab his trouser bottoms as I went down, so I was able to pull myself back up to the surface.

Unfortunately the sewer pipe not thirty feet upstream from us discharged its untreated contents into the outgoing tide at regular intervals. We were scrambling to get up the slimy walls when these contents and their stench arrived, and began sticking to us.

Uncle John stood there grinning and said, 'The sewer's out. Hea, hea.' He made no move at all to try to rescue us. Dad started to shout at him to help, and at last he got his rod, lowered it down and I got hold of it. I managed to scramble up the wall, followed by Dad. All the while John just kept grinning, and when we got out he went back to his fishing.

We absolutely stank, so we packed up and headed home as fast as we could. People stared at us as we squelched along, and the stench was so bad that they held their noses as we passed. When we got back we were kept out in the back yard and the hosepipe was turned on us. That was the best we could do – there was no bathroom in which to wash, and no hot water. A great effort was made to dry my clothes before I went back to the home, but as all they had was the coal fire, I was still a bit damp and rather smelly when I got back. Everyone noticed a whiff in the air but they didn't immediately realise it was me.

As always happened, I was told to go and get changed and my clothes were sent to the laundry. What I didn't know was that they always checked in the pockets of my coat and trousers, in case I had anything they didn't want me to have. When they found my pockets were unusually wet for such a dry day, I was called into the office, and that's when they found out that the rotten smell was coming from me. I was careful not to mention the fishing, but I owned up to falling in the river and I was thrown in the bath and scrubbed.

A few days later, Uncle Kennedy called me into the office and told me I would not be permitted to visit home ever again. I felt devastated. How could they just take away my days with Dad and Anita and my brothers and little sisters? I felt that I must be a bad person, a criminal, for them to take away the people and the things I loved most.

I said nothing to Uncle Kennedy. I knew it wouldn't make any difference. I left his office and went up to the dormitory, where I sat on the side of my bed, my shoulders slumped. I felt so wounded I couldn't even cry. I thought of how much I loved fishing under the bridge with Dad, and how much it meant to me to leave the home and be in my family that one day a week. And the pain of loss hit me all over again. I had lost Irene, and now I was losing Dad and the rest of my family.

I was nine years old and it felt as if my world had ended – again.

It was to be eight years before I saw any of my family again. And for all of that time I heard nothing of my father, brothers, stepmother or sisters. I didn't know that my older brother, Michael, was eventually allowed to go home and live with Dad and Anita, while George and Brian, like me, had to stay in care.

It seemed to me that the people in charge would wait until I was happy and then ambush me, taking away whatever – or whoever – I cared for. In my grief and pain I declared a kind of war against them. I decided that I would behave myself until they took their eyes off me, then I would ambush them, so they would know how it felt. Of course, the problem with that plan was that the only one who was likely to get hurt was me. I just didn't know it yet.

10

Irene

Without Alan, it was as if time had stood still. I stopped being the brave, sparky little tomboy who would fight alongside the boys, and became quiet and withdrawn. I didn't play with the other children, I just wandered off on my own, and I became more and more isolated.

Rennie Road had always been unusually quiet. You'd expect a house with thirteen children in it to be filled with the sounds of laughter, happy chatter and even tantrums and tears. But the strict rules meant we had to keep quiet most of the time. We ate and did our chores in virtual silence.

Now that Alan had left, the house seemed somehow even quieter to me. A silent house. I moved around it silently, and it seemed to me as if everyone else did too.

Most of us children felt that we must be there as a punishment. We must have been bad, or naughty, to end up in a house with no mum and dad, and endless rules. I certainly felt that way. And the aunties reinforced this by ticking us off continually and punishing anyone who stepped out of line.

I used to listen to other children – the children with mums and dads and proper homes – playing out in the street in the evenings. Sometimes I would watch them through the windows, wishing I could be out there with them. I'd see their mums and dads going out to call them in, and giving them hugs, or ruffling their hair affectionately, and I'd ache with longing for a family.

I would wonder if Alan really had a family like that now. A nice, smiling mum and a dad who would kick a ball around with him, or take him fishing. And if Alan really did have new parents, could I have some too? I hardly dared to let myself hope that some kind people might want me.

A few weeks after Alan went, I turned ten. Birthdays were never very special, but this one was especially bleak. No one greeted me when I got up in the morning; I simply went to school as normal. Back at the home for tea, there were cupcakes – no one got a birthday cake unless a relative had brought it round. I didn't mind about the cake: the cupcakes were nice, and the children sang 'Happy Birthday to You'. Then Auntie Doris gave me a card and some sweets which Joan had brought over for me. The sweets had to be shared out between all of us – that was the rule – and I took the card up to my room and put it beside my bed.

I was so glad of Joan's card, but I couldn't help wishing that I'd had one from Alan. Secretly I had hoped that he would remember it was my birthday and find a way to contact me. Then I would know that he hadn't forgotten me. Surely his new family would let him send me a card – wouldn't they? That night I lay in bed, overwhelmed by sadness. I didn't think I would ever be happy again.

A few days later a new boy arrived – a small, dark-haired, nervous-looking lad of about eight, called Tom. He was taking Alan's place, and although it wasn't his fault I knew I just couldn't be friends with him. His arrival seemed to seal the fact that Alan wasn't coming back.

I might have got to know him in the end, but Tom didn't stay for long. After a few weeks he was gone – I never knew where. Perhaps he'd misbehaved and been moved on, or perhaps his family had taken him back. Of course, no one ever told us.

There were times when I thought of doing something really bad, so that I would be taken away too. I thought I might be sent to the place where Alan was, and then I could see him again. If I'd been sure of that I wouldn't have hesitated. I'd have done whatever it took – even stealing, if that would do it. But I knew that I probably wouldn't get sent to Whitby. In fact, as far as I knew there wasn't a children's home there. So my chances of ending up anywhere near Alan were pretty poor.

Besides, I had one very important reason for staying – my sister Joan. Now that Alan had gone I longed to be with Joan as much as possible – she was all I had to cling to, and the thought of being taken away from her was unbearable.

I would have loved to spend every spare moment at Joan's, but that would never have been allowed. I could be over at her house in twenty seconds, but that privilege had to be earned through good behaviour and officially arranged with the permission of the Children's Officer, who was based in the Weights and Measures building in the town centre.

The rule was that relatives had to telephone or call at the office with their request to take out the child in question for a few hours or for the day on a Saturday or Sunday – and this applied to Joan, even though she lived just yards from where I was. On Friday at teatime the telephone would ring and Auntie Doris or Auntie Nan would be given a list of those who had permission to go out that weekend. I would sit near the phone every Friday, waiting to see if I was one of the lucky ones.

The aunties knew how much it meant to me to go to Joan's, and it gave them a lot of power. Just one step out of line, they warned, and I would lose the great privilege of being able to visit my sister. So I spent my whole time trying as hard as I could to be good, in order not to lose those precious times with her.

I made a huge effort to always do as I was told and never put a foot out of line, so much so that I almost forgot I had a voice or a will of my own. This training in unquestioning obedience became so deeply ingrained that it coloured my life for many years. Even as an adult, I would find it hard to make my own decisions and not to let others control me.

Sometimes I was so desperate to see Joan and the children that I would sneak out and run around to Joan's and beg her to come back and ask Auntie Doris if I could come for a visit. I knew if Auntie Nan was on duty I'd have no chance, because she was so much stricter, but Auntie Doris was sometimes willing to waive the rules. After I'd sneaked back in, Joan would come round and, if she was in a good mood, Auntie Doris would say that it wasn't strictly allowed, but seeing that Joan was in the next street I could go. But it was only to be for a half hour or so, then I had to be back.

Half an hour wasn't much, but that taste of freedom often made life bearable. I loved going to Joan's and being part of a family. I'd play with Elaine, who was a toddler, and baby Alan, and help Joan to bath them and put them to bed. I always wished I could stay and go to bed there too, after sitting by the fire with Joan for a cup of hot chocolate. But I had to leave and go back to Rennie Road, where Auntie Doris would be waiting.

I was almost used to my loneliness when a new family arrived. There were two sisters and two brothers and they were to remain at Rennie Road for several years. The girls were Margaret, known as Margy, and Silvia, or Silvy, and they were put into a bedroom with me.

Margy had dark hair and blue eyes and was thick-set. She was always cheerful and everyone found it easy to get on with her. She was older than me, while her sister Silvy was younger. Silvy had blonde hair and was very pretty. She was a quiet child who followed Margy everywhere.

I liked Margy and Silvy, but I didn't know how to be real friends with them. They stuck together, and I was so quiet that I felt they barely noticed me. Being silent had become such a habit for me that I didn't know how to do anything else. Sometimes I walked to school with them, but even then I never felt able to say much. They probably thought I was boring, and I didn't blame them. I wanted to be friends, but after losing Alan I felt I just didn't know how to talk to other children.

Margy and Silvy's brothers were really tough kids. The elder was Joe, who had dark hair just like Margy, and a reputation for being hard. The younger boy, Kenny, was blond, with the same blue eyes all four of them shared. He was sweet-looking, but his looks were deceptive – he would fight anyone, anywhere, at any time! Whenever there was a battle on the hill with the Castlers, it would be Kenny at the front leading the fight, and he could be reckless to the point of endangering himself and others.

The two brothers became the leaders of the Redhousers and the boys in the home, and even those living in the surrounding streets would follow Joe and Kenny wherever they went. The two of them would march right into the Castlers' home ground, below the hill, with their gang behind them.

Once the Redhousers attacked the Castlers while they were sitting around a big bonfire they had built, in between the building sites below the hill. There must have been about thirty of them around the fire when our lot, with Kenny at the front as usual, bombarded them with stones. I was on the hill at the time when I saw our little army, outnumbered by at least ten, retreating up the hill as fast as they could, stones flying past them as the Castlers followed in hot pursuit.

It was the girls who saved the day. Several of us, from the home as well as the street, joined in, hurling stones at the pursuers, which gave the lads a chance to regroup and stand their ground on the hill. We all cheered when the Castlers retreated, shouting and swearing at us.

Life in Rennie Road was predictable and dull, and outings were few and far between. But occasionally we would be taken to visit other children's homes for an evening. I'm not sure why, but it was probably thought that meeting other children would do us good. We would all be sent to the playroom of whatever home we were in, where the younger kids would play with the toys from the box and the older children would stand about, bored.

There was no excitement for us older ones in watching the very young ones play, and we all longed just to go back and get on with the things we were used to. In between the awkward silences we would ask each other half-hearted questions: 'What's your auntie like?' 'What school do you go to?' But none of us really wanted to be in another children's home just like ours, and we all felt like prisoners going for a day out to another prison. The real enjoyment was for the aunties, who would chat over a cup of tea, with the radio playing light music in the background, and swap anecdotes of their children's escapades.

Sad and inadequate as they were, these visits to other children's homes were almost the only opportunity we got to mix with other children socially. The children at school all knew we were from 'the homes' and that made us different. And if we were able to get past this barrier, any budding friendship was doomed because we weren't allowed to go to the other children's houses, or to bring them back for tea.

When Christmas came, three and a half months after Alan left, I had no heart for celebrations. We had a tree and some decorations, but somehow there was never a sense of fun or excitement in Rennie Road. It was business as usual, even at Christmas.

I used to walk up the street, looking though the windows of the other houses at their trees covered in sparkly decorations, piles of presents and cosy family scenes, and wonder why we were different. I so wanted to be in those homes, with those families, that it was like an ache inside.

For our big Christmas treat we were taken to a panto in the town theatre the week before Christmas. It was *Puss in Boots*, and for a couple of hours I was lost in the joys of yelling, 'He's behind you!' and laughing at the panto dame, with her rouged face and elaborate gowns. At moments like those I wished Alan could be there. We would have spent a happy half-hour afterwards, on the windowsill behind the curtain, reliving the delights of the show.

A few days later we all went to a party at the local Working Men's Club, along with children from other care homes. There was jelly and ice-cream and we played games, but my heart wasn't in it. I missed Alan too much, and besides, I knew this party wasn't the same as the ones girls at school had with their families and friends. It was meant kindly, but somehow I knew it wasn't the same.

One of the things I really did like about that Christmas was the carol singers. People from the local church or children out with their mums and dads would come up the street, singing carols, and I would watch them through the window, longing to be out there with them.

Our only chance to sing carols came when we were all marched down to church for the annual carol service. We Rennie Road children were led to the front and made to sing our carols to the congregation. I hated this, and so did most of the others. Having to be on show and pretend to be happy, joyful children enjoying Christmas was something we all resented. It was bad enough being in care, but having everyone stare at us in church, knowing that we were in care, felt awful. I couldn't wait to get back to my seat afterwards and try to sink down, out of sight.

The day before Christmas Auntie Doris called me to one side and told me that I was to be allowed to go to Joan's on Christmas Day in the afternoon for a couple of hours. That changed everything for me – suddenly there was something special to look forward to, and I couldn't wait.

On Christmas Day we had a roast dinner, which we all helped to prepare, and afterwards we were each given a present. Mine was a little musical box, with a ballerina who turned round as the music played. I thought it was lovely, but I knew I mustn't get too attached to it because, like all the other toys, it had to go into the toy box, to be shared by all of us.

The aunties did their best to make Christmas nice for us. But there was an overwhelming sense of sadness among us children, because every single one of us longed to be living with our families. I knew I was one of the lucky ones: at least I was going to see my sister. A few of the other children were allowed visits too, but that only made it harder for the ones left behind.

That Christmas there was a little girl called Julie who had only been in Rennie Road a couple of weeks. I didn't know why she was in care, but she couldn't go home for a visit and she cried for her mother and her brothers and sisters most of the day.

I wanted to comfort Julie. She was only seven, and she didn't understand why she had been taken away from her family. I knew the aunties disapproved of what they called 'fussing' over someone. They said that if you were fussed over the pain only lasted longer, and they discouraged any hugs for the younger ones, saying, 'They'll get used to it soon enough.' But that didn't seem right to me – I couldn't help feeling that if you were unhappy, surely a hug would help. Especially on Christmas Day. So when Auntie Doris and Auntie Nan were having their cup of tea after lunch and the rest of us were in the playroom, I gave Julie a little cuddle. She sniffed back her tears and managed a shy smile. And after that I smiled at her to try to cheer her up whenever the aunties' backs were turned.

Mostly we older children didn't try to comfort any of the younger or newer children when they were upset. We weren't being purposely unkind: it was just that we'd been treated in the same way. We were always encouraged by the aunties to brush aside sad feelings. Their attitude was that you should 'get on with it'. They saw it as their mission to make us children strong enough to cope with life's difficulties, and they thought the best way to do that was not to dwell on unhappy feelings. But perhaps those of us who had been there for some time were also a little afraid that comforting a younger child might remind us of our own sadness and sense of loss.

After dinner we cleared up and then played some games. I had one eye on the clock, which seemed to me to be going at half-speed. But eventually three o'clock came and I was allowed to go round to Joan's – on the strict understanding that I would be back by five. I'd got my coat on and shot out of the door before Auntie Doris could check that I'd buttoned it up or remind me to walk in a ladylike way.

A few seconds later I was tapping on Joan's door. She was just clearing the meal away, and her husband was snoozing in his chair, so I settled down to play with Elaine and look at her new toys. Joan made a cup of tea and came and sat with us, and she gave me a box of chocolates to take back with me. She and I both knew that if I was even a minute late I wouldn't be allowed to come back for a long time. So at five to five I put on my coat, hugged Joan and the children and, my feet dragging, walked reluctantly back to Rennie Road.

11

Alan

After I was stopped from going to my dad's I kept my head down, trying to avoid too much attention. I had lost all interest in school and mostly daydreamed or stared out of the window until the teacher spoke to me. The pain of losing my family again went very deep. By now I didn't trust anyone. All I could think about was running away again, to find Irene, or my dad, or both. It was just a question of when, and how to avoid being caught.

Then I had a brainwave. I could head back to the bridge where I had been fishing with Dad. I didn't know the way to where he lived, and even if I had known I didn't want to get him into trouble. But I knew the bridge. Perhaps I would find him there. And I could shelter under it for a while, and then head over to find Irene when they stopped looking for me. I was getting excited. Maybe I could even catch fish to eat. The thought that I might need to cook them never entered my mind.

I took off again a couple of days later, and headed for the bridge. I hoped I might see Dad fishing from the quay, but there was no sign of him. Thinking that I'd better get out of sight, I decided to climb the huge pipe that was attached to the concrete wall. I was very agile, so it wasn't too difficult: I just held on to the brackets that fixed it to the wall and walked up, as if it was a ladder.

When I got to the top, some thirty feet up, I climbed over the edge on to a wide flat area of concrete. From there the steel supports for the bridge, criss-crossing like a vast Meccano set, reached right up to the bridge, another fifty feet above me. I could see that if I climbed the steel girders I would eventually be underneath the curve of the bridge, where there was a narrow walkway. I was sure that if I got up there I would be safe, as no one would guess where I was.

I was small and nimble and determined, but even so the climb was extremely tricky. The steel was cold on my fingers and my feet had to rest in awkward v-shaped angles. Careful not to look down at the death-defying drop, I climbed steadily up and made it to the walkway.

I felt as if I had conquered Everest. I stood and looked at the spectacular view down the river on either side, gazing down at the boats passing beneath me and across to the shipyards on the banks. The loud rumble of traffic crossing the bridge above my head was swollen by the constant hooting of the ships below.

I walked right across to the other side of the river, then climbed down the girders that side to where there was a ledge and two small square openings in the wall, fifty feet above the ground. This climb was much more difficult, because these girders, more exposed to the weather than the others, were wet and slippery. A couple of times I almost lost my grip, clinging on precariously until I got a footing.

Eventually I reached the two holes. I crawled in and found a huge dark cavernous area of stone and concrete. The only light came in through a manhole cover up on the bridge road, thirty feet above. It was freezing in there and very eerie, so I crawled out and climbed back up the girders to the bridge.

Crossing the bridge again, I spotted two similar holes in the foundation wall on that side. I climbed down to them, and crawled in. The cavern inside was smaller, and because this side of the bridge was more sheltered it was warmer too. I decided that this was where I would stay. This would be my secret world.

All I needed now was a source of food, and I didn't have to look far. Every eight hours the horns would sound, to signal a change of shift in the shipyards. First one horn would sound, then another and another, and the sound would travel up the river, shipyard by shipyard. Within minutes, thousands of men would stream up the banks to the bridge, heading home. Along with two or three other dirty little boys, I would gather near the road and as the men, in their mufflers and flat caps, passed by, we asked them if they had 'Any bait, mister?'

We were always given loads of scraps the men had left in their lunchboxes. I'd grab the bits of sandwich and go back under the bridge, where I'd stuff it all in my mouth. None of us grubby hungry little boys spoke to each other. I've often wondered who the others were, and if they were in care like me.

Now and then I'd ask the men if they had any change, and though the majority said, 'Bugger off,' sometimes one of them would give me a few pennies or a thruppenny bit and I'd go to the shop and buy pop to wash my sandwiches down.

I lived under the bridge as a scavenger for two weeks. It was cold at night, huddled in the corner of a concrete room under the road, but I still preferred it to the children's home where I was at the mercy of Uncle Kennedy.

By the end of that fortnight I was sure they would have forgotten about me. It seemed like such a long time. I decided it was safe to come out and head for Rennie Road and Irene, so when it got dark I made my way along the little path beside the bridge and began to climb over the railings, peering around me to make sure no one was there. As I got to the top of the railings, a hand grabbed my collar. A policeman had been standing right there when I'd popped up next to him. I think he was more surprised than I was. Holding my arm very tightly he dragged me off to the police station, a short distance away. I knew it was no good putting up a fight, but I was heartbroken. All that time in hiding, and I'd got caught the minute I stuck my head out. It was a bitter blow.

In the station a friendly desk-sergeant called Emerson, who had come to know me well by then, sat me down with a mug of tea and tried to talk me out of being a bother to people. Despite my upset I really liked him, as he always smiled, called me by my first name and took the time to see if I was OK. Years later I met a girl with the same name. She was his daughter and she told me he had become a detective, a promotion I'm sure he deserved.

As usual, Uncle was waiting for me on my return. He was furious that I had managed to evade capture for so long and the beating he gave me left me in no doubt about his frustration. He was determined to find out who had helped me to stay out so long, and despite me telling him that no one had helped me; he tried to beat the information out of me. By the time he'd finished, I was black and blue.

At this point Matron took charge of the situation, and she appeared distressed. I got the impression that she had thought I'd gone for ever, or was even dead. She patted my head and put me to bed with tears in her eyes. A part of me wanted to open up to her, but I didn't dare trust her. I was too afraid that she would tell Uncle Kennedy and I'd be in more trouble. Better to say nothing, I thought.

Though I still felt a deep sadness inside, at this point in my life I was introduced to two new activities that really made a difference to me – the church choir and the Cubs. No doubt I was enrolled in both in the hope that they would be a positive influence on me, and for a while this strategy worked.

The Cubs met in the church hall, and most of the younger boys from the home joined. Unlike school there was lots of action and fun, and I enjoyed earning my badges through accomplishing tasks. I was proud of my uniform, and as I got each new badge Matron would sew it on to my shirt-sleeve; it gave me a sense of pride in myself that I had never experienced before.

When we sat around the campfires on dark nights, roasting potatoes and sausages and singing campfire songs, I felt I was a part of something special. I loved the sense of sharing with the other boys, who came from all sorts of backgrounds. In the Cubs we were all the same, all brothers, and I didn't feel like the kid from care.

After I'd been in the Cubs for a few months, some new boys, whose families had just moved into the area, joined our group. I found the new boys very different to most of the boys I knew. They were well-spoken and talked of having interests in areas that were completely unfamiliar to me. One had a telescope and watched the stars, while another went sailing. They all talked of holidays to places I'd never heard of, and I was fascinated. In the playground I might not have mixed with them, because different social groups tended to play separately. But in the Cubs, once each boy had sworn his oath of allegiance he became one of us, and as far as we were concerned we were in it together.

One of our favourite games was British Bulldog. All the boys had to race from one end of the hall to the other, while one or two 'defenders' had to try to catch them. Each time someone was caught they joined in the catching, and the last boy left uncaught was the winner. The game could get very boisterous and rough at times, because we would often hurl one another to the ground with flying rugby tackles, as some boys, even when they'd been caught, pushed on through the defenders to reach the other side. But it was all good fun and generally no one got hurt.

Soon after the new boys joined, the day came for a game of Bulldog and, bursting with energy, as small boys so often are, in we piled. I was keen to demonstrate to one of the new boys that I was good at the game, so as he ran towards me I grabbed him and flung him to the floor. It must have hurt because he shouted out, then jumped up and called me a name. I don't remember what it was – I probably didn't even understand what he'd said – I just felt angry that he was hurt so easily when he was supposed to be one of us. So, in a panic, I lashed out and gave him a black eye.

I was grabbed by the ear and led out in disgrace, and when the boy's mother made a formal complaint I was told I had to leave the Cubs. My precious uniform was returned to them a few days later, minus the badges, which were thrown away.

There was no appeal. No one wanted to hear my side or was interested in how I felt. I was the rough naughty little boy who'd hit the good boy. I missed my uniform and the other boys so much. Cubs had given me a sense of purpose and belonging, and when it was taken away I felt very bleak. And I never saw most of the boys again, apart from the few who were also in the church choir.

I was still in the choir, and although it wasn't as good as Cubs I really enjoyed it. I loved singing and, as with Cubs, it provided a sense of belonging and achievement that meant a great deal to a small boy who had lost so much. But this was not to last either.

This time my crime was sniggering at a funeral. I didn't mean any disrespect, but something sent me into a laughing fit and I just couldn't control it. I struggled to stop and tried to sing louder to drown out whatever thought was giving me the giggles. But it kept coming. I held my hymn-book in front of my face so the choirmaster couldn't see me. The trouble was that the choirmaster always wanted to look at us, so that he could direct us with his eyes as well as his hands. At appropriate moments, while mouthing the words in an exaggerated way, he would raise his eyebrows to raise the pitch or frown to lower it. When he looked at me and saw a shuddering hymn-book in front of my face, he nodded to the boy next to me, who nudged me with his elbow. I slowly lowered my hymn-book, and when the choirmaster saw my face, puce with the effort of struggling not to laugh, his own face turned red and he grimaced angrily at me.

After the service some members of the grieving family approached the vicar and mentioned to him that they had noticed how some of the younger choirboys had been 'upset' during the funeral. The family had found it very moving that such young boys could feel so deeply for them. They donated a half-crown to each of the younger choirboys in appreciation.

Shortly after that I was given my half-crown with one hand, a good 'clout' round the lug with the other, stripped of my cassock and told not to come back. The other boys cheered me for having earned them a good tip for that day. But, as with the Cubs, I never got to see any of them again.

It felt as if I had lost just about everything – and everyone. Life was at its bleakest, until one day a couple who were probably in their late twenties arrived at the home dressed in motorbike gear – leather jackets and helmets. I was told that the man was my Uncle Rex and that they had driven all the way up from Kent just to see me. I was surprised, because I didn't know I had an Uncle Rex. But when they asked to take me out for the day I was quite happy to go along.

They had arrived on a motorbike with a sidecar, and they popped me into the sidecar with the lady. At first Uncle Rex suggested a run up to Scotland, but the lady said it was too far and they needed time to get back, so we went around the town and the local park.

Uncle Rex told me that they lived in the countryside and had large apple orchards in Kent, and they'd come to see me because they wanted to take me home with them. He said I would love it there, and that the orchards were mine anyway and they were just looking after them for me. I had never felt more exited. Was I really going to live with these nice people, in an apple orchard? The idea was so good it was almost unbearable.

At the end of the day they dropped me back and off they went. I wondered how long it would be before they could take me, and dreamed of living with them. But days passed, and then weeks, and finally months. I waited and waited for them to come back, but they never did. When I eventually asked Matron about it, I was told that they were not allowed to take me because of my bad behaviour. I felt gutted, because I'd wanted to go with them so very much.

This painful let-down, coming after losing Irene and being banned from seeing Dad, taught me that the more you want something, the greater the pain when you don't get it. After that I tried not to hope for anything; I never wanted to feel such terrible disappointment again.

As for what Uncle Rex had said about the apple orchards being mine, I had no idea what that meant until many years later, when I was told that my brothers and I had a very wealthy grandfather on our mother's side. It seemed he'd had a terrible accident on a motorbike and ended his days in a mental institution. My eldest brother Michael was able to visit him before he died, though by then our grandfather wasn't able to have a meaningful conversation. There were many rumours about a missing will and large investments, including apple orchards in Kent. But it may all have been just that, a rumour, because no one had ever heard of an Uncle Rex.

After this let-down my behaviour deteriorated. Hurt and angry at yet more loss and rejection, I became wilder, and the other boys at school began to shy clear of me because of the trouble I would land them in. I was caught in the garden shed of one boy and he was given a good hiding because of it, while another was punished for being consistently late because he was playing with me after school.

I became more and more isolated, often playing on my own and drifting into my own little world. Once or twice I went on the run again, sleeping under trees and bushes. One winter night, when it was snowing, I was lying under a bush in the dark, feeling colder and wetter than I ever had before. Then suddenly it was daytime, bright and sunny, and a friend from school was next to me chatting away. I was warm again and it was great chatting to him about the things we had done and games we had played. Then, just as suddenly, he was gone and it was dark and I was freezing again.

I didn't know it then, but I was hallucinating and showing signs of hypothermia. Not only was I bitterly cold, but I hadn't eaten for two days, so I was starving hungry too. As I lay there in the dark, wondering what to do, I remembered that the bakery was only a few streets away. And the delivery van that came early every morning would soon be standing in the lane at the back of the shop.

Drooling at the thought of a hot pie, I got up and set off. That probably saved me from freezing to death that night. I made my way to the back lane and waited down an alleyway nearby, and it didn't seem to be too long before the delivery van arrived.

The driver got out and went into the back of the bakery, then he came out and opened the double doors of the van. What a heavenly sight! I could see tray after tray of bread, pies and cakes. He pulled out a tray of bread, lifted it on to his shoulder and went into the shop. I began counting to see how many seconds it took him to come back. By the time I got to twenty, there he was.

He collected another tray and went back into the shop, and I ran to the van and grabbed a big pie with both hands – but it was so hot that I dropped it!

I grabbed a smaller one from the tray above, and thankfully it was cooler. I stuffed it into my mouth, but it was very hot inside and burned my mouth, so I was blowing like mad to try to cool it while trying to eat it at the same time.

'OY!' shouted the driver, and I began running, stuffing pie into my mouth as I went. I didn't get far before he collared me, but even as he hung on to me and bellowed that he'd got me at last, I kept stuffing in the pie.

It turned out that his van had been regularly raided about twice a week. The kids from the local school knew all about it and had taken turns grabbing pies and cakes for months. But it was me he'd caught. I was frog-marched back up the road to a small police office on the corner.

I was sent back to the home but this time, because I was so badly chilled, I avoided a beating and was put to bed and kept there for about three days while I recovered. I hoped that was the end of the matter. But a couple of weeks later I found myself in the magistrates' court. As I sat, looking at the coat of arms on the wall and dreaming of knights in armour, the court ordered them to bring in a child psychologist to get to the bottom of what was wrong with me. The first I knew of it was when I was taken to the other Esplanade, across the road – the one where we went for our medicals.

I was taken into a big room with toys in it and left there alone. There was a large fort on one side and a doll's house on the other, with bits of puzzles scattered around the floor. Somehow I knew that I was being watched through the large mirror on the wall. I thought I'd be clever, so I knocked the fort over, peered into the doll's house – I saw it had patchwork quilts on the beds, which for a brief moment reminded me of a home – and scattered the puzzles across the floor. Then I got bored and just sat in the corner watching the big mirror, waiting until they let me out.

I went to the house every week for the next couple of months. The sessions always started the same way – I was put at a desk in a small office and given a large questionnaire to fill in. I wasn't allowed out of the room until I'd completed it, and it seemed to take for ever. I don't remember any of the questions, just the length of time I was kept in that tiny room. It was worse than school! I ticked some of the boxes without even reading the questions, just so that I could be finished and get out.

After that I had to see a man I didn't like very much. He was rather scary, and he asked me lots and lots of questions, about the homes I'd been in and school and Dad and my brothers. It was really boring, and I didn't have much to say. I couldn't understand why I had to be there with him. When I'd seen him I would be put back in the playroom, where I'd sit and watch the mirror and think, 'I'm not telling them about Irene.'

Then one day the visits to see the man stopped, and a black car arrived at the door of The Esplanade. The driver came in, and when he glanced in my direction I knew he'd come about me. He had a long discussion with Uncle in his study, and a little while later Matron came and got me and took me upstairs, where we began to pack my things. Close to tears, she told me I was going away for a while. It was not for long, she said, but I must try to behave, as this was my last chance for things to work out right.

I had absolutely no idea what she meant. When we'd finished packing we went downstairs and the driver led me to the car, where he stowed me in the back, with my things. Matron waved goodbye from the steps, as we headed off to heaven knew where.

12

Irene

I missed my mum terribly, even though I didn't remember her. Aunt Jane had once told me, when I was only four or five, that Mum had become a star in the sky. That comforted me, and through all the years in care, whenever I felt sad or lonely I would look for the brightest star and then talk to her and ask her to come and get me.

I often tried to imagine what Mum had been like and wonder if I was like her. I used to think sadly that if she hadn't died my family would all have lived together, sharing cuddles and toys and happy times. I dreamed of living with my sisters, especially Pat, who was so close to me in age. Instead I had to settle for visits, whenever one of the family was able to take me out on a Saturday or Sunday. Uncle Bob or Dad or Greta would all make formal requests to the Children's Officer. But it could take days to obtain permission, so sometimes they'd promise me a visit and then it wouldn't be granted in time, and they'd have to give up and try again the following week.

Every Friday I waited anxiously to see if someone had permission to take me out that weekend. If they had I was thrilled, but all too often they hadn't, and I sat sadly in the playroom, on the windowsill behind the curtain, hating Rennie Road and wishing I could be in Whitby with Alan.

Even if a visit had been arranged, any misbehaviour would result in the aunties cancelling. When this happened my disappointment was terrible. One week I was told I couldn't go out with Uncle Bob because I hadn't washed up properly – Auntie Nan found two dirty dishes. And another time a visit to Greta's was banned because I hadn't finished my homework. Each time I begged for another chance, offering to do extra chores or homework to make up for it, but a stony-faced Auntie Nan refused and I wept bitter tears of frustration.

I liked it best when Uncle Bob came. He was great fun to be with, always kind and jolly. In many ways Uncle Bob had been more of a father figure to me than Dad. He had always visited me regularly, wherever I was, and he brought me little gifts and made me feel I was his special girl. Usually the two of us got the train to Seaham Harbour, where we spent the day with Pat; I looked forward to these visits so much. While Uncle Bob had a cup of tea with Aunt Jen and Uncle Charlie, Pat and I would play in the garden, or in her pretty bedroom. Secretly, I'd pretend that I lived there too. And when the time came to go I would try to put it off, wishing that Aunt Jen would offer to keep me, and that I could stay and never have to go back to Rennie Road.

On the train going back I was always a little quiet and Uncle Bob would pat my hand, understanding how hard it was for me.

When Greta came she would take me home to her husband Ken and their new baby boy, Paul. They had moved from the cottage they had shared with Ken's mum, and had their own little home. Greta was always concerned for me and wanted to know how I was. She would take me and Paul out to the local park for walks, and I was delighted when she let me push Paul around in his pram. Some days she would take us on the bus to the park at South Shields, along the coast.

It was always full of flowers, and we would feed the ducks and swans in the lake. At other times she would take us to Durham and we would walk along the riverbank and stop at a little café for tea and a buttered scone. It always reminded me of the riverbank by the bluebell woods and the chapel that Alan and I had played in.

I loved these outings and longed to live with Greta, just as I longed to stay with Pat when I was at Seaham. But I didn't say anything to Greta. Like Joan, she lived in a tiny house and was struggling to raise a family. She couldn't take me in too.

If Dad came it was always on a Saturday. I would be in my best dress, waiting for him in the playroom. For an hour before he arrived I'd sit on the windowsill, watching for him. But Auntie Doris or Auntie Nan would often turn him away because he had been drinking. When this happened I had to go back upstairs, take off my nice clothes and put on everyday ones again, and return to my chores, weighed down with disappointment. But worse still were the days when he never arrived at all, and there were plenty of those. On those days I would sit and wait, knowing that he was in a pub somewhere, drowning his sorrows in pint after pint of ale.

When he did arrive to take me out, we went straight to the railway station, an old Victorian building with a huge domed glass roof. Not much light shone through, as it was coated with the grime of many years, not to mention soot from the steam trains. Just inside the station was a pub, and this is where Dad always went. He would sit me on a bench with crisps and a lemonade while he stood at the bar chatting with the many visitors passing through, always willing to buy a pint for a new-found friend.

The air in the pub was always thick with the blue haze of cigarette smoke. The light in there was very dim, because so much nicotine had stuck to all the windows that you couldn't tell if it was day or night outside. Hundreds of sailors would pour into the station, heading home from the Merchant Navy and the occasional Royal Navy ship visiting the port, or from the many merchant ships and colliers berthed along the river. Plenty of them would stop for a pint before boarding their trains, and when Dad got chatting to one of them he would tell me I had to touch the sailor's collar for luck. I did as he asked, but I often wondered why, as it never seemed to bring me any luck. I thought that perhaps it made Dad feel lucky.

It was hard to hear in the pub as it was always so full that everyone had to shout to be heard. I would sit on my bench, listening to the hubbub of many voices, the clanking of glasses and the occasional sudden shout of laughter. After a while I'd slip out into the station, where I'd stand and watch the people and trains coming and going. It was always full of people rushing on and off the many trains and up the steps to the roadside where taxis and buses were waiting to whisk them away. On top of the chatter of the crowds there was the noise of the old steam trains chugging in and out of the station, the shouts of the guards on the trains and the piercing shrills of their whistles as they waved their flags, signalling for the trains to go. There were porters in those days, and they pushed luggage trolleys with wheels that made clacking sounds as they rattled across the platforms.

Inside the entrance to the station, there stood a big cast-iron machine that looked very much like a large weighing machine. It had a dial with the letters of the alphabet in a circle around its face and a lever on one side. It was a luggage-labelling machine. You put a penny in the slot and turned the dial to the letter you required, then pulled the lever. The machine stamped the letter on to a small metal plate. You kept doing this until the name you wanted was stamped on to the plate, which the machine would then eject. Each plate had holes in it at either end. These were to put string through, so that you could tie it to your luggage.

I loved that machine. I would stand next to it and watch as groups of sailors with their heavy kitbags gathered around to get their tags. If Dad had given me a few pennies I would stamp out my name on a metal plate. And sometimes I stamped out Alan's name on a plate. I took all the tags back to Rennie Road, and with a little piece of string I made a bracelet out of them, alternating my name with Alan's. I kept it secret. I knew I would be in big trouble if the aunties found it. I could only wear it when I was outside the home, or now and then at night under the covers. I kept it hidden under my pillow, and when I knew the sheets were going to the laundry I would move it to another hiding place. To me that bracelet was so special it was as if it had magical powers. It was one of my very few private possessions, and it made me feel protected when I wore it.

After Dad finally left the station pub, a little the worse for wear, he would walk me into Jackie White's market nearby and stuff a handful of change into my hand. This, or a cheap toy from one of the market stalls, was the closest he got to showing me affection.

Anything Dad gave me would be taken away from me when I got back. So I preferred it when he gave me money, as I could buy a handful of sweets and hide what I didn't eat. Of course, sweets were supposed to be shared out too, but sweets were easier to hide. And when I had one of the sweets Dad had bought me in my pocket it felt as though I had a little bit of his love there. I would put my hand around it and imagine that he was still with me.

Sometimes, when Dad had given me a handful of change, I slipped into Joan's on the way back to Rennie Road and left it there to spend in the travelling shop that came down her street on Sundays. This was an old single-decker bus that had been fitted with shelves and a counter. It sold all kinds of things housewives might need, as well as food and sweets. On a Sunday afternoon when we were outside playing I would sneak around to Joan's, get some of the change and buy a few sweets, biscuits or my favourite Oxo-flavoured crisps.

While I was still ten my periods began. It came as a shock to me, and to the aunties too. No one had told me anything, so I had no idea what it all meant and thought I must have something wrong with me. Nor was I enlightened! The aunties simply told me to use sanitary towels and to 'stay away from boys', and that was it. Being so young, I took it literally and believed that I shouldn't play games with boys at all and had to avoid their company. It was only over the next few years that I began to learn the facts of life from the other girls at school, and even then most of it was myth rather than fact. We were all convinced you could get pregnant just by kissing a boy.

Every month I had to knock on the office door to get sanitary items from the auntie on duty, which was very embarrassing. I wasn't allowed to keep them in my room and had to go through the ordeal of asking for them. Like all young girls I was deeply sensitive about such matters and I hated being denied this simple privacy.

During termtime the aunties would take it in turn to go on leave. Each of them went for at least a month and another auntie would move in to share the duties. These temporary aunties were often more affectionate than Doris and Nan. Perhaps it was because they were usually still trainees, and hadn't yet learned to distance themselves emotionally from us children. It made a nice change: it was good to have someone around who was a little warmer and softer, and I'd miss them when they left.

As spring became summer and the days became warmer, my spirits rose. Soon we would be going back to Whitby and I would find Alan, I was certain of it. The school term ended and the long summer holidays arrived and we children were all allowed to go out and play on Bunny Hill most days. I didn't go down the hill. I never went to the bluebell woods again after Alan left. But I would go with the other children to play on the top of the hill, and to the air-raid shelter. Sometimes I would watch as the smaller boys squeezed through the narrow slits, and once they were in I could hear their voices echoing. I never went in; it looked so dark inside that it scared me.

Sometimes I played skipping or ball games with Margy and Silvy, though if their brothers came over they would pester and tease us to a point where I would end up getting angry and fighting with them. Fortunately it only happened well out of sight of the aunties, so I avoided getting into trouble.

When the aunties didn't want us going out on to the hill we were sent out into the back yard, which was surrounded by a high brick wall and paved with red flagstones. We hung out the washing there, and the girls and I would play two-ball on the wall or do handstands and play skippies. But more often than not I didn't join in the others' games. I wandered off on my own, or found a quiet spot where I sat on the hill and felt the breeze on my face and remembered the fun we'd had. And I dreamed of messing about in boats, eating fish and chips and running up the 199 steps to the abbey with Alan, as we had done the summer before, when we thought we had all the time in the world together.

I dreamed of sunny days playing in the sand on our beach, burying each other and picking shells on the shoreline. I had so many questions I wanted to ask him about his new family. I knew he would ask them if I could stay with them too, and secretly I imagined us both living with a loving, kind family.

At last the day came when we packed our small bags and boarded the coach. I watched the streets and houses and fields passing out of the window and joined in the same songs we had sung the year before, singing my heart out because with every passing mile that took me closer to Alan my spirits lifted higher. We stayed in the same ex-army huts in Staithes that we had been in the previous summer – girls in one, boys in the other, as before. We were all excited about being on holiday, and couldn't wait to go down to the beach, or over to Whitby.

For me, it was tinged with an extra joy. It was a whole year since I had been there with Alan, and yet I felt I was going to turn around at any moment and find him there, with a big grin on his face, waiting to play with me. Everywhere I looked I saw the two of us, as we had been, side by side, exploring, laughing, climbing the steps, picking up shells.

I was sure I would find him easily, because Whitby wasn't a very big place. Word would get round that the kids in care were there, and he would come looking for me. Or someone there would be able to tell me who had adopted a little boy from the care home.

I started with the fishermen down on the beach. They were still mending their nets, as if they'd never moved from the spot while we'd been gone. I described Alan, in the clothes he had been wearing then, not thinking that he might be wearing something different by now. When the fishermen didn't know him, I moved on to the people in the town. I stopped in shops, at ice-cream stalls and beside the old men making ships to put into bottles. I asked deckchair attendants, fish and chip sellers and women doing their shopping. But everywhere I went, people shook their heads. 'No, love, I'm sorry,' they all said.

Where was he? The people I didn't dare ask were the aunties – Doris and Nan. They must know, but I knew I'd be in trouble if I told them I was looking for Alan.

As the week went by I felt more and more worried. Why hadn't I found him? Where was he? It never occurred to me that he might be somewhere else or even that the family who had adopted him might have moved. Auntie Doris had said he was in Whitby, and in my mind he had been there for a whole year, playing on the beach every day.

On the last day I sat on the beach, just waiting, willing Alan to come before I had to go. I sat for as long as I could, until Margy was yelling at me to come back quickly because the aunties were looking for me. And even then I waited a few more minutes. When the time came to get on the bus, I climbed on board with my shoulders drooping. While the other children sang loudly all the way home, I stared out of the window, thinking that it would be a whole year until I could look for Alan again.

I felt so dreadfully disappointed that I hadn't found him. I had secretly hoped that I might not be coming back to Rennie Road; that instead I might be going to live with Alan's new family. To find myself back there again, having found no sign of Alan, felt awful.

To comfort myself I checked to see if my metal tag bracelet was still where I'd hidden it, at the back of my shoe locker. Thankfully it was – it meant such a lot to me. I put it back under my pillow and held it tightly in my hand as I went to sleep. Sad as I was, I still felt sure in my heart that Alan and I would find each other again. One day.

On my next visit to Joan I decided to confide in her about Alan. I needed to tell someone how much I had wanted to find him. Joan was the person I trusted most in the world, so while I was helping her bath the little ones I told her all about Alan. Joan smiled and said, 'I've always known he was your special friend – you never stopped talking about him.' I was shocked; I'd had no idea that I'd talked about him.

The new school year began the following week: my last year of primary school before I transferred to secondary school. Like the rest of my year, I was due to sit the eleven plus exam which would determine whether I went to the grammar school or the local comprehensive.

I had no real interest in the eleven plus and didn't much care what school I went to. Joan's husband Alan offered me five pounds if I passed, and I was impressed because that was an enormous sum of money then. But my enthusiasm soon fizzled out when I realised that the money would be taken from me by the aunties, and saved.

I had a couple of friends at school but we weren't especially close. I remember one of them struggling to understand what I meant when I told her I lived in a house with twelve other children and that we weren't allowed to play out, apart from at certain times, or to visit anyone or have visitors, apart from family. She thought I was in a prison and wondered what my crime had been, and I felt she wasn't far wrong.

At school my attention was focused on staying out of trouble and being obedient. To me this was far more important than learning, as I felt I had so much to lose if I misbehaved or broke the rules. I was one of those children who didn't really get noticed in class. I didn't stand out in any way, and although I got by I didn't do well. No one really cared how I did at school, as long as I didn't get into trouble. There was no one to encourage me, help me or believe in me. I wasn't expected to make anything of my life or to achieve much. After all, I was the kid from the care home. And that said it all.

13

Alan

Sitting in the back of yet another black car, I wondered where I would end up this time. An hour later we arrived at what looked like several large buildings, surrounded by a high wall. We went through the front gate and stopped outside the largest of the buildings, where I was led into a kind of waiting room, with posters on the wall, chairs and a coffee table with magazines on it.

After I had been sitting there on my own for some time, the door opened and a large lady in a nurse's uniform walked in. She stood in front of me with her arms crossed, looking pretty fearsome.

'I'm the matron,' she said, 'and here are the rules. You will be silent at all times and you will only speak when you are spoken to. You will do as you are told immediately and without question. You will refer to members of staff as either Sir or Miss at all times, apart from me; you call me Matron. Disobedience will not be tolerated and the punishments for breaking these rules will be swift and harsh. Now get up and follow me.'

By now scared, and wondering what sort of place this was, I followed her into a room containing shelves full of bottles and jars, where she ordered me to strip and put my clothes into a bag. She examined me all over, wrote some notes and made me put on a uniform of grey shirt and trousers. Pushing me down on to a wooden chair, she put on a pair of rubber gloves and took a handful of white cream from a big jar. 'Remember,' she said, smearing the cream roughly into my scalp, 'no noise or you will be punished.'

Combing the cream roughly through my hair, she added; 'You mustn't touch this cream. It has to stay on for at least four hours, do you understand?'

'Yes, Miss.'

'You call me Matron,' she barked.

'Yes, Matron.'

She led me to a large room where another twenty boys, aged between eight and fifteen, were standing silently in a line. An uncle – or was it a master now, I wondered – was at one end of the room sitting behind a desk. Two other boys in front of me had the same white cream in their hair and the younger one was crying, while the other was grimacing as if something was hurting him. The master shouted at the crying boy to 'stop that noise'. I wondered why he was crying and what this cream was.

We waited in that line for about ten minutes, during which time I could feel my scalp getting itchier and beginning to burn. By the time we were led through to the dining room for tea a few minutes later my scalp was on fire, but I was determined that I wouldn't give them the satisfaction of seeing me cry. I thought the cream was punishment for my misdeeds. I had no idea that I had been sent to a remand home for young boys, and that the dreadful cream was the nit treatment given to every boy on arrival.

We had to eat in silence, after which I was taken to my bedroom to unpack my things. I endured the next few hours with my scalp in agony, and when we were taken to the showers I raced in to get the stuff off my head. The younger boy, who was still crying, got in and began rubbing his head. He had hair so white that when he'd finished he almost looked as if the cream was still on. Except that now you could see his skin through his hair, and it was angry red and raw.

After the shower we were taken upstairs for a cup of tea and a biscuit before bed. I didn't sleep much because my head was still stinging, and I could hear the fair-haired boy in the next room still crying, no doubt for more than just the pain of his inflamed scalp.

The next morning after breakfast we were led, in silence, into a large schoolroom, with old-fashioned wooden desks and chairs. We were given pencils and exercise books, then told to complete the exercises in the books. At the front of the room a master sat behind a desk, reading a book while keeping an eagle eye on us. I was expecting lessons to begin, but I soon learned that this was our schooling. Whether we did the exercises or not didn't matter. Provided we sat there looking busy until lunchtime and then all afternoon to teatime, nothing was said. The books were only checked to see if they were filled in, and as long as your book had writing in it, all was well. I used to doodle in my book, and when the master wasn't looking I gazed out of the window and daydreamed about hills and fields and warm days in the sun.

These were long, long days for young boys, and inevitably someone would be caught looking out of the window, whispering or sniggering. As soon as someone made a noise – coughing or dropping a pencil was enough – the master would shout 'UP!' and we had to get up and move all of the desks to the side of the room. Then each of us picked up a chair and had to hold it above our heads while walking or running in a circle around the room. The master would stand, like a lion-tamer, with a cane in his hand, and as the weaker ones started to lower their chairs he would pounce and lash them across the back or legs with the cane. He would keep this going until the stronger ones lost their grip, then they got a whack too, so that everyone got a lash or two in the end, and more if you didn't get out of his way. After a month I had a lot of black, blue and yellow stripes across my back and legs.

I never made friends there, nor did any of the other boys. We got to know only a little about each other, because most of our time was spent in silence. It was a grim and frightening place that set out to terrify us boys into submission.

One day I was called out from tea and informed that Uncle Kennedy from The Esplanade had died of a heart attack. Though I hadn't got on with him I still felt sad, and a little guilty. And I wondered how Matron would feel now that he'd gone. I knew she would miss him. Would things be better there now, I wondered. I began to look forward to going back. Without Uncle there to punish me it would be so different. Matron had always cared for us and I liked her. I would make a big effort to be good, I decided, as I wouldn't want to hurt her.

About six weeks later I was taken to the medical room, where I was given my old clothes and told to change. A car arrived at the main gate, and the same man who had delivered me to the remand home took me out to the car and drove me away. I was relieved to be leaving. Nowhere could be worse, I was sure of that.

As we drove along I was asked the usual question, 'Do you know where you're going?'

'The Esplanade,' I said.

'No' the man said, before announcing that I was going to another home across town. I felt very sad. I had thought I was going back to Matron. Now I had to face yet another home, another school and another set of children.

When we arrived at the new home, in Grindon, the auntie and uncle were waiting to greet me. They seemed nice, and after the remand home it was like heaven – we were even allowed to play out in the street with the other children. There was just one hitch. Not long after I arrived one of the other boys said to me, 'Have you been seen by Uncle yet?'

I didn't know what he meant, so he told me to watch out because Uncle liked to 'inspect' the new boys. If you seemed OK to him he would 'adopt' you. 'Try not to be alone with him,' he said.

I had no idea what he was talking about, but I soon found out. The following day, when Auntie was out, Uncle called me upstairs to his study and explained that he worked at the hospital. That meant he was a bit like a doctor, and you trusted doctors. He told me that he always examined new boys to ensure that they were healthy, and he made me remove my short trousers. His 'examination' involved feeling my dangly bits, which made me very uncomfortable. Then he told me that he could tell when a boy played with himself and needed to make sure he didn't do this too much. He said I was to tell him when I did.

Well, at that point I didn't. I was nine years old and had no idea what he meant. But I knew I didn't like what he was doing, so I pulled away, yanked my trousers up and kicked him on the shin. He was furious and gave me the slipper across my behind. But he never bothered me again. Over the next few weeks I learned that some boys were in his study for a long time. One lad in particular was sometimes gone on evenings when Auntie was away, coming back very late and crying himself to sleep. Sometimes he was away for a whole weekend, and he never told us what happened to him.

Nobody dared tell on Uncle. How I wish we had, but we had no adult to confide in. We only met the people who worked in the system, and we knew that to tell would only heap more trouble on our heads. A few children visited their families, but they didn't dare tell them either because the likely outcome would have been loss of the visits. The authorities knew how to keep control.

At first Grindon seemed a lighter place. But I couldn't settle. I knew I shouldn't go off, because I'd get into trouble, but eventually the urge to wander and to look for Irene again became too strong.

Uncle and Auntie had gone on holiday and a new auntie had come to cover for them. She was very nice to us, but by then I had already decided to go, and one morning I walked out through the front door before anyone was up. I'd packed a school bag with nibbles from the kitchen and set off down the road.

Not far away there was a car park where a travelling shop used to stop. When I saw it was there I decided some sweets would be useful to keep me going. The shop was still locked up, as it was so early, so I had a go at the back door and got it open. Inside I rummaged through the sweet shelves and filled my school bag to the brim. I also took a nice-looking cake and off I went across the road, cramming chunks of it into my mouth. I didn't think of it as stealing, only a means of sustaining the journey ahead.

I headed across the cornfields leading down to the river and then walked through the woods, enjoying the warmth of summer. I watched as the skimmers flew inches above the water, calling to one another, the occasional wing-tip causing a ripple as they passed. Sometimes a trout would leap out of the water. I thought it was so happy it couldn't contain itself and just had to jump. And that's how I felt then, as I ran through the fields: free as a bird, or a fish.

I sat on the riverbank and thought of Irene, wondering where she was now. It had been almost two years since we had last seen each other, so I felt sure they would probably have moved her to somewhere else by now. But I knew that, wherever she was, she could still look up and see the same blue sky as me.

I wandered through the woods and fields, sleeping in the warm cornfields. I wondered where the butterflies came from and how they managed to survive when high winds blew. I watched the sunlight sparkling on the water, dazzling me, so that when I stared at it I couldn't see properly for ages. All around me were the smells and sounds of summer, and I drank them in.

I had been gone for four days when two policemen picked me up as I was walking through the little riverbank hamlet of Coxgreen – my old haunt. I was taken to the police station, where they found some of the stolen sweets in my bag. The owner of the travelling shop had reported the break-in, and I owned up and was charged before they took me back to Grindon.

The new auntie was waiting at the door and as I got to the doorstep she raised her hands. I closed my eyes, waiting for the slap. When she grabbed me and gave me a great big hug, I was dumbstruck. It was the first time I had ever had a hug since being put in care. You could have caught fish with my mouth it was so wide open with surprise. When she let me go she said, 'Don't look so surprised – you'd think you'd never had a hug before!'

'Thank goodness you're all right,' she continued. 'I've been so worried about you.' That was another surprise; no one had ever expressed any worry about me before either. I was in love!

One of the policemen who'd returned me said, 'How could you run away from here with such a nice lady to look after you?' I was in total agreement.

Apparently the auntie hadn't slept since finding me gone. At that moment I swore to myself that I would never go astray again. I wanted to stay with her and try to be good. She didn't punish me. She didn't need to, because seeing her hurt was enough. I began to think of ways to please her and improve my behaviour.

The next day it was back to the normal routine, but with a difference: I felt happy. I got on with my chores as usual and I decided that when I went back to school on Monday I'd ask the teacher for help with my reading and writing. That was a huge thing for me, as I never asked for help. But before school even started, a black car drove up and a tall man got out. Auntie was in tears and I realised what was happening. She came over and gave me another of those brilliant hugs. 'I'm so sorry,' was all she managed to say.

I was soon in the car and we drove off. Then came the usual question, 'Do you know where you're going?
'No,' I said.

'You're going to where you won't be any trouble to anyone else again,' he said, and he leaned back and tried to slap me with one hand while trying to steer with the other.

I was scared. What could he mean? Was I going to prison?

Not long after, we arrived at the remand home again. My heart sank. Prison couldn't be any worse. I steeled myself for what I knew would be the hard days ahead, beginning with another dose of Matron's 'cream'.

The boy with the white hair was still there, and I nicknamed him Whitehead. He didn't cry any more. He had changed, his face had hardened and he'd become an angry, tough kid. That day we had the first of many scraps. There was no real reason: it was simply that most of us found fighting was a good way to let off steam.

The weeks passed by, and back in the schoolroom I hardly noticed the caning any more. Then one day they brought in a television and told us we would be allowed to watch it for one hour each evening. Brilliant! We were led into a small dark room with chairs positioned in a semi-circle around a brown television set with a tiny screen. We were under the usual orders to keep silent, but with a treat in store it didn't matter. Until the television was turned on. At the hour when we were allowed to watch, there were only two programmes: the news and a brand new show called *Coronation Street*. We had to sit and watch Ena Sharples in her hairnet, in glorious black and white. Hardly the stuff of young boys' imagination. At least in The Esplanade and Grindon we'd been allowed to watch *The Lone Ranger* or *Robin Hood*. But here we were forced to sit in silence and watch Ena until time for cocoa and bed.

Some days we were taken outside to play football. After the many hours of regimented silence it was great being outdoors. We used to play with an old casey, a football made of leather, and if it was raining it got heavier and heavier. The first time I got a header the ball was soaking, and I went down like a ton of bricks, almost knocking myself out. It was the same when I kicked it; I ended up with a limp. After that my strategy was to run around shouting, 'Here, here!' then dodge before the ball was passed, so I wouldn't have to kick it.

As the weeks passed new boys regularly arrived, their hair soaked in cream, tears running down their cheeks. There were two kinds of boys who came. There were those who didn't really belong, who had got into trouble but would soon go home and not come back. And there were those who were in the care system and who were being hardened and would turn to crime – most of it petty – as a way of life.

Most of these boys in care were harmless and only acted tough to protect themselves. But there were a few who seemed to have a darkness locked inside them. These boys would hurt you for no reason at all, and seemed to take pleasure in it. Whitehead was one of those. Though he was only nine years old, we could all see the fury in him and avoided him if we possibly could.

None of us had any idea how long we were there for, or where we were going afterwards. But six weeks after I had been sent back, I was taken to the medical room one morning and told to change, then with no goodbyes to anyone I was led to a car waiting outside and off we went.

The driver was a middle-aged man who had the window open and smoked the whole way. He didn't speak to me, so I watched the fields out of the window and wondered what was coming next.

The place where we eventually arrived seemed just like a hospital. It had a long corridor with a shiny floor that stretched the whole length of the building, with lots of doors on either side. I was led to the headmaster's office, where it was explained to me that this was the Aycliff Assessment Centre, and where I was going next would depend on how I behaved while I was here. I was amazed that someone was actually explaining to me where I was and what it was about. It had never happened before.

The whole place looked new. At one end was what I soon learned was a secure unit for youngsters who had committed terrible crimes such as murder. At the other end were several large houses linked by concrete paths. In the middle were the schoolrooms and a football pitch.

I was led to my house by a master. He asked me about my journey, and I was so unused to being talked to in a pleasant way that I hardly knew what to say.

There were about ten boys in the house, all about the same age. Each of us had our own small bedroom and each night our bedroom doors were locked. Each master carried a set of keys on a chain attached to their belts, and each night a master would be posted downstairs. If you needed the toilet you had a button to press. At one end of the house there was a detention room with a steel door and a narrow glass window. Inside were a blanket and a bare mattress. Occasionally a boy would go crazy or start fighting, and when this happened he would be stripped naked and put in the room for several hours, or in some cases, even days.

I managed to avoid the detention room. I didn't want to go back to the remand home or anywhere worse, if that were possible. I wanted to go somewhere better, so I was determined to keep my nose clean and be good.

14

Irene

I finished my last year of primary school and, having failed the eleven plus, was told I would be going to the comprehensive. But before that the whole summer holiday stretched ahead and, best of all, there was another trip to Whitby.

Once again, I counted the days. Two years on I still longed to see Alan again. This time, I promised myself, I would find him. I would ask every person in Whitby, if I had to.

I spent every spare moment during that week searching. Whenever I could slip away from the other children and the aunties, I walked the cobbled streets and the beaches, peering into shops, talking to the fishermen and running after any fair-haired boy who looked about ten years old – only to feel a pang of disappointment when I reached him. It was with a sore heart that I left at the end of that week, knowing it would be yet another year before I could look for him again. And there was no one to help me in my quest.

So it was back to Rennie Road, to endless dull routine, chores and school.

Before I started at my new school, Auntie Doris took me to the school outfitters in the city centre to be kitted out in the uniform: navy-blue blazer with the school badge on the breast pocket and a matching navy pleated skirt which hung to just below the knee. The badge had a castle in the centre of it, probable based on Hylton Castle at the bottom of Bunny

Hill. I also had a pale blue shirt and a navy tie with pale blue, red, yellow and green stripes. Each stripe represented one of the four houses of the school; mine was North House, I had been told, and our colour was pale blue. To complete the ensemble I had a pair of hard black lace-up shoes, which I absolutely hated.

Margy was already at the comprehensive so on my first morning I walked with her. It was about two miles away, but we weren't allowed to take the bus unless it was raining. The walk took the best part of an hour, so I was glad when Margy showed me a short cut that saved us at least fifteen minutes. The only problem was that it meant going across fields, so I had to be careful not to get my horrid shoes too dirty or I'd be in trouble with the aunties.

I arrived on my first morning at Redhouse Comprehensive, in September 1962 in my smart new uniform, hoping that this might be my chance to make some real friends. The school was so big that it took me several days to find my way around. We had different teachers for different subjects now, and I struggled to keep up. I had never found schoolwork easy, so I was in the lower sets for most subjects, along with the troublemakers and struggling learners.

I longed to be one of the in-crowd. The older girls wore tatty uniforms which they personalised by hitching up their skirts and sewing badges on their jackets. They left their hair loose and swung brightly coloured bags over their shoulders. I would have given anything to join them and to let my uniform take on the 'worn' look that marked you out as cool and a bit of a rebel. But the aunties insisted I look spick and span each day, not a crease out of line, shoes gleaming and hair still cut into the regulation pudding-basin style. While others wore hand-me-down uniforms that had lasted for years, the Local Authority, much to my disgust, provided funds for me to have a whole new uniform every year.

The only way I could make friends, given my miserably un-cool appearance, was to prove that I was tougher than I looked. I homed in on the most unruly of the girls, attracted by their rebel status, and persuaded them to let me hang out with them by acting as lookout when they were smoking behind the swimming-baths wall. I was still too much of a goody-goody to do anything really naughty myself – I certainly didn't dare smoke – but I tried desperately to be accepted by the in-crowd by pretending that I didn't care about getting into trouble.

After school the girls would meet up at the sweet shop near the school and talk about music and fashion while eyeing up the boys. I struggled to be part of it all, following them to the sweet shop. But I could only stay a few minutes, as I had to get back to Rennie Road or face trouble.

Badges were all the rage. The most popular was 'Ban the Bomb' with its upside-down Y-shaped sign, used by all the hippies as a symbol for peace. How I longed to sew one on my uniform, but the aunties wouldn't hear of it.

Eventually, I found my own way round the problem. I made myself a little 'Ban the Bomb' badge out of tin, painting the 'Ban the Bomb' sign on it and attaching a safety pin to the back. I wore it under the lapel of my blazer, so that it could only be seen when I turned my collar up, and it looked real enough. The rest of the girls kept getting caught wearing theirs and got into trouble, but not me!

I wasn't allowed to have friends round to the home, or to stay over at their houses, and I found this really hard. How could I be part of the crowd when I couldn't go to a girlfriend's house, even for an hour or two? Other girls would make arrangements every day after school, while I had to walk away, back to the endless dreary routines. It made me feel sad and angry and sometimes very lonely.

Margy had the same problem. She was in the year above me, but she was under the same restrictions and could never stay out with the other girls or personalise her uniform. I know she shared my frustrations about being excluded from this exciting, changing world. But, strangely perhaps, we never talked about it with one another. Each of us went through our private miseries alone.

That Christmas, after I had turned twelve, I was given a small bottle of cheap perfume at one of the Working Men's Club Christmas parties. I was thrilled; just owning it made me feel a little bit sophisticated and grown up. Desperate not to have to surrender my gift, I hid it under my pillow. I knew the aunties would take it away from me if I actually wore it, so instead I used to open it in bed at night, and sniff its fragrance. It reminded me of the glamorous women who walked around town in high heels, carrying bags from the most fashionable stores in Sunderland.

I hung on to that perfume for years, hidden alongside the precious metal tag bracelet. Those two treasured things were all I had that were truly mine, and I guarded them zealously, moving them into one of my slippers on laundry day each week until I could replace them safely under my pillow.

As we became teenagers the other girls at school started to go out together for evenings at the community centre, or to dances and parties and discos. They would talk about these events all the time – what they wore, who they danced with and so on. I was envious, hearing about the good times they were having, and tried to imagine the things they were describing. They knew I was from 'the homes' so they never asked me to go with them: they knew the answer would be no. And I resigned myself to the dull monotony of my existence as a bystander, while it seemed to me the whole world partied and danced and rocked.

There was new music everywhere for a new social group that had emerged – teenagers! The big bands of the fifties had given way to groups like Freddy and the Dreamers, and in the wake of Elvis, who was rocking the States, crooners had given way to singers like Billy Fury and Adam Faith, who oozed sex-appeal.

Until the late fifties there had only been one television channel, but then a second channel, called ITV, appeared, and now it was running pop shows like *Ready Steady Go!* and *Thank Your Lucky Stars*. This was a hugely exciting development, because it brought our pop heroes right into our living rooms.

Mostly we weren't allowed to watch them in Rennie Road, but I managed to get permission go around to Joan's on many a Friday night, where we watched *Ready Steady Go!* together, jumping around the floor, dancing and shaking our heads to the music. When I visited on other days Joan always had the radio on and we listened to pop music being played. Some of the girls in the street got hold of the new transistor radios: for the first time radios had batteries and were portable, so that you could use them outside. They would sit on top of Bunny Hill listening to Radio Luxembourg, and later to Radio Caroline, one of the many pirate pop stations being broadcast from ships floating out on the sea.

On New Year's Day in 1964, not to be outdone, the BBC launched *Top of the Pops*. It was an instant hit, and had all the best bands on it, including a couple that really grabbed me – the Rolling Stones and the Animals. With their wild looks and raw sounds they were both groups that appealed to that part of me longing to rebel.

And then there were the Beatles, the group that shot to number one in 1963 and reigned supreme for the next few years. They weren't my favourites, but no one could ignore the Fab Four and everyone had a soft spot for Paul, John, Ringo or George.

Unlike all the girls we knew, those of us in Rennie Road weren't allowed to put anything on our bedroom walls, so posters of our idols were out of the question. So were make-up and mini-skirts. While hemlines were rocketing all around us, even talking about wearing a mini-skirt would send the aunties into frenzied outbursts of moralising about 'that type of girl'. The best I could manage was to turn over the waistband on my school skirt once I was out of sight of the aunties each morning. A couple of turns got it to just above my knees, but it was frustrating as it took a while to sort out the pleats so that they looked straight. With my skirt hitched I felt a little more in tune with the other girls, but that was as adventurous as it got for me. So while the girls at school partied, wore mini-skirts and plastered black eye-liner around their eyes like Dusty Springfield, my world barely changed.

The only concession I won as I grew a little older was that the aunties would let me watch a little extra telly, when the pop shows were on. In compensation for this I was given extra jobs to do, helping to look after the younger children. I didn't mind this – I liked bathing the little girls and getting them ready for bed. Knowing I wasn't supposed to get too close to them or show affection, I tried to hold back. But they were so young and I felt so sad that they had lost their mothers, so sometimes I gave them a big hug before they went to bed, while swearing them to secrecy.

Around this time there was a great sadness in my life. One afternoon I looked out of the playroom window and saw Dad and Uncle Bob walking very slowly past, on the other side of the road. Normally if they passed by, on the way to or from Joan's, they would look up and wave, but this time they didn't. I was puzzled, and worried. Why were they going so slowly? And why hadn't they looked up to see if I was watching?

A few days later I was looking out of the window when I saw Greta coming up the street. I ran to Auntie Doris and asked to go out and meet her, and when Auntie Doris agreed I ran out to Greta.

She put her arms around me, and I sensed that something was wrong. Then she told me that Uncle Bob had died. I was heartbroken. I had loved Uncle Bob so much. I couldn't get used to the idea that he wasn't there any longer. I went back indoors in tears and was left alone in my bedroom until the tears stopped.

No one told me what Uncle Bob had died of and I wasn't taken to his funeral. As so often happened when someone died in those days, no one spoke of him again. But I thought of him every single day, and often wished I could see him walking up the street again, coming to take me out for the day, his cap on his head and a broad smile on his gentle face.

15

Alan

After the horrors of the remand home, Aycliff was almost human. And my determination to behave well paid off; for the next few months life seemed to be getting better for me.

We went to classes in the school buildings and were given proper lessons. We played games on the pitch, which was floodlit so that we could carry on when the evenings grew dark. And a group of us even went to one of the masters' homes, where his wife baked cakes for us and played us jazz music. One lad knew every jazz sound and song they could name. I was puzzled by some of the crazy sounds and never really enjoyed it. But sitting in the master's home, eating my fill of his wife's cooking, I was happy to listen.

One day I was sent for by the headmaster and told about the new 'school' I would be going to. It sounded great! It was somewhere in Wales and everything about it sounded nice, but the bit that stuck in my head was that it had its own miniature railway system. I had been well-behaved, the headmaster said, and if I kept up my good behaviour it was likely that this was where I'd be going. Picturing that miniature railway, I headed back to my lessons with a big grin on my face. Of course I was going to carry on being good, if that was where I was headed.

When we were introduced to rugby for the first time I loved it. I thought it was a bit like British Bulldog, but better. We played on the floodlit pitch on the evening of Hallowe'en, and to my amazement one of the new boys on the other team was Whitehead. We clashed when I brought him down just before he made it to the line – and boy, was he steaming mad! Not a good thing where he was concerned, even though it was a game.

The next day about five of us were waiting for a master over at the main block when Whitehead appeared. When he saw me he snarled and ran at me. There was a small wall between us, but he was so mad he just didn't see it and he jumped in the air, aiming a flying kick at me. His lower leg caught the wall and he hit the concrete with a thud and a squeal. Another boy close to him burst out laughing, and in an instant Whitehead was up and on him and began to kick him furiously. Now Whitehead was famed for wearing very hard shoes with which he would kick the living daylights out of anyone he didn't like, and once he started on someone he wouldn't stop.

We had to intervene as quickly as we could so we all jumped on him, grabbing his feet and arms to keep him still. He was screaming in frustration but we hung on to him until he wore himself out. The boy he'd kicked was bleeding badly from his face, and unfortunately while we still had tight hold of Whitehead the boy ran at him and kicked him in the leg – just as the headmaster walked out.

Whitehead went loony, and with his mad strength he broke free and we all got kicked or fisted somewhere. The headmaster was shouting at us all when Whitehead attacked him, too, and bit his leg. Two other masters who were passing got hold of him and pinned him down until the school doctor arrived and gave him an injection, after which they carried him away to the secure block.

That was the last we saw of him. We all knew Whitehead was dangerous and mad but, as we found out when we were summoned to the headmaster's study the next day, the adults wouldn't listen to us. The headmaster, whose leg was bandaged, was furious; his interpretation of events was that we had held down a defenceless boy and made him have a fit – it turned out that Whitehead was also epileptic. We tried to protest our innocence, but he refused to listen and we were locked in the detention rooms. I spent my eleventh birthday alone, lying on a foam mattress, naked and wrapped in a grey itchy blanket.

After forty-eight hours I was taken back to the headmaster's office and he informed me that the 'school' I was going to had been changed: I would now be going somewhere more suited to me. The other boys had the same story; their allocated school had been changed too, but none of us had been told where we were going.

I felt gutted. I had worked so hard to be well-behaved through my time there, only for it all to be blown by one incident – and even then I was trying to do the right thing. Now I was going to go somewhere that was probably awful – and I would never see the miniature railway in Wales.

Days later I was called in to see the head, who told me I was being transferred that day. I had one hour to say my goodbyes. I was amazed – I'd never been given notice before. I went back to my house and said goodbye to the other boys, before I was put into yet another black car to set off to my eighth destination in seven years.

It was Friday 9 November 1963. I always remembered the date because it was one week after my eleventh birthday and just two weeks before President Kennedy was assassinated.

This time I had a very chatty driver, who worked at the school where I was going. He told me I was going to live in a castle, and painted a warm and inviting picture of my new home. It sounded magical, like something out of a story book: a castle on a hill overlooking a river and a green valley, surrounded by high hills. And the boys there went camping each year. To think I'd been worried! I could hardly wait to get there.

It took us a few hours, driving along winding country lanes, over hills and moors, passing stone walls, forests, small villages, little bridges and sheep and cattle in the fields. I enjoyed the journey; it really did seem right out of a story book.

It was afternoon when we arrived at a small village with a market square and an old church with a square tower to one side. We followed the narrow road under a low stone bridge to a gateway, with a gatehouse. The wheels crunched on the gravelled drive as we drove slowly up to the castle.

One end of the building really did look like a castle. The rest was a large three-storey building covered in Virginia creeper. There was a circular lawn on our right, surrounded by large trees, with pathways leading through them. The whole place was built on a hill, and it certainly did look out across the valley and surrounding hills.

We got out of the car and I was led to a large set of wooden gates, like the castle gates you see in books. One side of the gate had a door in it with a large metal ring. We went through and into a dark tunnel, which opened out into a courtyard surrounded by grey stone walls four storeys high with small windows set in them.

I really felt as if I was in a castle when some of the boys marched by and their voices echoed around the walls. I noticed they were wearing the same old short pants, long grey socks to the knee and V-necked jumpers. And they had black boots with studs set into the soles, so that they sounded noisily on the ground when they walked. Was this the fairytale castle the driver had described? I wasn't at all sure – the boys had looked as though they were in an army camp. I felt very nervous as I waited to see what would happen next.

Minutes later my housemaster arrived. He led me to the clothing store in the basement, where I was kitted out in the uniform and given black shoes as well as the hard boots, a navy blue raincoat, a pair of striped pyjamas and a school cap with a badge on it. The housemaster took out a set of cobbler's steel stencils with figures on them and hammered the number 45 into the leather of my shoes and boots. That was to be my number from now on, he said.

I discovered that I was now in Stanhope Castle Approved School, which was run like a cross between a public school and an army camp. The headmaster was an ex-public schoolboy and an army major who had fought in the war. My housemaster, who was called Mr Maddison, had been his regimental sergeant-major, and most of the masters had a military background and had served with him.

That evening I was taken into my houseroom to meet the other boys. There were about twenty in each house – around eighty boys in all. Each house was named after a local hill; ours was Horsley.

Friday turned out to be 'roll' night. That meant a full kit inspection. You had to wear all your clothes, including raincoat and cap, and report to the houseroom, where the housemaster was sitting behind his desk with some older boys standing beside him. One by one we had to go and stand at attention in front of the desk and give our full name and number. The boys would inspect our clothing for damage and the housemaster would inform us of any punishments or rewards due for that week; he would then tally our pocket money, after first deducting savings and fines for any damage to clothing or the building.

The remaining amount was credited to each boy. But we didn't get any actual money. Beside him the housemaster had a large box full of sweets and comics from which he would issue you with what he thought was appropriate, according to the amount of pocket money you had.

We had to stay in silence on roll night until the housemaster had finished. But on that first night no one told me about it. I had no idea what was going on, as each boy went up to the desk when he was called. I asked the boy next to me what was happening. He looked at me, eyes wide like a frightened rabbit, and whispered 'Sshhh.'

One of the older boys standing next to the housemaster came over and shouted, 'Quiet!' and, without warning, hit me over the head with a bunch of heavy keys. Furious and in pain, I jumped up and punched him on the nose. For a moment he looked startled. Then he grabbed me, and the next minute we were rolling around the floor, trying to punch or kick and bite and sending chairs flying.

It all came to an end when a hand grabbed my collar and I was dragged into the air, legs dangling. It was the housemaster, highly annoyed at this disturbance. 'I'll teach you to be disobedient!' he said, and I was dragged into his study, where he gave me six of the best with a springy bamboo cane.

I could hardly believe that another boy had been permitted to hit me. Everywhere else I'd been, boys couldn't hit other boys. But later I learned that the boy had been the house leader and that the house leaders almost ran the place; if any of them gave you an order, you obeyed them, as they had full authority to mete out any corporal punishments other than caning.

So my first night was a disaster. I lay in bed that night, bruised and miserable, thinking that this castle on the hill was more a Sheriff-of-Nottingham-type prison than the Camelot I'd imagined.

After lights out some of the boys crept out of bed and came over. They told me what the place was like and who to avoid. The main thing was to do as you were told to avoid punishments from masters and the older boys. And watch out for the headmaster, they whispered.

Breakfast the next morning was in the vast, wood-panelled dining hall. The long tables were laid with cutlery and serving dishes, toast racks and jugs of orange juice. I was shown to my place by another boy and we had to sit to attention with crossed arms, in complete silence.

At one end of the hall was a large Georgian window looking out across the lawn, and in front of it was a wooden rostrum about a foot high with a dining table on it. On the table was a silver coffee-pot and a carefully rolled newspaper. Beside them was a springy walking stick.

The doors opened and a large middle-aged lady walked in. This was Matron, wife of the headmaster. She was, I learned, in charge of all medical matters, the laundry, the kitchens, the sewing rooms, and all the staff who ran them.

'Good morning, boys,' she said.

'Good morning, Matron,' we all replied.

The doors opened again and in strode the headmaster. He was short, bald and plump, with thick pebble glasses. He walked with his feet pointing outwards, like a duck, and his arms swinging high, marching style, and he had a cheery grin on his face. I thought he seemed rather jolly.

'Good morning, boys,' he boomed.

'Good morning, Sir,' we repeated.

He strode up to the rostrum and sat down at the table, with Matron.

On the opposite side of the hall from the window was a wide door that led into the kitchens, and through it came some of the best food I had ever tasted – wonderful roasts, pies, hot-pots and puddings. It seemed the head insisted that the cook should always cater to the highest standards. He would go into the kitchen each day and taste the samples prepared for him by the cook although, strangely, he didn't eat the same food as the boys. Lunch and supper were prepared separately for him and Matron, and delivered to their living quarters on a trolley. The only time he ate with us was at breakfast, when he had toast, marmalade, coffee and prunes!

As for the walking stick on the table, I didn't know what it was for until two or three days after my arrival, when a boy dropped a fork on the floor. He began scrambling about under the table for it, and the other boys had to move, scraping their chairs on the wooden floor.

'Come here, boy!' the head shouted.

Everyone stopped eating and froze. The boy was obviously terrified as he walked over to the rostrum. The headmaster got up, grabbed the stick and began to beat him around the legs and behind while shouting, 'You – will – be – silent!' in time with his strikes. He repeated it twice – eight very painful strokes. The boy fell down, crying his eyes out, and the headmaster shouted, 'Get up, boy, and be a man.' The boy got up and said, 'Thank you, Sir,' through his tears.

Matron took the sobbing boy by the arm and led him out of the hall. Apparently if she didn't his sobbing could set the head off again. Meanwhile the head returned to his breakfast as if nothing had happened and we slowly returned to ours. I wondered what he'd do if you did something really bad.

I learned from the other boys that it was fairly common for the head to lose his temper. The little corridor outside his office was, they told me, often host to a queue of boys awaiting 'judgement' from him in the mornings before breakfast. Perhaps it helped his appetite. And he expected every boy to say 'thank you' for the punishment that helped him to recognise his wrongdoing, or there would be a repeat performance.

We were certainly well fed. We even had a supper, which consisted of cocoa and a piece of cake or a scone before bed. But the food turned out to be just about the only good thing about the place.

Later that first day the house leader and his friends decided that I should be shown where I stood in the pecking order. That was usual in all the homes I'd been in; I'd long ago learned that taking on the leader earned the other boys' esteem, but it also meant taking a hiding, unless you could beat him. Which I couldn't, on this occasion. I was to end up with several bruises and a large black eye.

16

Irene

By the time I turned thirteen I had begun to realise that I would probably never be moved from Rennie Road. I was both sorry and relieved about that. Sorry that I would never be moved to wherever Alan was. But relieved, too, that I wouldn't be suddenly whisked away to a home that was cold and cruel, as I had heard some were. And then, of course, there was Joan, around the corner. She and the children gave me an escape route that made everything so much more bearable, and I was grateful to be able to remain close to them.

For better or worse, it seemed that Rennie Road was my home, and would be until I left, as all children did then, at the age of fifteen. Of course, no one ever told me I was staying – and I wouldn't have dared to ask. It was simply that, as time went by, I realised I might never be moved. But there was always a chance that I could be wrong and would be woken one day and told to pack, so I was still careful to behave as obediently as possible.

The only other children who remained long-term were Margy and Silvy and their brothers Joe and Kenny. So many others arrived and then vanished again that their faces just became a blur in my memory.

Now that I was thirteen I was told to help Margaret the cleaner with the domestic chores whenever I had free time after school. So I would vacuum, dust and tidy up with her, while the younger children went out to play. At the weekends I helped the aunties by peeling the veg for dinner, making sandwiches and setting the table. I also spent more time helping with the younger girls, getting them ready for bed and helping them dress in the mornings. I always enjoyed doing this, because it gave me a chance to mother them a little.

I liked being given more responsibility. But although I had more chores, there was no more freedom. I still couldn't even go to a friend's house for tea after school, and my life was just as restricted as it had been when I was nine. The only small concession was that I was allowed to walk back to the church alone on Sunday afternoons, to help out at the Sunday school. Normally we were marched everywhere by the aunties, which immediately identified us as the kids from the home. Walking alone, for the few minutes it took to get to church, I had a brief taste of how it felt to be like other teenagers.

I used to love telling people I was a Sunday school teacher. Helping there made me feel grown up. I read the younger children stories from the Bible about Jesus and Mary, or helped the little ones with their prayers or with colouring pictures to take home to their mums and dads. I was determined not to be bossy or order them about in the way the aunties treated us.

Auntie Nan had been at Rennie Road ever since I'd arrived, and I think for a long time before that. So it was a huge surprise when we were told that she was leaving. We children didn't hear about it until the day she went, so there was no time at all to get used to the idea. And of course we weren't told where she was going, though perhaps she was simply retiring.

Nan had been the strictest auntie, cold and distant and always a stickler for rules. It was Nan who had pulled me and Alan apart at the holiday camp, and who had no doubt set things in motion for him to be taken away. She could have overlooked two children playing together on the last day of their holiday, but Nan overlooked nothing, reprimanding us for the tiniest misdeed. So perhaps it wasn't surprising that, the moment she left, the atmosphere lightened. No one commented on it – we wouldn't have dared – but it was as though we could all breathe a little easier without her standing over us.

For me, especially, there was a great sense of relief. I had never forgiven Nan for sending Alan away. Four years later I still felt angry and upset about it. I'd had to swallow those feelings for all that time, never daring to show her how I felt. When she left, a lot of my hurt and anger seemed to dissolve, and I felt suddenly happier. My only worry was that she might be replaced by someone worse. But to all our delight, the new auntie who arrived was entirely different.

Auntie Joyce was much younger and friendlier and far less strict than Auntie Nan had been. I liked her immediately, and so did the other children. She had a ready smile, and instead of barking orders she asked us politely to do things. With Auntie Joyce it was possible to feel like a human being instead of a little robot. She would often sit and talk to us and even give some of the younger ones a hug, and before long I was missing her every time she went off duty and longing for her to come back.

Auntie Doris had never been as tough as Auntie Nan, but she was very much of the old order. She would take Auntie Joyce to one side and mutter to her that she should 'stay clear' of getting involved with the children. As the months passed by, the strain between them began to show as they spent more and more time having talks in the office, from which Auntie Joyce would emerge looking flushed and upset. I was very afraid that she would be made to leave, but in fact she never was: she was still at Rennie Road when I left, two years later, so perhaps Auntie Doris realised that Auntie Joyce's more relaxed, warm style was not entirely a bad thing.

The next person to leave Rennie Road was Margy, who was now fifteen. She had an older sister who hadn't been in care, and one day this sister turned up to collect her and took her home to live with her. I knew how lucky Margy was, because most of those who left care had nowhere to go. I wondered what would happen when it was my turn to leave, because I knew none of my sisters had room for me.

Silvy missed Margy a lot, and so did I. We began to get much friendlier and I asked Auntie Doris if Silvy could help me with some of the chores. Silvy and I would chat together while we made sandwiches, washed up and mopped the kitchen floor. She was the closest thing I had to a best friend, and after feeling friendless for so long it was a real joy for me to have someone to talk to.

Nan's departure, the arrival of Auntie Joyce and my blossoming friendship with Silvy all helped to bring about a shift in me. I became more outgoing and cheerful, and though I was still rather serious and very responsible, I felt lighter and happier.

Despite so often feeling that I was the odd one out, the care-home girl the others looked down on, I even managed to make three good friends at school – Denise, or Denny, as we called her, and the two Margies, neither of whom was the Margy who had been at Rennie Road. Denny was quiet and well-behaved, and our friendship lasted long after I left school. The two Margies were rebellious and often in trouble, which is what attracted me to them. I would watch out for them when they were smoking behind the wall or getting up to other forbidden pranks.

I was longing to grow up and be more fashionable, like the other girls. But Auntie Doris was determined to resist. I asked her if I could grow my hair a little longer, as I was older now and would soon be leaving. But she said it was the rule that we had to have it cut short because of head lice and there could be no exceptions. I felt very frustrated as I had never known anyone in the home to have nits, and I was sure it was just a ploy to force me to have the usual awful cut. The hairdresser would arrive every six weeks and all of us, girls and boys, would be lined up in the playroom to have our hair cut. We all came out looking exactly the same – the girls with the universally unflattering pudding-basin cut and the boys with a short back and sides.

Apart from the extra chores I was given, I was still treated in just the same way as the younger children and I felt more and more upset and frustrated about it. Worst of all was the bath-time routine that took place every night. All of us had to queue in two lines on the landing outside the two bathrooms, wrapped in towels and waiting for our turn. We girls would take swipes at the boys, who were always trying to pull at our towels when the auntie in charge wasn't looking. I would grip mine tightly round my blossoming figure, desperate to get the bath over with.

Once the bath was run the smallest child went in first, followed by the next, and so on. The water wasn't changed, so the older children, who went in last, got the dirtiest water. By the time I was fourteen I was waiting an hour or more on the landing in my towel, and then bathing in water that had already been used five or six times. And I was still not allowed to lock the door. The only exception to this was during my monthly cycle, when I was allowed a little privacy.

This bath-time routine became more and more humiliating and awful. But it was made clear that it would not be changed. The same applied to bedtime: I still had to go to bed at 8.30 every night. It seemed like torture, especially in the summer. I would lie awake for a couple of hours, frustrated at being treated the same way as the seven-year-olds.

The only change in our routine was that we were now allowed to watch TV for an hour in the evening, provided we had hand-washed our underclothes and completed our chores before getting bathed and ready for bed. This, I suspected, was the result of Auntie Joyce's influence, and even though there wasn't a lot of choice about what we watched, it was a treat.

At school my studies were as poor as ever. I found it very hard to concentrate on anything for long and spent most of my time daydreaming and looking out of the window. I couldn't see the point of schoolwork. No one had ever talked to me about what I might like to do with my life, or helped me to improve my work. I just drifted through school, without any direction, ambition or thought of what the future held.

That year another piece of news absorbed a lot of my attention. My sister Joan was pregnant for the third time. I was so excited. I loved going round to Joan's house to see how big her bump was getting, and as she got nearer to the end of her pregnancy I helped out as much as I could with Elaine and Alan. Elaine had blonde hair and piercing blue eyes. She was a beautiful child, always smiling and giggling, and everyone adored her. Alan had the same blond hair and blue eyes, and though a little quieter he was always a very happy child.

The baby was born in October 1964, just before my fourteenth birthday. It was another little girl, and they called her Joan, after her mum. I went round to their house as often as I was allowed, to see the baby and help with the other two while Joan nursed her. She was a gorgeous little thing, and whenever I was allowed to hold her I gazed at her tiny face and little curled fists in wonder.

My sister was only twenty-seven, but tragically she began to develop serious health problems and was diagnosed with rheumatoid arthritis. It became hard for her to hold on to things, and gradually her hands began to twist out of shape and became increasingly painful. It was a struggle for her to look after the children, and I wished that I lived with her and could help all the time. At least I was now allowed to go round to Joan's more often, so, if I had done my chores, while the other children played outside I would nip over to Joan's to see what I could do to help. Fifteen months later, in January 1966, Joan gave birth to her fourth child, a son named Robert. He was another adorable baby, and I loved him as much as I had the other three.

My second sister Greta, who was twenty-four when little Joan was born, had two children by this time – Paul and Sue. She had moved from the cottage to a bigger house in Carley Hill. She sometimes came to see me, with the children, and at other times Dad or Joan would come and take me to visit her. I loved seeing Greta and her children.

Pat was now seventeen and had left school and started work in the Sunderland branch of Woolworths, as a sales assistant. She still lived in Seaham with Aunt Jen, and she would get the bus from Seaham to work each day. She loved her job, and now that she had money of her own, and the freedom that went with it, she would come to meet me and Dad at the Railway pub whenever he collected me on a Saturday. While Dad sat over his pint, Pat and I would walk around town together and visit the shops. Pat was always dressed in the latest fashion, with her hair beautifully styled; she was very popular, and we would often bump into her friends in town. I loved these outings, even though I felt like the frumpy little sister: I loved being with Pat, listening to the tales she told of her friendships and her nights out, and wandering through the shops, looking at the latest fashions.

This was all another world to me. I still didn't have any of my own clothes, and when I was out of school uniform I had to wear the clothes they dished out at the weekends. Silvy and I, who were a similar size, would rummage through and swap the clothes around, trying to put a reasonable outfit together and to find the best fit. But no matter how hard we tried, we still looked as though we were wearing a hotch-potch of second-hand clothes. It was rare that we found anything we liked to wear, and if we did, it wouldn't be there the next time we sorted through the clothes, or someone else would snatch it first.

One Saturday Dad told me he'd decided I was old enough to have a few of my own clothes now. We both knew this would have to be a secret mission because if the aunties got wind of it the things would be taken away from me, and we agreed that the clothes would have to be left at Joan's. But I didn't care – even if I had to hide them, just to have my own, new clothes would be wonderful.

Dad took me around to the market and asked me what I wanted. I chose a pair of tanned patent leather shoes with Cuban heels and a little cotton mini-dress with multi-coloured circles on it. It was the latest look, and for the first time in my life I felt really with it. All I needed was somewhere special to wear them.

In town a club for teenagers had opened, called the Rink. All the girls at school were talking about it, and it had instantly become the place to be seen. The Rink was open on Saturday afternoons, and Pat often went there after our shopping trips to meet her friends. The two Margies had started going there too and I longed to go with them, so we hatched a plan.

The next time Dad took me out on a Saturday I asked him if I could go to the Rink and meet Pat. He said yes, but not to tell the aunties about it. He didn't have to tell me – I knew they would go mad if they found out. He took me to the Railway pub, as usual, and I went into the toilets and got changed into my new mini-dress and smart shoes. I gave Dad my other clothes in a carrier bag and set off to the Rink, which was only five minutes away. It was the dawning of a new world for me. I felt like a different girl as I headed for the club in my new outfit. When I went in there were stairs leading down to the dance floor and I stood at the top, feeling so excited, listening to the throb and pulse of the music, which was incredibly loud. On the dance floor, lights were flashing and hundreds of kids were doing the twist and lots of other dances that I'd seen on TV.

The two Margies arrived and we all went in together. I was so glad we'd arranged to meet – I wouldn't have dared to go in without them. Inside I found Pat with her friends. They were all older than me so I stayed with my school friends and danced all afternoon. I did the twist and jumped up and down and spun around like everyone else, and I just didn't want to stop. It was fantastic.

Eventually I had to go back to the pub to meet Dad. Pat walked me back, and all the way the music was still playing in my head. I slipped into the loo and changed back into my awful care-home clothes and put my new things in the bag. Then Dad and I went round to Joan's and I left the bag with my precious new things at her house.

Back at Rennie Road I replayed the afternoon over and over in my head. I had felt alive for the first time since Alan had gone. At last I was one of the girls, accepted, normal and like every other teenager out on a Saturday afternoon. After that I begged Dad to come and get me every Saturday, and most weeks he did. We'd go through the same routine – collecting the bag with my dress and shoes from Joan's, heading to the Railway pub where I'd change, and then Dad would nurse his pint while I sprinted off to the Rink to join my friends. Those Saturdays made all the awful childlike rules and routines of Rennie Road bearable. I had a wonderful time, and the music would stay in my head right through to Monday morning.

The following year Auntie Doris finally made two real concessions. She allowed me to skip the dreaded hairdresser's visit and grow my hair a little longer. And, to my amazement, she allowed me to buy some coloured underwear instead of the regulation white cotton. She used to take me to Joplings department store in the town twice a year to buy undies, and there was usually no question of choice. But on our last visit she allowed me to buy a pink bra and knickers set and a lemon one, while she muttered that she would have to put it in the book as white so the Children's Office, which oversaw such things, wouldn't know we had broken the rules.

In the summer of 1965 I went on what was to be my last holiday to Whitby. By this time we had stopped staying in the army huts in Staithes and had moved to a hotel on West Cliff, in Whitby itself. This was much nicer than staying in the draughty old huts. We all shared large hotel rooms with big comfortable beds, wardrobes for our clothes and a chest of drawers beside each bed. The curtains hung to the floor and were tied back with fancy rope that had tassels on the ends, and the whole thing made us feel very special.

All the homes were sending their children to this hotel, so the place was packed with us and there were, thankfully, no other guests to disturb. And unlike the old days, when we were marched everywhere in silence, the staff appeared far more relaxed and let us run about.

During that week I often sat on the window seat in my room, looking out across the harbour, and watched the boats sailing by and the people below, sitting on benches or on the sand with their ice creams. I was still looking out for Alan, still certain that he was there somewhere and that if I kept looking I would eventually spot him.

For five years I had looked forward to the annual holiday, so that I could search for Alan. And for five years I had failed to find him. It was hard to accept, as we left that last time, that I might never go back, or find my special friend again.

17

Alan

On my first morning at Stanhope the headmaster called me to his study after breakfast. He told me that my behaviour the previous evening demonstrated that a firm hand was needed to control me, and it would be applied. After the caning I'd been given by the housemaster, and the head's performance at breakfast, I believed him.

I spent the day being introduced to rules, rules and more rules – and trying to find my way around. The school was a bit of a maze and it took a while to learn the layout, though if you remembered that the courtyard was in the centre and everything else was in a circle around it, it was easier. The dormitories ran right around the building on the first floor, each one linked to the next by an open doorway, so that to get to one room you walked through the others.

Every morning all the boys gathered in the assembly hall, standing to attention in our four house groups and in size order, little ones at the front, so that the head could see us all. The younger boys then went to their classrooms, where we were taught the basics of reading, writing, science and maths using wooden-shafted pens with nibs, inkwells and blotting paper. There were no exams taken at Stanhope, so boys left without qualifications. It was assumed that we would all take up manual trades. Once we reached thirteen, formal education was cut back and each boy was given jobs to do in the school – working in the laundry, kitchens or gardens, or on maintenance, repair and cleaning – which was presumably considered to be some kind of preparation for work in the outside world.

There was plenty of exercise – the head obviously believed in keeping young boys active. We had a huge playing field with three football pitches on it, and most of the boys played regularly. But Mr Maddison loved to walk, so when the other houses were playing football or games, we were walking – no matter what the weather. He believed, as did the head, that boys needed strict discipline and hard work to toughen them up. I sometimes wondered if the two of them didn't think they were preparing us for another war.

We'd go on great long treks that frequently lasted several hours. Mr Maddison used to wear an old-fashioned full-length raincoat with stout brown walking shoes and a hat right out of a 1930s movie. He always wore his suit and tie underneath, of course; proper attire was vital at all times.

Much of the time we had to march, especially through the village. We were lined up in size order, smallest boys at the front, with the house leader to one side, shouting, 'Left! Right! Left! Right!' Mr Maddison would take up the rear with his walking stick in hand. The villagers thought it was a walking aid, but we knew its real purpose.

Once we reached open countryside we were allowed to stop marching and walk more freely. And tough as many of these walks were, they did have a lasting effect on me. I fell in love with the hills and streams and watching the shadows of clouds racing across the hillsides. We visited waterfalls, and out across the moors we watched the hawks swooping down for prey and listened to the lonely sound of curlews and the panic of disturbed grouse. Occasional owls swooped by and we'd catch the bark of a distant dog fox. This was all magic to my ears, and I came to know the hills and valleys and the changing seasons intimately.

Just outside the village there was a hill so steep that the road going up it curved from side to side, like the roads we'd seen in pictures of the Swiss Alps. It led up to the high moors and Bollihope Common, and then around to the next small hamlet, up the valley, before dropping back to the school. On an average day this round trip would take us three to four hours. But one cold winter's day Mr Maddison decided to take us on this route despite the fact that snow was falling as we set out.

All we boys were wearing was our rain macs, with a vest, shirt, jumper and short trousers underneath, no gloves and only our school caps. As soon as we saw where we were heading, there were quiet murmurs among the boys, because we knew it was going to be hard and cold. As we climbed the snow got heavier, so that by the time we stopped to rest in a disused quarry, high up on the grouse moor, we were in blizzard conditions.

Mr Maddison must have realised it was getting hazardous so we were rapidly called into line and marched onwards. This didn't last long as it was impossible to march through snow. We had to break ranks and walk as best we could. The road disappeared and we struggled on, using old stone walls and the marker poles set along the moors road to guide us. But with a four-mile stretch of road still ahead and the blizzard still raging, we were frozen and exhausted. We pressed on, heads down to keep the snow out of our eyes, but it was an immense struggle to go forward into the wind, sinking into deep snow with every step. The skin on our knees got scraped by the icy crust on top of the snow and we longed to stop, but it would have been fatal. The older lads kept the youngest going by singing songs, yelling words of encouragement and linking arms with them.

It took us nearly six hours to get back to the school. Exhausted, terribly hungry and rigid with cold, we headed to the dining hall, where one dinner lady had stayed on to serve tea – by this time several hours late. However, instead of the hot meal we longed for, we were presented with plates of congealed and unappetising cold food. And to add to our dismay, when we attempted to eat, our fingers were so frozen that we couldn't use our knives and forks.

We went to bed hungry, sore and cold that night. Our knees, cheeks and hands were burned and chapped for weeks after; we had to go to the sick-bay each morning so that the nurse could put iodine on the worse bits. That stung so badly that you could hear our squeals down the road. Though we were taken on plenty of other tough walks, none was quite as harsh as that one.

In keeping with their belief that the more time we spent outside the better, the staff organised camping trips for the boys every June. We always went to a little campsite up the valley from the school, close to a wide stream. We had two army-style ridge tents made of canvas for the boys and one for the master. We had an old sleeping bag each, one itchy blanket, a change of clothes, plimsolls with no socks, our usual shorts and pyjamas, and unless the weather was unusually warm we spent most of the time shivering.

Breakfast was hot porridge. But to get it we had to run down the hill, across a stream and up the hill on the other side. This was harder than you might imagine, as the hillside was covered in a tangle of heather and we had to scramble up it, our bare legs being scratched and scoured by the foliage.

If we were too slow the master would hand out other tasks, which often involved carrying heavy rocks about.

The opposite hillside curved round, out of sight of the master waiting at the bottom. So to prove we had been right up, we were supposed to bring back a leaf from a tree there. We soon came up with a strategy to get around this. One boy was chosen to run up and complete the task, bringing a handful of leaves back to share out, while the rest of us waited, out of sight. When he got back, a couple of boys would carry him back as he was too tired to run all the way. This worked beautifully and the master never caught on, despite the fact that one boy's legs would be scratched to bits while the rest of us were fine.

There were the occasional treats at Stanhope, to break the harsh regime. One was our weekly trip to the swimming pool in Durham city. We made the hour-long journey in an old-fashioned single-decker bus. Its bonnet stuck out at the front, and between the big headlights there was a hole for the crank-handle. If the battery was flat – as frequently happened – we would watch the driver working up a sweat as he furiously wound the handle to start the thing up. It was a wonderfully picturesque and slow journey as we chugged along, through the dales and across the hills. But God help you if you needed a pee, because the driver didn't dare stop in case the bus failed to start again.

Our biggest treat of all was a trip to the pictures once a month, on a Saturday evening. We were lined up and checked for proper dress, which meant boots, raincoat and cap if it was raining, or boots and a jumper if not. Then we were marched out to the main gate and up the road to the town hall, where rows of wooden benches like church pews had been set out. In front was a stage, above which a large screen was lowered from the ceiling.

All the children in the village went to the pictures too. They always sat at the front, while we filed into the seats at the back. Before we went we were told not to talk with any of them. If asked a question we would reply with a simple yes or no without further discussion, and a master would be present there to prevent any contact.

One day the kids from the village decided to have some fun, so some of them sat in the back seats, where we were supposed to be. This meant that we had to spread out, and some of us had to sit next to village boys and even – heaven forbid! – girls. The masters weren't happy, but they could hardly tell the village children what to do so, grim-faced, they said nothing.

I was one of the lucky ones that day; I sat in the middle of the front row next to a local girl who looked about the same age as me. Sitting on the bench next to her, all her friends were whispering and giggling among themselves as I took my place.

The lights went out and the film started. Shortly afterwards the girl turned to me and whispered, 'Do you like the film?' and put her hand on my bare knee. I could feel the heat rising in my face as I squeaked out a high-pitched, 'Yes.' She removed her hand and turned to her friends to carry on whispering and giggling. But a few minutes later she put her hand back on my knee, and once again my temperature soared so high that I must have been glowing in the dark.

As soon as the interval arrived there was a scramble from the older boys and deals were done to change places with those of us sitting at the front. Relegated to a back seat by a senior boy, I basked in the memory of my illicit encounter.

Back at school word spread to the headmaster that there had been fraternisation with the local children. Action would have to be taken, but what? We soon found out. In assembly the head announced, 'Instead of going to the cinema, the cinema will be coming to us!' At that point a large projector was wheeled in on a tea-trolley. 'In future we will be showing our own films each month in the assembly hall. Won't that be good, boys?' he boomed. 'Yes, Sir,' we all said, our hearts sinking.

On the appointed evening the large drapes in the assembly hall were drawn and we were seated in rows, facing a projector screen. We sat in silent anticipation as one of the masters fumbled with the projector, trying to load the first reel. Just as the film was about to begin the head stood up and announced, 'I know you will enjoy this film. I chose it especially for you and I am arranging for some of you to use it as a school project.' You could feel the sudden onset of depression ripple through the audience. If he chose it then it had to be the most boring film known to man.

In total silence we watched as the projector flickered into life and the title of the film appeared on the screen: *Man of Arran*. It was a black and white documentary about life on the Isle of Arran in the Scottish Hebrides. A brilliant educational documentary, no doubt. But not exactly what we had in mind for our Saturday night treat.

We were afraid that this meant the end of film-night fun, but fortunately for us the head never made an appearance at the film show again and the housemasters were given a list of reasonably decent films to choose from.

I had been at the school for about eighteen months when I made another bid to escape and find Irene.

Two older boys approached me, planning to escape. Knowing that I had walked for miles around the area, they asked me if I could tell them how to get across the hills to

Gateshead. I knew the route, and I also knew where the key was to the locked window which gave access to the school roof, so I promised to help. Then I decided to go one better, and go with them. I had dreamed of trying to make it back to Sunderland to find Irene. This was my chance.

A few nights later the three of us climbed out of the window and into the cold night air. I remember pausing for a moment to look at the myriad stars gleaming in the blackness and the feeling of space it gave me. We crept past the headmaster's window, slid down the drainpipe and carefully made our way across the drive and out of the main gates. Using the back lanes, we got up to the high moor.

Once on the moor road we started running. It was windy up on the tops and I lost my cap somewhere on the moor, but I was hot with running and the cool air felt good. The night was clear, and in the starry sky I saw a meteor. And it was in that moment that I realised I was on a fool's errand. It had been five years since I'd seen Irene, and it began to dawn on me that she would almost certainly be long gone from Rennie Road by now. I was also exhausted from trying to keep up with the two bigger lads and probably wouldn't have made it a lot further. So I stopped them, and after a short discussion we agreed that I would return and try to cover their tracks.

It took a little less time to get back, as it was all downhill. The dawn was breaking by then, so I hurried back up the drainpipe and through the window, locking it behind me, before quietly making my way back to bed. I could have slept for a week, but minutes later the master walked into the dorm to wake us. Although I was completely shattered, I felt almost victorious as I ate my breakfast. I had managed the near-impossible.

All day the only talk was about the night's escape and the news that the police were scouring the moors for the missing boys. I felt so relieved that I'd made it back. But the following day, during breakfast, two masters came into the hall and whispered to the headmaster. Then one of them held out a school cap, and I knew I was done for.

It was not long before I was standing outside the head's office. He called me in, and as I turned to close the door behind me I saw a sudden flash of light as a searing pain hit me on the back of my neck, then on my back. The shock of it disoriented me and I fell forwards on to my hands and knees. I felt more thuds on my back and legs, and then a loud crack and a splintering noise as an indescribable pain shot up my back and down my legs.

I heard the head shouting in the distance and some other noise I couldn't make out. Then the full weight of the pain hit me and I began screaming. There was a stinging numbness from my lower spine all the way down to my feet. The thuds stopped and I caught a glimpse of the walking stick in his hand. It had broken in two.

I don't remember much after that, apart from a master trying to put me on to the sick bed, which made me scream even harder than before. I had no medical attention and was left to recover alone. It was an agonising, terrifying time. I knew that real damage had been done to my back, but there was nothing I could do. Somehow I managed to get to my feet and keep going, but I walked with a limp for many weeks and was left with permanent pain in my neck and spine.

That was the last time I ever tried to get back to Irene. My injuries meant I wasn't able to go anywhere for some time, and now she was probably not at Rennie Road any longer I wouldn't know where to search for her. Though somehow, deep inside, I still felt sure I would see her one day.

Weeks after the escape we heard that the other two boys had been caught in Newcastle, but they never came back to the school so we could only guess what happened to them.

One day a new science teacher arrived at the school. He was introduced to us as Mr Bumby and we could see straight away that he was different. His hair was much longer than the usual short back and sides of the other masters, and his manner was far more relaxed. This was the sixties, and out in the big world beyond the gates a social revolution was taking place. And he brought a breath of it with him. He believed in talking to us and explaining things, instead of handing us something to learn then thrashing us when we didn't. He inspired us and showed us that the world was filled with people who knew things and with others who didn't, and that the ones who had knowledge were in charge, so to have any kind of power over your own life you had to know things. We had thought our lessons were boring and pointless, but he made us see that we needed to understand the world around us. Suddenly we all wanted to learn, but most of us didn't even know the basics, so we all started to study harder.

We loved Mr Bumby, but the older masters weren't so happy. We once saw him grab the hand of another teacher who was on the brink of hitting a boy with his walking stick. They walked away, but we heard the ensuing argument about children and abuse, and it being a different world now.

Shortly after that another new teacher arrived. This one was a physical education instructor, and he was different too. Until then we'd only had football in winter and cricket in summer, but the new teacher introduced rugby and the javelin, high jump and long jump, and pressed for new facilities, which we eventually got. About a year later an indoor gym was built, with facilities for badminton and tennis as well as a five-a-side pitch.

Other schools were invited for football matches, something that would have been unimaginable a year before. Sadly, our school football team was rubbish, so we came up with a scheme to improve our game. A herd of sheep was kept on the pitch, and when it was needed we would round them up and put them in a kind of corral at the far end. As a result there were piles of sheep muck all over the place and you had to watch out for it when you were playing. If we were losing a game to another team, we'd roll the ball in the muck before kicking it at the other side. There would be cries of 'Shit!' when the ball hit them, and worse if some poor unfortunate headed the ball. After that their goalies often dived *away* from the ball. This method actually brought us success on a couple of occasions.

When it came to the long summer holidays most boys spent ten days on home leave. But I had lost all contact with my family, and presumably the authorities had decided it was not to be resumed, so I had to stay at school. At the time I didn't feel bothered by this; I had got used to being alone, with no family contact. But with hindsight I think my sense of loss was enormous, and I had simply buried it deep inside in order to cope.

The same thing happened at Christmas, when most boys went home. That's when the headmaster showed his more generous side, producing an enormous turkey and inviting all the pensioners from the village for a free Christmas dinner, which we would help to serve.

In the summer holidays, once all the boys came back from home leave, we went camping. I shuddered at the thought of our earlier camp in the hills, but to my surprise and delight we were told that we would be going to Whitby. I hoped, wild with excitement, that Irene would be on holiday there too, and I would be able to find her.

We arrived by coach and camped on the Boys' Brigade field on a hill overlooking the town. We stayed in bell tents, like wigwams but with thick centre poles, sleeping eight to a tent with our heads to the outside and feet to the pole. It reminded me of Custer and the Indians, with our wigwams in a large circle around the edge of the field and in the centre a white flagpole with the Union Jack flying. Every morning we had assembly there, when we were given pocket money and any instructions before being sent out for the day 'on patrol'.

We had a whale of a time – it was wonderful to have some freedom, even though we stood out wherever we went, as we were dressed in green from head to toe. Green shorts, green shirts and green socks.

I loved wandering through the little cobbled streets and quaint shops. We climbed the famous steps to the Abbey, stood under the whalebone arch on the other side of the town, and played on the beach. Everywhere I went I looked for Irene, hoping to spot her. I used to try to imagine what she would look like by now, and looked out for all the red-haired girls just in case one was her, but sadly it never was.

We travelled to Whitby every summer for the five years I was at Stanhope – from 1963 to 1967. And every year I sat on the beach thinking of Irene and wondering where she was. But despite not finding her, those holidays were the highlight of our year.

Afterwards it was back to the tough Stanhope regime. And by the time I was thirteen I was being given jobs around the school. This meant fetching and carrying for the ladies in the sewing rooms and laundry, or working in the kitchen or in the school gardens. Maintenance jobs included helping fetch and carry for the caretaker, shovelling coal for the boilers, painting and decorating, cutting grass on the fields, sweeping leaves and helping with the plumbing and the electrical maintenance.

The nicest job was working in the gardens. The school had a Victorian walled garden the size of three or four football pitches, where all the school's vegetables and most of the fruit were grown. We used to pick apples from the trees lining the garden walls, and then lay them out to store on large wooden trays in the large gazebo. The work was hard; we spent hours weeding and digging, but it was the closest we got to being 'somewhere else', and that helped to make the time there more bearable. I spent many hours labouring in the gardens, my hands dirty, my head in the clouds and my heart where it had always been – with Irene.

18

Irene

I was due to leave school at the end of the Easter term after I had turned fifteen. It was 1966 and my classmates talked excitedly about what they were going to do. Most of them had jobs to go to and were looking forward to being out in the world. But when they asked me where I was going I said I wasn't sure yet. In fact I had no idea what I was going to do. No one had discussed it with me, and I wasn't sure how to go about getting a job, or even what kind of job I might be able to do. I worried about it and wondered whether I should broach the subject with the aunties.

Before I could, Auntie Doris dropped a bombshell. 'You'll be leaving us when you leave school,' she told me one morning.

I stared at her, dumbfounded. 'Where will I go?' I asked her.

'You'll need to find a place to live,' she told me. 'Once you leave school you're no longer the responsibility of the Local Authority.'

I felt shocked. Of course I knew that I wouldn't be staying at Rennie Road for ever, but until that moment I had thought of leaving as something that would happen one day in the future. Now suddenly the future had arrived. And I had absolutely no idea where I would head for.

Life in Rennie Road had prepared me for very little. I had no formal qualifications and no knowledge or understanding of the world. I didn't know how to cook, manage a budget, shop or run a home. All I had learned in six years, apart from how to do as I was told without question, was how to clean and wash up – something I longed never ever to have to do again. Apart from that, I knew how to sew; one of my jobs in the later years had been to help the aunties with the mending, and I had become very adept with a needle and thread.

I had no plans and no picture of my future. While other girls looked forward to going to college, getting jobs and finding husbands, I couldn't imagine what the future held for me. Neither Auntie Doris nor Auntie Joyce ever sat me down and discussed the implications of leaving the home or what the future might bring. It was all a bit of a blur in my mind, and I had no real perception of the dramatic changes that lay ahead. I felt panicky when I thought about it, so I did nothing and simply tried to push the thought away.

A couple of weeks before I was due to leave school, Auntie Doris told me an interview had been arranged for me at Jackson's the tailors, a local firm that made men's suits. I didn't know whether I wanted to work for a tailor's, but it was a job and I knew I had to take what I was given. A few days later Auntie Doris took me shopping for the last time and I was allowed to choose a dress, a blouse and skirt, a cardigan, some shoes and some underwear. I had never owned so many clothes before.

On the day of the interview I put on my new dress and got the bus to the factory, which was down towards the East End of town. It was a large place which employed around three hundred girls. I went to the interviewer's office and sat outside with five or six other girls. When my turn came I was asked whether I could sew, and when I said yes I was told that I had the job. I would begin work as a trainee seamstress the week after I left school.

I was proud of having got the job, and I was delighted by the idea of earning my own money – the vast sum of £13 a week, which in those days wasn't a bad starting wage. But I was still terrified of living on my own. Where would I go? Most of the other girls I knew would still live at home when they went out to work, but I had to leave the only home I knew.

Auntie Doris handed me a list of landlords who were approved by the Local Authority and told me to find out which of them had a vacancy. I phoned a few, and was told that one of them had a bedsit available if I wanted it. I said I did. A few days later I went to see my new home. It was a tiny attic bedsit at the top of a large four-storey Victorian house in an area full of bedsits and flats. My little room would cost me £5 a week to rent.

I got the bus back to Rennie Road feeling very scared. In a few days' time I would have to pack my things and move to that tiny room and live there all alone, going out to work every day and managing everything for myself. That evening, as I queued for the bathroom with the other children and got into bed as usual at 8.30, I thought that at least I would be able to choose when to go to bed. That thought comforted me as I tried to push away the fear I felt about being alone in the world.

A couple of days before I left Rennie Road I got out my precious metal tag bracelet. The tags had become bent and broken, the thin metal had worn and snapped, but it was still possible to make out my name and Alan's, engraved in the metal. I would always remember those happy days when I was a little girl and Alan was my friend. But now it was time to grow up and move on, and to let the bracelet go. I couldn't bear the idea of throwing it away, so I took it to the top of Bunny Hill and buried it. As I did so, I looked out across the hill for the last time, to the far woods, and for a brief moment remembered warm days and bluebells.

The day I left I woke early and found Silvy crying. She said that I was her only friend and after I was gone she would have no one to talk to or be with. I understood just how she felt. I was frightened of leaving her too, and of knowing no one in my new world. But I felt I must be strong and brave, so I gave her a big hug and told her that soon she would be leaving too and when she left we would meet up and have fun, and she cheered up at that prospect.

I packed my few things into a small brown leather bag, went downstairs and put my bag in the hall before going into breakfast with the other children. As always, we weren't allowed to speak at breakfast. The other children looked at me, in my new blouse and skirt, and I could see their sadness. I felt sad too. I wished I could talk to them, say a proper goodbye, promise to see them again. But I didn't dare: we were never allowed to speak at meals, and this day was no exception. After breakfast the other children all went about their chores. For the first time since I had arrived there, another child was told to do the washing up while I went with Auntie Doris to the office and was given a little money to take with me.

Not long after, a black car arrived outside. Doris gave me a hug – my first ever from her – and told me to take care of myself, then sent me out to the car with my bag. I felt a lump in my throat as I waved at the small faces looking out from the playroom window. I wanted to cry. I felt fear, excitement and sadness, but most of all I felt as if I was being thrown away. This was the closest I had ever had to a home. Yet after the six long years I'd been there, there was nothing to mark my passing through its doors and out into the world.

It took about half an hour to reach my new home. I sat in the back, with butterflies in my stomach, as we wound through the city. When we got there the driver dropped me off, nodded and drove away. I got out the keys which the landlord had sent me, let myself into the house and climbed the stairs.

I sat in my bedsit, my bags on the floor beside me, and wondered what to do next. This was it. I was grown up now and alone in the world. This small room – with its bed, chair, table, tiny coal fire and single small window overlooking the roof – was my home now. The trouble was, I didn't want to be there. I felt so alone, I was desolate. What was I to do next? I had no idea. So I sat in my room for hours, until eventually I realised I would have to go and get myself some food and plucked up the courage to go downstairs and out into the street. I went to the little corner shop and bought some tins of soup and a loaf of bread with the money Doris had given me, and went back up to my room.

Ten or twelve other people lived in the house, three or four to a floor, all in separate rooms. And we all had to share a kitchen on the ground floor. It was late in the day before I eventually traipsed downstairs with the small bag of food I had brought, only to find there was a queue for the kitchen and I was last. An hour later I was finally able to warm up my soup and cut some bread and butter, after which I carried it back up to my room and ate it sitting at my small table. Then I got undressed and climbed into bed. I lay awake for a long time, jumping at every small sound in the house, feeling frightened and lonely and wondering what my life was going to be like now.

The next morning I put on my dress and new shoes, had a piece of bread and butter for breakfast and went out to get the bus to work. I'd been told to bring a pinnie with me, and I'd got a new blue one tucked into my bag. I was due to start at 8 a.m. and I arrived a few minutes early. I was shown how to clock in, in the big entrance hall, and I put on my pinnie before being taken into a huge room called the training room, where I was introduced to Dorothy, who would be showing me the ropes. She explained that my job would be helping to make the pockets for the men's suits. I had to sit beside her while a big basket arrived next to us on a conveyor belt. It was our job to take out the pockets, turn the flaps down and sew them along the top, and then put them back in the basket.

At twelve we got half an hour for lunch, which we ate in the canteen. I met some of the other girls there, and although I was shy they chatted to me and were very friendly.

By the time I finished work at four I was getting the hang of how to do the pockets. I'd enjoyed my first day and the company: the other girls seemed friendly and I didn't mind the work.

I got the bus back to my bedsit and spent another lonely evening wondering what to do with myself. I slipped downstairs to make myself some beans on toast, passing a man on the stairs who smelled of beer and winked suggestively at me. I blushed bright red and almost ran to the kitchen. He followed me in there and asked if I wanted to go for a drink with him. Scared, I said, 'No, thank you,' grabbed my food and shot back upstairs, locking myself into my room.

It turned out that the house where I was living had a fast turnover of residents. Students and foreign sailors passed through, some staying months, others only a few days or weeks, so there were often strange men from the docks hanging about on the stairs or in the kitchen. They would eye me every time I passed, so that I had to run a gauntlet of unwanted attention each time I came home or made a meal. I often had to cook my food while fending off advances, then, carrying my plate, run up the stairs and lock myself in my room to eat. I hated it, and often felt frightened that one of these men would break into my room in the night.

On my first weekend in the bedsit, Joan came to visit. She brought me sheets and a few towels and told me where to go to buy some of the household things I needed. And she advised me on budgeting to make my money last and the sort of food to buy. I needed every scrap of advice. I was fifteen, very innocent, and I knew nothing of life. I had never shopped for food, managed my own money or paid a bill. I didn't know what clothes I should buy or where, how much money I should save each week for necessities, or how much things should cost.

But I was enjoying my job. I learned fast, and after a week I was moved from the training rooms into the factory proper, where I was turning out four hundred pockets a day. Every man dressed in a suit in those days, no matter how poor, so suits were in great demand and three hundred of us girls worked eight hours a day, our sewing machines creating a huge clatter, turning them out in vast numbers. The girls at work were always nice to me, but I was so shy and unsure of myself that it took me a long time to make real friends and I didn't see any of them outside work. Every Friday, which was pay day, we finished work an hour early and a big group of the girls would go along to the local sweet shop and buy sweets to share out between them. They invited me to join them and, happy to be part of something at last, I bought a big bag of liquorice and lime sweets to contribute. After that I looked forward to that Friday treat all week.

But while work was fine, the unwanted attention from the men in the house where I lived terrified me so much that I hardly dared to leave my room. The worst culprit was the Turkish man living in a ground-floor room beside the front door. He would pounce on me as I came in, trying to coax me into his room. I rushed up the stairs to shake him off. Then one day he introduced me to his friend, who seemed pleasant and polite. Lulled into a false sense of security, I agreed to have a cup of tea with them. What a mistake! As soon as I was through the door the amorous one made a lunge at me. I jumped on to the table, lashing out with my feet to keep him at bay, while shouting at his friend to help me. He was still standing by the door, looking surprised and more than a little worried by these goings-on. He opened the door and I leaped down and bolted out. After that I shot in and out of the front door as fast as I could.

Those were lonely days for me. Once I had finished work I had nowhere to go. I spent evening after evening in my little room. My only company was a little mouse that lived in a hole behind the fireplace. It would come out when all was quiet, and scamper around the room looking for tit-bits. Over the weeks it became bolder and ignored me as I lay on the bed or sat in front of the fire, and I would chat quietly to it. I grew very fond of my little mouse.

Winter arrived and it was freezing. I had a small wrought-iron fireplace in one corner and I had to buy a bag of coal from the corner shop and carry it up the four flights of stairs to my room, avoiding the volunteers who offered to carry it for me – at a price. The girls at work used to say how great it must be to have my own place and the freedom to do whatever I liked. Most of them still lived at home and had to stick to their parents' rules. But they had no idea how lonely I was and how much I would have loved to belong to a family.

Things changed for me when I got to know a girl called Pauline. She was my age and very pretty, with tousled blonde hair. She was outgoing and confident, and she invited me back to her home, where I met her parents, who were welcoming and kind.

Pauline began to teach me a lot about the world. She gave me make-up and clothes to try on and we'd go to town together on Saturdays, where she would show me the right shops to go to. At last I began to feel that I was living a normal life, like other girls. I had a friend, and we had fun together. We went to the cinema, shopping and for walks, and my loneliness eased. Sometimes we went to the Rink, where I'd meet up with old school friends like the two Margies. But more often, now that we considered ourselves grown up, we went to a couple of the town's night clubs, Annabel's and Wetherall's, where we danced for hours and drank cider and Cherry Bs.

One day Pauline told me that her mum and dad were going away and she was having a party, and I could come and stay the night. I was so excited. I went round early and we got ready together and made sandwiches. She had all the latest records, and when her friends arrived we danced the night away.

It was Pauline who told me about boys and how to talk to them, and a little about the birds and bees, though I was still very naive and didn't really understand some of the things she was telling me. One evening, when Pauline and I went out dancing with some other friends, a young man came over and asked me to dance. He was tall and slim with lots of dark hair in a Beatle cut. We had a nice time, so when he asked me out the following weekend, I agreed. His name was Robert, he was two years older than me and he was charming and very attentive. Over the following few weeks he called to take me out every Friday and Saturday night. I was very flattered as there were always lots of girls who were interested in him.

I was delighted to have a boyfriend. It made me feel so grown up and special. So when Robert asked me to stay over at his little flat, I did, without really understanding what I was doing or what the consequences might be. I was still very naive, and I slept with him to please him, thinking that this was what I was supposed to do.

A few weeks later I woke up feeling very sick, and retched several times before work. I thought I was going down with something, but I felt all right later in the day, only to feel sick again the following morning – and the one after that too. I had no idea what was going on, but that weekend I mentioned it to Joan. She told me I was probably pregnant. I was so shocked I could barely speak. I was seventeen and felt my world was about to cave in. In those days, despite the advent of the Pill, which was just becoming available, pregnancy still meant marriage or disgrace. I had never heard of abortion, so I didn't even consider the idea. My head spun. I liked Robert, but I didn't love him. What was I to do?

Joan was quite clear on the subject. She said I must tell him straight away and see whether he would marry me. She was a powerful influence, the closest person to a mother that I had, and I didn't think to question her. Putting aside my doubts, I phoned him and we met him by the church near his flat.

Despite my own shock, I was hoping he would be happy about the news, but he stood looking at the ground and then said, 'You'll have to meet my mum and tell her.' I realised he was as reluctant as I was, but the wheels were in motion and we had to see it through. We went round to his parents' house and found his mother baking in the kitchen and his father reading the paper. Robert introduced me, then announced that we were going to have a baby. His dad gave us his congratulations, but his mother didn't raise her eyes from the pastry she was making on the wooden table as she said coldly, 'You're not the first and you'll not be the last to cross my door.' I was very shocked. I knew the news might not please her, but those cutting words were to haunt me for years to come.

Despite his mother's disapproval, Robert agreed to marry me and we began to make plans to set up home together, both of us making the best of a situation we didn't want to be in. Robert worked at the local Pyrex Glass factory and his salary would be enough for us to live on, if we were careful, so we found a tiny two-up and two-down house just outside the town centre and arranged to rent it.

We both needed parental consent to marry, as we were under twenty-one. I hadn't seen Dad, who was by this time living in a bedsit on his own, for a few months. He'd never met Robert and didn't know I was pregnant, and I was very nervous about seeing him in case he refused me permission. Robert and I went together to see him, and fortunately all went well and he signed the papers. Robert's parents had already given their permission, so we went to the Register Office to arrange a date. There was only Christmas Eve left and we didn't want to wait until the New Year, so we took it.

We invited Dad, my sisters and Robert's parents, plus a few of Robert's friends. Both Pat and Greta told me that they had already made plans for Christmas Eve. I was upset and wanted to change the date, but in the name of respectability I knew we couldn't. We had to marry before my pregnancy showed.

Despite the circumstances, as the wedding drew near I felt excited about the idea of becoming a wife and mother and starting a new life. I was very glad to be leaving the grim little room where I'd lived for two and a half years and looked forward to having a home of my own. I bought a beautiful white lace mini-dress from a girl at work and, as Robert said he didn't have time to come with me, I bought my own wedding ring from the jeweller's for two pounds and fifteen shillings. It was clear that Robert's heart wasn't in it. But I put my concerns about his lack of interest to the back of my mind and told myself all would be well.

I spent the night before the wedding at Joan's. She was excited for me, so I set aside any last misgivings and did my best to look forward to my new life. We spent a quiet evening, and the next day we got a taxi down to the Register Office, me in my mini-dress and Joan with all the children. When we got there I looked around, hoping Greta and Pat might have changed their minds. But they hadn't come, and neither had Dad. I shouldn't have been surprised, because he was never reliable. But I was so very hurt that my own father didn't make it to my wedding.

Robert's parents didn't come either, but at least their excuse was that they were preparing the buffet they had offered to lay on for the guests afterwards.

I swallowed my tears of disappointment and we went ahead and married in a quiet and brief ceremony, with only

Joan and her children and a couple of Robert's friends there. Afterwards we got a taxi to Robert's parents' home for the meal and a few simple toasts. And when Joan had taken the children home we had a night out in town with Robert's friends.

At the end of the evening we went to our new little house for the first time. From the very start Robert was distant and cool towards me. But despite all that had gone wrong, in my naivety I told myself that things would be fine. I was eighteen years old and full of hope, and there was a baby on the way. Surely that would make everything all right.

19

Alan

Harsh discipline and constant bullying by masters and older boys was a way of life at Stanhope. But under the surface we boys were angry and desperate to protest. So when yet another boy was seriously hurt, things came to a head.

He was a new boy, just nine years old, and he was thrashed by the headmaster for some minor offence. We heard him sobbing after lights out, and the following morning we woke to find he'd gone. He'd got out of a window on to the roof, down a drainpipe and away, wearing only his pyjamas, with a blizzard blowing outside. He was found the next day in the hills, curled up in the snow, barely alive, and was taken to hospital with hypothermia and frostbite.

That was the trigger. We boys had no one to fight our corner or even listen to grievances, and we decided that enough was enough. A few of us held a secret meeting to talk about how we could fight back. We decided that we would mount a campaign of disruption in an attempt to bring the normal running of the school to a halt, and we began a secret recruitment drive and enlisted several more boys we could trust.

The campaign got off to a good start. We left windows open, power switches off, doors open or closed, equipment in the wrong places, water taps running and light bulbs missing. After a few days the teaching staff realised that the problems were more than mere coincidence and the headmaster made the first of many announcements. 'Someone is playing funny games in the school. Well, I say to those responsible, and you know who you are, you will stop these games immediately. If you do not then we will catch you and you will be severely punished. Do you get my message?' he thundered. 'Yes, Sir,' we all replied. But the campaign went on.

More and more boys joined in, so the headmaster retaliated by punishing the whole school. He started by removing privileges such as playing games in our houserooms during the evening, or sweets on pocket money day. We had to sit all evening in silence, polishing shoes or floors before being sent to bed early. A silence rule was imposed which meant you could only speak when spoken to, and many boys were slapped or caned for breaking the rule.

The headmaster expected that, through his punishing all the boys, the majority would pressure those responsible to stop. But he was wrong: we all became even more determined to stand together and carry on.

It reminded me of the film *Spartacus*. When the Roman leaders demanded that the crowd of prisoners identify the rebel leader Spartacus or they would all die, they stood up one by one, crying out, 'I'm Spartacus.' We were the same; we stood together and no one gave in.

One morning at breakfast the headmaster tried a different tack. He announced that we could watch TV that night, and he would lift the silence rule the following day. He added that from then on we would all be able to vote on which film we'd like to see each month. He finished by saying, 'Let's all get back to normal and stop this nonsense and we'll forget all about it.'

We knew from that moment that we were winning. We had another meeting where we decided to carry out one big final mission. Our target was the boilers which fed the school heating system, including the headmaster's living quarters. We all knew how he liked to keep a constant temperature there for his beloved houseplants.

The boiler rooms were at the back of the school under the kitchens and were kept locked. But I had a way in. At the back of the courtyard there was a coal chute, with a heavy steel lid, where coal was delivered once a fortnight. It was only about fourteen inches in diameter, but it led directly into the boiler rooms.

The school was asleep when four of us sprang into action. We borrowed pillows and stuffed our beds, then went to the cleaning cupboard where we had hidden some old torn pyjamas and changed, leaving our good ones there. We climbed out of a second-floor window and down a drainpipe into the courtyard, and opened the steel hatch over the coal chute with a piece of metal I'd hidden earlier in the day.

I was first to slide down the chute, keeping my arms above my head to avoid getting jammed in it. I had no idea how long the chute was, so it was a relief to find it was only about a foot long with a five-foot drop on to the coal pile. Once we were all in we raked around in the pitch dark, on our hands and knees in the coal, for the door. When we pushed it open we all slid out, with the coal, on to the boiler room floor. We'd made it.

There were two large boilers with dials on them and the sounds of ticking clocks. We decided to reset the clocks, thinking that the heating would come on or turn off at different times to those planned. We also turned most of the wheels on the big pipes to new positions, hoping that what had been on was now off, and what had been off was now on.

Getting out of the hole was much trickier than getting in. The smallest boy climbed up the rest of us and squeezed though the hole. Then he lay on the ground and put his arms though for the next boy and we managed to shove him through. They tied their pyjamas together and lowered them down the hole and I went up next and, with a great deal of pulling, got back up, and we heaved the last boy after me.

There we stood, naked and as black as the coalhole we had just climbed out of. Our eyes and teeth gleamed white in the moonlight, and looking at each other we had to stifle our laughter.

We carefully repositioned the steel hatch, then disentangled the pyjamas and dressed. Climbing back up to the window was the hardest part. We were tired, and climbing thirty feet up a drainpipe in your slippers isn't easy at the best of times, but somehow we managed it. We got through the window and headed for the shower room, where we showered and washed the pyjamas and slippers. Then we went back to the window and, using a mop and cloths from the cleaning cupboard, we cleaned the coal dust from everything, including the trail to the showers.

Finally we put on our clean pyjamas and put the wet ones in the laundry basket used for the boys who wet the bed, for the laundry lads to recover. We spent a bit of time towel-drying our hair and then got back into bed.

I had barely shut my eyes when a master walked in and shouted that it was time to get up. It was unusually cold that morning and when we went to wash, the water was cold. Word travelled fast, and the boys realised that someone had made it to the boiler rooms, which had been considered impossible.

The head began ranting the moment he came into the dining hall. 'Someone nearly killed us all last night. Some fool moved the boiler controls and could have blown us all up. Only a safety device saved us. Who was it! I want to know, NOW!' Then halfway through breakfast a master entered the dining hall, went to the headmaster's table and whispered something in his ear. His face lit up. My stomach lurched with fear. We must have missed something, but what?

At the end of breakfast the dining-hall doors were opened and the four housemasters walked in. Each of them was carrying a pair of slippers. My heart was pounding. We learned later that when a search was made of eighty pairs of slippers, four were found with tiny traces of coal dust deep in the grooves of the sole. Not much, but just enough to convict us.

The headmaster used two canes, swapping them if he thought he wasn't getting enough response from the squealing boy in front of him, and pushing his desk to one side to get a bigger swing as he laid twelve strokes on each of us. The four of us couldn't sit down for many days or lie on our backs in bed or sleep for the stinging. For me it was especially bad, as my back was still damaged from the last beating. After that we were made to spend every evening from six to eleven cleaning the corridors.

Despite this, the campaign went on. The headmaster was out of his mind because he thought he had got the ringleaders, but he was with the four of us when the washrooms flooded.

A week or two later, while on corridor duty, I dropped my polisher and nipped around the corner with another boy to where there was a strange power switch up in one corner right against the ceiling. I was on the other lad's shoulders with my hand on the switch, about to turn it off, when the head walked around the corner. I had never seen him so happy. He was mumbling, 'Yes! Yes!' and holding his fists together on his chest.

We were given yet another beating. Then a few days later, as I was once again polishing floors, the head suddenly appeared from around the corner, looking very jolly again. 'Ah, there you are,' he said. 'I want you come with me. I've got a surprise for you.'

He hummed cheerily as we walked the short distance to his office. I went in and stood by his desk as he went rummaging in the big cupboard where he kept his canes. He found what he was looking for and turned to me. 'You like wires, don't you?' he said, and in a flash he moved his arm and I heard a whoosh and felt a sting across my neck. He had whipped me with a wire flex, and before I could react, he did it again. He must have been simmering for days, and he'd finally snapped.

He managed to whip me a few more times, and I could feel agonising pain and the blood running down my neck. That's when I too snapped. I flung my full weight at him and we both tumbled over his desk, knocking the chairs over. I knew I'd hurt him by the sound he made when we landed, and I could see the surprise in his eyes. We struggled up and I punched his left eye. He went even wilder then, lashing out at me with the wire. At that point the door burst open and Mr Maddison ran in, took a look at me and grabbed the head by the collar, shouting, 'What are you doing?'

He turned to me and said, 'Get outside quickly.' I did, and as I stood in the corridor I could hear a lot of shouting going on inside the office. I looked down and saw that my shirt was covered in blood, and I took it off and held it against my neck to stop the bleeding. After a while it went quiet and my housemaster came out and took me to the sick room. I was expecting to be punished for hitting the head, but nothing happened. Mr Maddison cleaned me up, bandaged my neck – and that was that. The subject was never brought up again.

The following day the deputy headmaster stood in at breakfast, and for many weeks after. He was a more moderate man, whose attitude was one of sensible discipline, and he used the opportunity to bring in more flexibility. We no longer had to sit to attention at mealtimes and were allowed to talk quietly among ourselves, like normal children. I heard that when he took over the school, after I had left, he gathered all the boys in the assembly hall and had them strip to their underwear. Laundry baskets were brought in and all of the clothes, including those hated corduroy short trousers, were removed. More baskets were brought in and new clothes were issued, including denims and long trousers, to the cheers of all the boys!

The disruption ceased on the same day. After six weeks the rebellion was over, and it was never mentioned by any of the masters again. We didn't see the headmaster for some weeks. A few of the boys thought he might have had a black eye and wanted it gone before appearing in front of us again. As for me, the cuts in my neck weren't too deep and healed quickly.

About two months after the incident, soon after the head had returned, I was called to his office again. I was on my guard as I knocked on his door. 'Come in,' he said, 'have a seat. I think it's time you got out a bit as you don't go on home leave, like the rest of the boys, so I've got an idea. You're a big lad now, so how would you like to go out for a day?'

I was stunned. 'Yes, Sir,' I blurted.

So every Saturday, from then on, I was given a couple of quid and caught the bus to Bishop Auckland. For the next few months I spent the afternoons just wandering in the park, not really doing anything at all, as I had no idea what to do. But just being there, and being free for a few hours, felt good.

In November 1967 I turned fifteen and I was informed that the following May I would be leaving the school. Glad as I was to be going, I had no idea what I would do next, and the prospect was daunting.

Shortly before I was due to leave it was announced that the headmaster was retiring, and Mr Maddison announced that he too would be leaving soon. Both he and the headmaster were old-fashioned men whose time had passed, and they knew it.

The day of my own departure came with more of a fizzle than a bang. No one really took much notice of just another boy leaving. After five and a half years at Stanhope, being punished for crimes I'd long forgotten, I knew nothing else. And as I packed my small bag with a change of underwear and the old-fashioned suit I had been given for my new life, and said goodbye to a few friends, I wondered what would become of me.

I was barely educated and without any skills or direction in life. How would I manage now that, suddenly, I was expected to cope as an adult? I hadn't been taught self-discipline, independent thought, decision-making or a real trade. I was immature, naive and impulsive. I longed to have a job, a home and a family – but I had no idea how I would achieve that.

This was 1968 and the world was changing. The Beatles and the Stones had exploded on to the scene, hippies ruled, there was a war in Vietnam and a race for the moon. But I knew nothing of all this. I had been imprisoned in the system for so long, shut away from the outside world, that I had no idea of the cultural revolution that was taking place all around me.

Mr Maddison drove me to Sunderland with my belongings at my feet and five pounds in my pocket – the sum deemed adequate to see me on my way. I had no idea where we were going, as I hadn't been told and dared not ask. It felt just like all the other journeys I had made in the past, never knowing what lay ahead.

We pulled up outside a terraced house in the west of the city and Mr Maddison knocked on the front door, which was opened by a tall, scruffy-looking man in his late sixties. He looked exactly like Fagin from *Oliver Twist*, with his stooped posture and threadbare jumper. I looked at Mr Maddison and thought, 'He can't be leaving me here, can he?' But he could, and did. With a hasty 'Goodbye, and good luck,' he got back into the van and drove off.

The landlord showed me up to a double bedroom on the second floor, which he told me I would be sharing with another boy. The room, like its owner, was scruffy and none too clean. The wallpaper was so old that the patterns on it had long since faded, and the carpet was threadbare. But at least the beds were of a good size and turned out to be surprisingly comfortable. My rent, he announced, would be five pounds a week, payable in advance, to include breakfast and an evening meal. So that was my fiver gone.

The house was large and full of tenants. Most of the rooms were rented out to sailors passing through the port, who stayed no more than a week or two. But the room I was given was reserved for boys like me, newly released from approved schools and with nowhere else to go. The landlord had a bedridden wife, tucked away in a room on the second floor, but I didn't set eyes on her during the entire time I lived there. The house had a small kitchen with an ancient cooker and a dining table with four chairs. There was a radio on the side, and the first time I walked in Louis Armstrong was singing 'Wonderful World'. There was also a living room, with a television in it, but he made it clear that it was reserved for the other guests and not the likes of me.

That afternoon I was dispatched to the Youth Labour Exchange to sign on. After taking my details the lady there gave me my National Insurance card. I had no idea what it was or what it was for, but she said not to lose it so I stashed it away. She then rifled through a pile of cards on her desk, picked one out and said, 'Ah! Here's a job for you, apprentice upholsterer.' She filled in the relevant details on a piece of paper, gave it to me with some brief instructions on how to get there, then shouted, 'Next!' and that was me done.

I headed for the quayside, where she had told me to go, and was directed to an old, very tall warehouse, of the sort you would see on any Victorian wharf. I met the foreman, who pointed to a heavy wooden box on the floor and said, 'Lift that.' I did, and he said, 'You've got the job. Start tomorrow, at eight o'clock sharp.'

That evening I met my room-mate, a boy of my age who was called Robinson. He had been there for a few days longer than me, and had also come from approved school. He had ginger hair and was very skinny, and he had a kind of nasal twang to his voice which gave the impression that he was nervous whenever he spoke.

I reported for work the next morning at eight sharp. My morning job was to operate the 'teasing' machine. I had to pack in the stuffing used to fill the chairs and settees, and this very noisy machine would tear at it with spinning rods with teeth on them, to tease the stuffing apart. My other morning task was drilling holes into small wooden blocks used to fix parts of the chairs together. My afternoon job was to manhandle the finished chairs and settees down three storeys to the basement with another boy of my age, then collect the bare wooden frames for the next job and carry them back up. It was heavy, hot work, and even though I was young and healthy – apart from the twinges of pain I still had in my back – by the end of the day I was worn out.

The workshop was warmed by old gas fires up on the walls which were turned on by pulling chains – one to turn the gas on and off, the other to ignite it. The air was full of dust and particles of inflammable stuffing, and I always thought it would be very dangerous if someone forgot to turn the fires off. Unfortunately, after I had left the job, someone did forget and the whole place burned down.

Friday was pay day and my wage packet contained five pounds. That was my rent paid, but obviously I needed a little cash for other things. To get round the problem it was arranged that I would be given ten shillings a week by the Probation Service. I had to finish work on Fridays and run to the town in time to get to the Probation Office before it closed. I was greeted by a man with a chitty to sign and was handed a ten shilling note before he locked up.

My work clothes were also provided by the Probation Service. I was given a slip of paper to take to a local store where they kitted me out with overalls, boots and a donkey jacket. I wore these all the time, as I hated the old-fashioned suit given to me by the school and I had no other clothes to wear. My ten bob a week didn't allow for luxury items such as clothes.

I had to work just as hard at weekends as I did during the week. The landlord ordered me and Robinson to clean the other guests' rooms, the landings, stairways, kitchen and living room, make the beds, go and get his cigars and his wife's pack of 200 cigarettes from the shop, and any other chores that needed doing. While the other guests sat around in front of the telly drinking bottles of beer, we were the unpaid slaves in the house.

Why didn't we just walk out? Because, after so many years living in institutions, we had no idea that we were actually free to go. Even though we were paying rent, we didn't see that we were the same as the other paying guests and could take our custom elsewhere if we wished. We were ignorant and there was no one to enlighten us. So we toiled on, handing over our wages to the landlord and then working for him all day on Saturdays. Our only day off was Sunday, but in those days everything was closed on a Sunday, so all we could do was wander through the empty town or sit in the parks even if it was raining, just to be out of the house.

I had been living in the lodging house for several months when one Saturday, as Robinson and I went about our chores, he spotted some cash lying on the bed in one of the sailors' rooms. He rushed in to tell me and we both went and looked at the row of twenty pound notes on the bed. I had never seen one before, and now I was looking at ten of them. Two hundred pounds was a small fortune to us, the equivalent of forty weeks' wages. Robinson and I looked at one another and had the same thought – freedom! It wasn't just the money we saw: it was our chance to escape. We could take the money and put all the slave labour behind us.

Within minutes we had stashed the money in our pockets, packed our things and left the house. We ran as fast as we could to the bus stop and got on the first bus into town.

20

Irene

Robert worked in the local Pyrex Glass factory, packing plates, cups and casserole dishes, and from the start I saw very little of him. He worked a round-the-clock shift system, and it seemed he was always either asleep, at work or in the pub, where he went whenever his shifts allowed.

Even when he was at home he was moody, distant and cold towards me. He'd often spend all evening in the pub before coming home, eating and going to bed, barely exchanging a word with me. I used to wonder if every young married woman felt as lonely as I did.

Our new home was tiny and very basic, but I set about making it as comfortable and pretty as I could, scrimping and saving for second-hand furniture and new bedding and curtains. I stayed on at work until I was six months pregnant and then left, as every woman did then, and after that I began to prepare for the birth, collecting all the things I would need. I bought a cot and filled it with all the essentials, from nappies to bottles. And I splashed out on a Silver Cross two-tone green pram. My friends thought it was odd buying a green pram – perhaps because green cars were considered unlucky – but it was my favourite colour and Silver Cross was the very best make.

Once the morning sickness passed I ate for two. My favourite meal was fish fingers and bacon – together! And I tried to occupy the long hours I spent alone. I lived close to Sunderland town centre so I could walk a lot to the shops and around the park to feed the ducks when it was warm. I looked forward to being a mum, but I missed my friends at work and the social life that went with it. Sometimes some of the girls would call in for a cuppa and a chat, and I really looked forward to those brief times together.

I saw my sisters whenever I could, and they helped me by talking about their own experiences and promising to visit and show me what to do once the baby came. They were all mothers now – a year earlier Pat had given birth to her first baby, a boy called Gary.

But despite my efforts to keep busy and get out of the house, I spent most of the day at home alone, and often all evening too. I longed for Robert to be the loving husband I had hoped for, but I often felt I was the last person he wanted to be around.

I became more and more upset and we started to argue a lot. I thought he was drinking too much and told him we needed the money for the baby, and that I wanted him to be with me. I knew he needed to see his friends and let off steam, but couldn't he make time for me too? Robert would explode, shouting at me and throwing things across the room before storming out, and I would be left feeling shaken and very upset.

On Sundays we would go to his parents' for lunch. I got on very well with his dad but his mum always stayed distant and snappy. One day when I was helping her in the kitchen she said to me, 'If you had a mum you wouldn't be so nice to me.' That hurt, because I'd made such an effort to get on with her.

By chance Robert was home when I went into labour and a neighbour – one of the few with a car – drove us to

Sunderland General Hospital. Men weren't present at births in those days, so Robert went off to pace up and down a corridor. After a labour of six or seven hours I had a beautiful boy. He had lots of black hair and pale blue eyes and looked the image of Robert, who arrived back to see him soon afterwards. We called him Michael.

They used to keep you in hospital for a week or even longer then, and I was glad of that time, to learn how to feed and look after our son. Even so, I felt a little panicky at first when I brought him home. But I soon got into a routine. And the pregnancy weight dropped away – within a couple of weeks I was eight and a half stone again, and back into my mini-dresses.

I loved being a mum. I felt really proud when I dressed Michael up and took him out in his pram. I took him to see my sisters regularly. And when he was a few months old I took him to see Dad. I hadn't seen him since before our wedding, but by this time he had moved into a one-bedroom flat just around the corner from Greta. He cooed over the baby, and it gave us something to share, so after that I began to go and see him more often. His little flat was cosy, especially when he lit the small coal fire. He always kept a bucket of coal beside the fireplace, and beside it on the hearth there was always a large lump of coal. I asked him why he kept it there and he told me he'd been given it for luck one New Year by Paul, Greta's son.

A couple of years later, when Michael was a toddler, we were visiting Dad when Michael suddenly picked up Dad's lucky lump of coal and threw it on the fire. Dad was in the kitchen making a cup of tea, and I panicked. I rummaged through the coal bucket until I found a lump similar in size and put it on the hearth in its place. Dad never noticed – thankfully!

With only one income and a baby to feed, money was very tight. That meant less time in the pub for Robert. We still went to his parents' for Sunday lunch, and as we walked home in the late afternoon we passed Robert's favourite pubs, and he would get wound up because he couldn't afford to go in for a pint. By the time we got home we'd be arguing, and soon we were fighting almost every day. I dreaded these rows; I felt way out of my depth and didn't know what to do. I wanted Robert to be happy with his little family, but he wasn't and it seemed there was nothing I could do to change that.

When Robert was at work I spent many hours pushing my baby around in his pram, going to the park, visiting friends or going to the shops. One of my favourites was a little second-hand shop around the corner from our house. It was just one room on the ground floor of a three-storey house, on the corner of Laura Street, just opposite the brewery. It was an odd house, because it faced the corner and the door was around the side. I used to pop into the shop for second-hand baby clothes, and I became very friendly with the woman who ran it. She was called Anita, and we often used to stop for a chat or a cup of tea. She lived above the shop with her husband and their five children, and she often chatted to me about them.

Robert was close to his granddad, who was also called Robert, and when the old man became ill and needed someone to look after him, Robert's mum suggested that, as she worked and I was at home all day with the baby, we move in with him. I liked him and didn't mind at all, even though I knew it would be hard at times, with the baby to care for too.

Robert's granddad lived in the village of Silksworth, outside the city. It was a long way from the Pyrex factory, so Robert gave in his notice and went to work as a miner, at Dawdon pit, just a few miles away from Silksworth. The two-bedroom house had plenty of room and felt rather grand after the cramped conditions in our previous home. We had a coal fire, and in winter we left the fire burning during the night and it made the house warm and very cosy, unlike our last house, which always felt very cold.

Old Robert was a lovely man. He spent hours telling me stories of the old days and the way things used to be. We all chipped in to look after him. Robert would help him with bathing and shaving, while I cooked the meals, did the washing and sorted his medication. Robert's mum would do the shopping after work and the old man's niece Betty, who I was very fond of, would pop in two days a week to help out, so between us we managed. Sadly though, even though I was looking after her father-in-law, Robert's mother never warmed to me. She continued to be cool and distant, and nothing I did seemed to please her.

One day, while Robert was working a shift at the mine, I went into the living room and found the old man looking very ill. He was finding it hard to eat and swallow by then, so I gave him some ice-cream, which he normally enjoyed. But on this day even the ice-cream was too much for him. I said to him, 'You must be feeling a bit fed up,' and he replied, 'I wish I was dead.' I felt so sorry for him, so I sat for a while and stroked his head, which calmed him, and he began to nod off.

I went back into the kitchen to finish my chores. Half an hour later I looked in to check on him. His head was slumped back and his skin had turned a faint yellow. I rushed to call an ambulance, but as I waited, trying to warm his cold hands, I knew that it was too late. The old man had died, sitting in

his chair by the fire, just as he had wished. I felt heartbroken.
I'd never known my own grandparents, and I had become
very fond of him.

We stayed on in the Silksworth house and I missed the old
man a lot. I was lonelier without him.

On the surface my life was fine. I had a husband who was
in a decent job – Robert earned more in the pit than in the
Pyrex factory – a lovely son and a nice home. We started
to go out to the local club on Saturday nights and became
friendly with some of our neighbours. Dad would regularly
baby-sit for us at weekends and often stayed over, and I liked
having him around.

But all was not well. While we were out Robert was
cheerful, outgoing and the life and soul of the party, but once
we were home his mood would change and he would become
quiet and sullen, and prone to angry outbursts. I worried
that he was still drinking too much, and tried hard to get him
to cut back. It was alcohol that made him angry and violent –
it was almost as if he became another person when he'd had
a few drinks.

I longed for him to show me more love and affection, but
a lot of the time he virtually ignored me. I began to feel I
was a failure as a wife and my confidence, never very high,
plummeted. I blamed myself for our differences because I
knew in my heart that I didn't really love him, and I felt I
should. I tried hard to put things right between us, but the
gulf was too great.

I hoped that another baby might bring us closer. We
agreed to try, and when Michael was five we had a daughter,
Joanne, born in November 1974. She was blonde with blue
eyes, and very beautiful. Robert went with me to hospital,
but when it was time for his shift to start at the pit he had

to leave – there was no time off for the birth of a child. He phoned the hospital later and a neighbour who was with me told him he had a daughter. I was told that he shouted it out at the top of his voice, so everyone knew!

I wondered why I had waited so long for a second baby, because she was a joy. But while I was very happy to be a mum again, it didn't help my marriage at all. Robert and I were further apart than ever, both of us wishing we could be somewhere else while trying to keep up the pretence of a happy family.

Robert was drinking so heavily that he would sometimes miss work to go to the pub. Not only was he often drunk, but he was drinking away most of our money. I began to feel that things were hopeless. I couldn't make him happy and I was tired, lonely and miserable, managing alone and putting up with his awful temper. When he'd been drinking he'd pick fights and criticise everything I did before exploding. I would grab the kids and we would huddle together as he attacked the furniture, terrified that it would be us next. Fortunately he never raised his hands to me or the children, but that didn't stop us being frightened.

The next morning he would be fine again, as though nothing had happened. The only evidence of what had gone on was the broken furniture.

I tried hard, for a long time, to make my marriage work. I often went out with Robert, in the vain hope that I might be able to get him to moderate his drinking or keep him cheerful so that when we came home he would be calm. I longed to be in a stable relationship and to bring up my children in a peaceful and loving home, giving them the things in life that I'd missed. I wanted my marriage to work for them, but it was hopeless and eventually I got tired of constantly trying to keep the peace and asked him to leave. He reluctantly agreed and found himself a flat.

In some ways it was a relief to break up. Without him the house was peaceful and calm. The fighting, rowing, protecting the children and then picking up the pieces was all over. But I was left with terrible feelings of guilt. The last things I had wanted, after my own childhood, was to take the children away from their father. I agonised over whether I'd done the right thing, whether I could have tried harder, done things better, worked it out somehow. I even tried getting back together with Robert briefly, when he pleaded for another chance. But nothing had changed, and within weeks things were worse than ever – with Robert drinking, me angry and both of us fighting.

This time when I asked him to leave, Robert agreed that it really was over. But after he moved out he still tried his best to win me back and said he wouldn't give in until he had the divorce papers in his hand. That made the guilt, and doubt harder for me. But I knew I had to go through with it, even though I felt desperately sad about ending my marriage. I had never, ever imagined getting divorced or bringing up my children alone, and there were times when I sat in the kitchen, once the children were in bed, and cried bitter tears of loneliness and failure and loss.

21

Alan

I'd been on the bus no more than ten minutes when I began to regret the whole thing, and so did Robinson. We looked at each other and wished we could turn the clock back and leave the money where it was. I knew no good could come of what we had done.

But it was already too late. We agreed that if we went back now we would get the same punishment as we would get if we were caught later. The landlord was not one to forgive.

We caught the train to Newcastle and spent the journey discussing where we should go from there. We thought we'd better get out of the country, so we decided to stow away on the cross-channel ferry from Dover to France and then to make our way to the warmer climes of the Med or across to Italy.

In Newcastle we bought a tent, sleeping bags, waterproofs and cooking utensils for our journey. I also bought my first pair of jeans. These were the latest fashion and had caught on in a big way. Wearing them, I felt that at last I looked like the people around me and blended in with the crowd. I felt normal for the first time that I could remember. And so, feeling on top of the world, we headed back to the railway station and caught the afternoon train to London.

It was evening when we arrived at King's Cross. We strode out of the station into a new world. City streets full of people, buses, cars, taxis and tall buildings. It was the first time I had been any distance out of Sunderland, and I was mesmerised by all that I saw. We found a small hotel and booked a room for the night, and spent the next day seeing the sights. I was impressed by the wide streets and tall buildings and imagined the Queen passing in her carriage, escorted by mounted guards and bands playing. We headed for the Post Office Tower, which was a main attraction then. The view from the top was spectacular and we stayed there for ages.

We would have liked to stay longer in London; there was so much to see and do. But we knew we'd better get on with the plan, so that afternoon we caught the train to Dover. We were alone in our compartment and I spent the journey looking out of the window to catch sight of the engine whenever we went around a curve in the line. It was a sunny day and I watched mile after mile of apple orchards passing by and lots of people among the trees picking the apples. I thought of Uncle Rex and the lady who visited me in The Esplanade and what he said about an orchard being mine, and I imagined me and Irene living among those trees full of golden and red apples.

When we arrived in Dover we climbed a hill to get a better view of the port, and then decided to camp there until we were ready to leave for France. For two weeks we lived on the hillside, gathering information about the boats and how to board one. One day, while having coffee in town, we met a guy who did casual work on one of the boats further down the coast at Folkestone. He told us that for ten pounds he could get us in the back of one of the wagons going on board and we could hide there for the crossing to France.

We'd already used some of our money travelling down there and living for two weeks, so we agreed to hitch to Folkestone and set off on our travels while we still had some cash left. That is, until Robinson decided he wanted to go back. It had all been a bit of a game to him, and the idea of leaving the country was too much. So we agreed to part, sharing what money was left. He agreed that I could keep the camping things, as he wouldn't need them, and off he went down the hill.

I'd bought a pair of binoculars from a second-hand shop in London, and I climbed the moat in which we'd pitched the tent and lay on the hill watching him walk down into town – and straight into the police station! I wondered if he'd given himself up to get a free lift back to Sunderland and a hot meal.

I kept on watching, and about an hour later I saw him again, this time accompanied by two tall policemen and heading for the hill. He'd told them about me! I couldn't believe it! But I had no intention of giving myself up, so I packed up my things and scarpered.

Out on the main road I stuck out my thumb and soon got a lift from one of the many trucks on the road heading for Folkestone. When I got there I headed for the beach to pitch my tent.

I spent the next couple of days lazing on the beach and listening to pop music on a small transistor radio I'd bought in Newcastle. Through the binoculars I watched the boats heading to France, thinking that I would soon be on one of them.

Friday came and I packed my kit and headed for town and the café where we'd agreed to meet the guy who was going to help us. I'd got there early and sat with my coffee, watching out for him. Then I had a sudden feeling. What if Robinson had told the police about this meeting? It seemed unthinkable, as he was a friend, but then he'd already turned me in. I decided I'd better leave and find a spot across the street to watch the place, just in case. I got outside and headed around the corner – straight into the arms of two plain-clothes policemen who were waiting there for me. I was gutted. I had dreamed of seeing France and then the world, and now I was back where I had always been – in trouble.

After an overnight stay in the cells, where I sat miserably on my bed, wishing I had never met Robinson and never taken the money, I was taken to the station and put on a train to Newcastle. I was handcuffed to the seat and had to endure stares from the passengers seated close by, who no doubt thought I was some kind of arch-villain from the north rather than a scared kid who wasn't yet sixteen.

Once in Newcastle I had to wait in a cell for officers from Sunderland to come and collect me. The two who arrived took me to the main station at Gill Bridge and put me in yet another cell to await my fate. The following day I was up in front of the magistrate, alongside Robinson. He wouldn't look at me and kept his head down the whole time. I didn't hate him. I just thought that, like me, he was trying to find a way through. But there was no way I could tell him, as we were separated by a couple of officers.

We were remanded in custody until a later date. One of the policemen had to explain to me what that meant: waiting in prison for our trial. I was put into a prison van divided into two rows of tiny compartments with metal doors and security locks. Each compartment consisted of a metal box with a metal seat and a tiny piece of opaque glass to let a little light in. It would have been a frightening experience at any time, but this was a hot day and the little metal compartment was getting hotter every minute. By the end of the journey I was desperate for water and cool air.

We were taken to Low Newton Remand Centre, a prison for young offenders. I was stripped, searched, given a uniform to wear and issued with a pillowcase full of various items for washing and shaving, and a pile of bedding to carry. The other new prisoners, plus Robinson and me, were led into the main area and up the stairs to small corridors with cell doors along one side. One by one we were locked into our cells.

When the door had slammed behind me I looked around and saw I was in a small rectangular room with a bed, a bedside cabinet, a chair and a small table. In one corner was a plastic toilet pot with a handle and lid on it, and there was a small window, set high in the wall.

I had been locked up many times in my life, but that was the worst night I'd ever spent. I felt so frightened, lost and alone, wondering what would happen to me and how long I would be there for. In the end I fell into a sleep filled with terrifying dreams, only to wake with a start when the warder banged on the door.

That morning I was taught the foul, almost medieval practice of 'slopping out', which meant emptying your toilet pot of its contents from the night before and rinsing it out in a large sink. The smell from all the pots being emptied at the same time was almost unbearable.

After that horrible chore we were given a larger bowl of hot water to wash with, back in the cell.

In the next few days I was given a job in the kitchens, cleaning and washing pans and serving meals. This cheered me up, as I liked the idea of cooking. There was chronic overcrowding even then, and as the kitchen staff had to be up long before the others, they put eight of us in one of the communal rooms along the corridor from the kitchen and gave us folding beds to sleep on.

At first this was fine, especially as the room had a telly in it. I preferred not to be alone and didn't mind the kitchen work, so life wasn't too bad. Until one awful day I discovered that Robinson, afraid of being labelled a grass, had got in first and told everyone that it was me who had gone to the police. This was almost like a death sentence, as most people in the prison system will sanction almost anything done to a grass.

So began months of torment at the hands of my room-mates. I was beaten up daily. Among our group was a very large and much older lad who weighed around seventeen stone to my ten. He was a nasty bully who loved wrestling, and every night he tried out his techniques on me, to see which one of his moves hurt most. And it wasn't just him I had to fear. If I fell asleep before the others, they would put a pillow over my head and rain down blows on me, without me being able to see who the perpetrators were. They found numerous ways to take out their aggression on me, and with no one to help me and unable to fight them all at once, I had no choice but to put up with the beatings. Many nights I lay awake with my body aching and bruised and my heart sore, feeling that no one in the world cared or even knew where I was, or that I was at the mercy of a bunch of thugs.

The one thing that kept me going was knowing my court date would come up and that when it did I would get away. Once I was given my date I kept it secret. On the day itself I found a way to be alone with each of my tormentors and gave each one a thrashing – even the seventeen-stone boy. I take no pride in what I did. I saw it as a necessity because the label would have stayed with me wherever I went, and if I had done nothing I would have been targeted for the rest of my days in those institutions. But from that day it stopped as the word went around about my retaliation.

A legal aid solicitor came to see me just before the case. He seemed very uninterested, and said there wasn't much choice but to plead guilty and tell them it was a first offence and I was sorry. I was, and he told the judge so, but I don't think it made a lot of difference. I was given a 'six to two', which meant I was sentenced to between six months and two years in borstal. The amount of time I actually served would depend on my behaviour, I was told, though as I later discovered, no one served six months, as it usually took that long to get there in the first place.

There was no place in a borstal available for me, so I was sent to Durham Prison to wait. It was a terrible place. I was led into what I can only describe as a birdcage for men. Four and five landings of rows of cells with a kind of chicken wire strung between each floor, which gave it the appearance of an aviary. There was a powerful smell of stale tobacco and urine in the air and the noise of hundreds of prisoners echoing around the walls.

I was shoved into an empty cell and the door was slammed shut and locked behind me. For the next three months I was only let out to slop out in the morning and at night, and to collect my meals. My cell was five feet wide and ten feet long, with a small window six feet from the floor. I could just see out of it if I stood on the chair, though it wasn't worth the bother because all I could see were other windows like mine around a large courtyard. There was a large heating pipe running through the cell, and the temperature was so high that previous occupants had smashed out all the glass in the window frames to let the air in, though it didn't help very much at all.

Every morning my bed had to be lifted up and placed against the wall, as there was no room to leave it down during the day. But even with the bed up, all I could do was pace restlessly a couple of steps up and down. I was given books to read from the prison library but they were all cowboy books, which were apparently the most popular but didn't really interest me. I had a prison-issue notebook and pencil, but I never wrote in it as on a regular basis the door would be opened and I would be made to stand on the landing while prison officers emptied my cell of everything and thumbed through the notebook.

I had no idea how long I would be there, and the time passed agonisingly slowly as I endured day after day of waiting in the stifling heat. It was utter torment. I was a boy, and was having to endure conditions men twice my age struggled with. Eventually it dawned on the prison authorities that they had made a terrible mistake. I was still under sixteen and should never have been kept in an adult prison. I was supposed to be on the young offenders' landing, which had separate rules, more appropriate for underage boys. I was quickly transferred to Strangeways Prison in Manchester, where there was an assessment centre for young prisoners.

Things weren't very different there. Again I was put in a cell on my own and left for many hours a day, with no work and nothing to occupy me. Desperate with boredom and loneliness, I managed to get hold of an elastic band to use as a catapult. Over the weeks that followed I perfected my aim and was able to shoot down flies, using bits of paper as ammunition. I also used my pencil to draw tiny figures on the wall in a kind of war game I invented.

It would have been easy to go mad. A sixteen-year-old boy along the landing from me cut his wrists with an old razor blade one morning, and when the guards arrived he ran along the landing with blood squirting out of his arms and peppering the walls as he went. They dragged him away and we never knew what became of him. It could have been any of us. But somehow I was determined to keep my mind occupied and stay sane. I knew that if I could get through it, I would have another chance at life, back on the outside.

It was while I was in Strangeways that I once again ran into Robinson, in the communal bath-house. The steam in the room made it hard to see clearly unless someone was a couple of feet away. So I didn't see him until I came around a pillar with a towel wrapped around me.

The anger I felt at his betrayal boiled up and I grabbed him by the throat before he could shout out.

I asked him why he'd said that I was the one who grassed when he knew it was a lie. His reply was that he thought that I might tell them it was him. He kept saying, 'Sorry, sorry,' and I realised that he was so afraid of the world he was in that he would say anything to protect himself. So I let him go and walked away. But the thirty or so lads in the bath-house had heard his confession, and a minute later the hissing chant of 'Grass, grass, grass,' started. I heard him cry for help and a prison officer ran in. Robinson was removed for his own safety and I never heard of him again.

After three long months my cell door opened one day and I was told I was leaving. A space had finally become available in a borstal in south Yorkshire and I would be finishing my sentence there. My spirits soared. It had to be a bit better than what I'd been through already.

It turned out that the borstal used converted army huts out in the fields, just like the ones we used in Staithes all those years ago, and many of the work duties involved helping out on a local farm. I hoped to be given work out in the fields, but I ended up working in the kitchens, cleaning pans and peeling potatoes by the dustbinful. Even that was far better that being locked in a tiny cell week after week. At least I could see the sky and talk freely to the others.

When I was released from borstal, after nine months, I was seventeen and had nowhere to go, no money, no skills and no hope of a decent future. With no one to believe in me or encourage me and no idea what I should do, I returned to Sunderland, where I drifted into bad company. I found myself in the underworld of misfits and lost souls, most of them not bad people but with no idea how to get out of the trap of poverty and petty crime. Like me, they had all been in care or prison, or both.

I moved in with some other lads and signed on the dole. It was almost impossible to get a job, with no training, no qualifications and a prison record. I wanted a way out, but I didn't know how to find it. They were the only 'family' I had and so, broke and with no direction in life, it was all too easy to join them on a raid to get 'easy' money from a factory safe. I knew deep down that it wasn't what I wanted, but I kidded myself that it would be just the once and then I could afford to make a fresh start. But, of course, there is no such thing as easy money; there is always a price to pay. We were fairly inept and were quickly caught, and I found myself back in the prison I hated so much.

I could easily have become one of those who would spend the rest of their lives in and out of prison. But when I arrived back there, facing a couple more years behind bars, something changed in me. I began to feel angry and frustrated that I had wasted so much of my life, and I became determined never to end up in trouble again. I realised that to make a genuinely fresh start I had to find a way to be free of all the influences that had got me into trouble, because everyone I knew – and I mean everyone – was involved in or had been involved in crime. I didn't know one honest soul who was 'normal' and who could advise me on how to live differently.

With long hours to think things over, I could see that I was the cause of my own troubles. No matter what had happened to me, I couldn't blame anyone else. I had spent my days trying to fit in with the wrong crowd and trying to please others at my own expense.

It was an epiphany. I realised that I wanted something more. A real family, a job that meant something, and a decent future. My thoughts drifted to Irene. When I looked back over my life she was the one bright thing that stood out in all of those dark years, and once again I wished with all my heart that I could find her. I had no idea where I would even start to look for her. I didn't even know her second name. But that didn't stop me thinking of her, wondering what she would be like, imagining how pretty she would be as a young woman and what it would be like to be with her again.

I made a list of the things I had to achieve in order to gain freedom and independence from all the stupid influences I had been following for so long. I needed to move away into my own place and not tell anyone where I was. To leave friends behind and go off to an uncertain future would be hard at first, but I had to do it. And I needed to come off benefits and get a job. Most importantly, I needed to get some form of training and education so that I could improve my lot and understand more about the world. The result of these aims, if I achieved them, would be that I was in control of my own life. No one would be in charge but me.

When I came out of prison for the last time, in early 1972, I was just over nineteen years old and had made up my mind that I would start life again. I kept the picture of Irene in my mind, to spur me on. If I ever found her again, I wanted her to be proud of me.

22

Irene

Though it wasn't what I had wanted, I was now on my own with my children, and more than anything I wanted to do my absolute best to be a good parent. I was twenty-seven, and the children were eight and three, when Robert moved out for the second time; I knew very little about life, but I promised myself that I would be there for my children, no matter what. And over the next twenty years I was, even though it was to be hard going at times, and I was to remain a single parent until the children were grown up.

After the split I stayed in the house at Silksworth, as Michael was settled in the local school and Joanne was going to the nursery and I didn't want to disrupt their lives by moving elsewhere. I had wanted to give them a stable home life, with a mum and dad. And now I had failed. I spent many hours wondering where I had gone wrong, and my confidence dived. I didn't think about Robert's unkindness, or that he had made my life almost intolerable. I blamed myself, and I often thought that his mother was no doubt blaming me too.

I found it hard being a single mum and money was very tight. Trying to make ends meet on benefits was a constant challenge. For the next five years I concentrated on being a mum. In front of others I hid behind a smile, never letting anyone come close. I just retreated inside myself, and my children were my comfort. I was often very lonely but I had no thoughts of becoming involved with anyone again. I had no intention of falling into another bad relationship.

Gradually I began to come back out of what had been quite a deep depression. Then one day I spotted an ad in the local paper for a cheap day trip to Whitby, on offer from the YMCA to local families. My heart leapt and suddenly I could see that long-ago summer holiday there with Alan. Was it possible that he was still there after all these years? I tried to imagine what he would be like. I was thirty-three by then, so he would be thirty-one. I thought he would probably be a fisherman with his own boat, and I wondered if he would remember me.

I signed up for the trip and took Michael and Joanne. We joined a coach full of parents and children, and I was a little shy at first as I wasn't used to being among a lot of people. But the children made friends and I was soon chatting to the other mums, many of whom were in a similar situation to me.

We had such a nice day that I wondered why I hadn't done something like that before. It was like a real holiday for the children, who were then fourteen and nine, and I was as excited as they were as we walked around the harbour and through the old cobbled streets. My heart raced when I saw the places where I had played with Alan. It was as though time had stood still in those little streets and, although I told myself I was being silly, I couldn't help looking out for him.

I never told anyone, not even the children, about the little boy I knew in care. It had become a precious secret I'd kept so long that I just didn't know how to share it.

That day trip was a turning point for me. I kept in touch with some of the other mums and became good friends with one in particular, Eileen. She owned a video rental shop and I offered to help out there, just for something to do. I wasn't paid, but she let me borrow the videos to take home for the children.

I began to look outward again, and to enjoy talking to the customers and the other girls who worked in the shop. So when, two years later, Eileen opened a beauty salon and asked me to come and work for her, I jumped at the chance to start earning a living again. The salon was equipped with exercise machines and toning tables, and the suppliers laid on training schemes for staff. I sailed through the courses and gained my certificates as a fitness instructor, and though it was a small beginning it was a positive one. At last I began to feel in charge of my own life, and the future was looking good. I even went on a couple of dates. I had a deep longing to fill that empty space inside, but a fear of getting it wrong again stopped me from getting really involved with anyone.

Money was still tight and I couldn't often afford to take the children anywhere. But every now and then I took them on day trips to Whitby. I told myself to forget about Alan, instead of hanging on to the hope that I would find him again and that the bond between us would still be there. But I couldn't help myself: I had to keep looking.

Sometimes I used to take the children to the beach at Seaburn. It was somewhere I was always drawn to. I used to go there when I was still married, to escape the difficult atmosphere at home, and I had once seen someone there who reminded me of Alan.

It had been when the children were only toddlers and we were playing and paddling by the water's edge, just like dozens of other families. The lifeguards, who wore red t-shirts and shorts, would patrol the beach, and they used to gather at the building where the first aid post was stationed. On that day I had noticed one of them standing looking out to sea and couldn't help feeling that there was something familiar about him. I could only see him in profile, from a distance, but I could see that he was tanned and had fair hair.

A moment later the children distracted me, and when I turned back he had gone. But fleeting as that sighting was, there was something about him that stayed with me for many years after that day, and I used to go back there, wondering if the lifeguard could have been Alan, and half-hoping that I would see him strolling down the beach.

The greatest sadness in my life, as the years passed, was the difficult relationship I had with my son. In his early teens he had become very disruptive and argumentative and I found it increasingly difficult to cope with him. As he reached the age of fifteen or sixteen he mixed with the wrong company, and whenever I was out he would let his friends into the house. I would come in from work to find the living room full of youngsters with beer cans and the house in a state. I was tired of having to chase them all out and worried that Michael might be drinking too much, like his father.

I tried everything to help my son but nothing worked, and I blamed myself because I'd parted from his father. After the divorce Michael and Joanne never got to see their dad regularly and I was convinced that Michael needed a father at home. That was the one thing I couldn't give him. So it was with a heavy heart that I asked Michael to move out, once he had left school and got a job as a labourer in a furniture store. He found himself a flat, and after that he led his own life and I saw very little of him. It was a source of terrible sadness to me, but I had to let go and accept his wish to do things his own way.

Joanne was still at school, and after Michael had moved out we settled into a peaceful routine. I continued to work as a fitness instructor, and although deep inside I was still lonely, I had a small circle of friends and family who helped to fill the void.

One of my greatest joys was seeing my sisters. The four of us used to meet up regularly, and we had a lot of fun. Joan had also parted from her husband. It had come as a surprise, and she would never talk about what had come between them. Greta, Pat and I always felt that she still loved him and missed him a lot. And sadly her health was deteriorating. Her arthritis was getting worse and her poor hands became so painful and distorted that she had to have an operation to replace the knuckles and joints. But despite this she retained a great sense of humour and was always a joker. She was an inspiration, and I felt that my problems were almost insignificant in comparison to hers.

Some days we would go shopping in town and meet up with Pat and Greta. Pat was working as the manageress of a night club, so on Friday mornings when she was preparing food and sorting deliveries we would pop in for coffee.

On Greta's birthday, Pat invited us all to the club to celebrate. Greta never drank alcohol, but that night we laced her coke with a little drop of vodka and Greta had a wonderful night and danced for hours. These were good times. We had spent so much time apart in the past that it was wonderful to be together, the four of us, laughing and having fun.

The years passed and Joanne grew up and met Dean, her future husband. They moved into a little house together when she was seventeen and I was happy for them, because I could see how in love they were.

By the time I turned forty I was living alone. I missed the children, especially Joanne. Still, I saw a lot of her and my job kept me busy. But unfortunately I was having health problems. I'd suffered from back trouble since my twenties, but had always ignored it. Eventually, though, it got so bad that I had to go to a doctor, and I was devastated when a specialist diagnosed osteoarthritis – inflammation of the joints – and spondylosis – inflammation of the vertebrae in my neck – as well as fibromyalgia – chronic muscle pain. The doctor told me that a lot of my ill health was the result of stress. There wasn't much to be done about any of it, apart from taking anti-inflammatory drugs. Despite these problems I was proud of having a job that involved being physically active and supple, and I was determined to keep it.

A year later, Joan was diagnosed with lung cancer. The news was devastating for all of us. Joan had moved to a house in Washington, just outside Sunderland, and now lived next door to her eldest daughter, Elaine. Greta, Pat and I went to visit her a lot and I often stayed overnight, to look after her. She died a few months later, aged just fifty-four, which seemed much too young, and we all felt heartbroken. Joan had been the closest family member to me throughout my childhood, and I missed her dreadfully.

Though we were never really close, I had always visited Dad from time to time over the years. Then, a few years after Joan died, he had a fall and, no longer able to cope alone, was admitted to a residential home for the elderly. By that time I was a grandmother. Joanne and Dean had a daughter, Faye, and a son, Liam, and together my two grandchildren brought a great deal of joy into my life.

Dad loved being a great grandfather, and so once a week I would bring him home for the day to see the children. He doted on them, and I believe the time he spent with them had a profound effect on the way he thought about things and gave him an insight into how it was for his own daughters when we were that age. His attitude towards all of us seemed to soften, yet it was still unexpected when, while I was visiting him one day, he told me how sorry he was for the years when we were all apart, and said how much he loved me.

It meant so much to me that I couldn't hold back my tears. I was filled to overflowing with emotion because I'd waited all my life to hear those words. It felt as though a dam of longing and loneliness burst inside me when he said, 'I love you.' I knew it couldn't change all the things that had happened, but hearing him say sorry released something inside me that I'd locked away for so many years.

It was a strange coincidence that, soon after that, I discovered from the staff in Dad's home that Auntie Doris from Rennie Road was in a home over on the other side of the river. I decided to visit her, in the hope that perhaps she would know what happened to Alan and could help me unravel the mystery after all this time.

When the day came I felt very nervous. I bought her some flowers and sat in the visitors' room, wondering what I'd find and how she'd react to me when we met.

She arrived in a motorised wheelchair. Thirty-two years after I had last seen her, she looked just the same as she had in the Rennie Road days, though her hair was now grey. She looked at me, puzzled, and when I told her my name she sat thinking for a few moments. Then it dawned on her who I was, and to my surprise she held out her arms to hug me. I was taken aback. I hadn't expected this. But I hugged her and we sat and talked for a while. I told her I had a nice job, children and grandchildren.

When I asked her about Alan, she said she had never heard of him again after he was taken away. I felt very downhearted as I'd so hoped that she might know what had happened to him. But, to her, Alan had been just one more child who passed through the home. It was yet another dead end, and I left feeling very sad.

23

Alan

Soon after I got back to Sunderland I decided to get in touch with my dad again. I hadn't seen him since I was nine, when my visits home from The Esplanade had been stopped after I'd fallen in the river. But I'd seen my brothers from time to time since I'd left care, and they told me where to find him.

It wasn't easy to walk back into Dad and Anita's lives, but I wanted to have more of a connection with my family. They had five children now: Sonia and Yvonne, who I'd met as babies, a third daughter, Alison, and two boys, Tony and Paul. Anita had a little second-hand shop where she sold small items like baby clothes, and they lived in the flat above, in a house on the corner of Laura Street.

They were surprised to see me, and a little wary. Anita wasn't very enthusiastic about me showing up and I understood why, given my reputation for getting into trouble. But despite the initial awkwardness on both sides, my visit went reasonably well. They were probably relieved when they discovered that I wasn't about to move in and only wanted to say hello.

After that I went to see them from time to time, nipping up the stairs to sit over a cup of tea with Dad. He was loving and cheerful with the younger kids and always keen to watch the racing on TV. But he was distant with me. I didn't feel a part of the family and always had to work very hard to get his attention.

About a year later Dad and Anita announced they were moving to a new council house, so I took over the flat above the shop and rented it for a while. I liked Laura Street, but the old crowd I had mixed with began coming round. They weren't bad people; most of them were a bit lost and simply looking for a way to get by. But they were into petty crime, and I knew that as long as I was around them I wouldn't make the new start I longed for. So I moved on again.

I found a bedsit on the other side of town, in a reasonably nice area called Belle View Park, and I moved in, feeling that this time it really was going to be a new beginning. The next day I went down to Roker beach and got a summer job working for the Local Authority as a beach cleaner. This involved walking along the sand all day picking up the rubbish left by visitors. My working tools were a black sack, a pair of gloves and a set of bright yellow waterproofs for wet days.

It was a modest beginning, but I'd managed two things off my wish list and I felt, for the first time, that the future was in my hands and I was standing on my own two feet. A bedsit and a cleaning job didn't seem like a lot, but I knew that if Irene had been there she would have understood how much it meant.

Unexciting as it was, I stuck with the job. I enjoyed being out in the open air and seeing holidaymakers playing on the beach. I must have picked up thousands of discarded chip cartons and drinks cans over the course of the summer.

At the end of September I was out of work – although I was promised the job again for the following March or April. I was quite happy to take the winter off, because I had other plans. First I got out my tent and went camping in the Lake District. All those hours walking and camping at Stanhope had given me a taste for the great outdoors. I can't describe the feeling of peace and contentment I got when I woke in the morning on top of some mountain ridge and looked out of the tent flap. I felt I could see the world. I often went into a small oak wood near Keswick, where I would light a fire, cook myself a meal and breathe in those wonderful moments of freedom.

After camping for a couple of weeks I came home and signed on at the local further education college to brush up on my English and maths. I was keenly aware that my education had been lacking, and I knew that to move up in the world I needed to start with the basics. I really enjoyed studying, now that I was doing it because I wanted to. I learned fast, and as a result the following summer, when I went back to work on the beach, I was promoted to the position of cashier, which meant hiring out deck chairs and beach tents. Even that modest step up was positively life-changing for me. I was overjoyed to be given responsibility.

I worked on Roker beach over the next few summers – moving up to take charge of a team of deck-chair attendants and beach cleaners, and then helping to run the car parks. And in the winters I went to college, taking the exams I'd missed at school. During the long hot summer of 1976 my sister Yvonne would come down to the beach with her friends. She was a stunning-looking girl and all the lads were keen on her, so I made a point of telling them she was my sister to keep them at bay. I was very protective of her, though I never told her, of course. She would probably have laughed.

After a few years I was moved to Seaburn beach, where I would stand on top of the steps behind the beach, in the red T-shirt and shorts we all wore, watching the swimmers and sunbathers. I used to look at all the mums and children playing on the sand and think of when Irene and I played together at Whitby.

In 1980, when I was twenty-eight, I married Julie – the daughter of a colleague I worked with in the car parks. She was nineteen and lovely, but I should never have married her. I wanted a companion, someone to share life with and be close to. But I didn't love her the way I should have, and in my heart of hearts I knew this even before we married. The trouble was, I found it extremely hard to say what I felt, and once I'd said yes to marriage I couldn't bring myself to change it to no. Today it would have been different. One moment's disappointment and hurt is better than a whole life that is untrue. But it can take a lot of harsh lessons in life to learn that.

Once I was married I was determined to make it work and be the responsible family man, so I left the beach to work in the Pyrex Glass factory. It was quite a change from working in the sun to working shifts indoors and in intense heat. I was trained to be a specification inspector, measuring and packing hundreds of very hot glass jars in a shift, alternating with two others to work around the clock. Then one of the other inspectors fell sick, leaving two of us to cover the three shifts. For week after week I worked in stifling conditions for twelve hours a day, six days a week.

Eventually I became ill with exhaustion and had to leave. I went back to working on the beach, where I was happy. More than anything I loved messing about in boats; I'd loved them ever since that first holiday in Whitby with Irene, and I spent every spare minute I could on the water. So when I was asked to do a little work with the in-shore rescue boat, as a stand-by crew member, I was thrilled. We were once called out in a terrible squall when red flares were fired from a large yacht.

It turned out it was a false alarm, but no one told us and we ended up in thirty-foot seas in our little semi-inflatable, being tossed about like a bobbing cork. The sea was like a boiling cauldron, and at one point we hit the middle of a huge wave and went right through it. I was hanging over the bow, using my weight to keep the nose down in the wind, and ended up with a large mouthful of sea water. It took us an hour and a half to cover the mile back to safety in the harbour.

To make ends meet I also took a weekend job as a watchman in a local factory unit just down the road, so, the lesson of the Pyrex factory forgotten, I ended up working seven days a week once again. The factory was being developed into small business units with grants available for those who were starting up new businesses, and I decided to have a go. With my brothers, Michael and George, I started a business making wooden toys for local nursery schools. We did well at first, but eventually we hit problems and I decided to go back to college.

By that time I had saved up and bought my own boat, a thirty-foot ex-ship's lifeboat with a diesel engine and a small cabin. It was painted blue and I called it *Sirius*, after the star. I loved it and it gave me the freedom of the river and the local coast. I kept it up-river at the little hamlet of Coxgreen – the same one I got caught in twice, when I ran away from The Esplanade to try to find Irene. At high tide, when the mist was in, navigating the seven miles up the river at night by the bright beam of the bow light was quite a journey.

In all my jobs I had worked incredibly hard, putting in long hours. So inevitably Julie and I didn't see much of one another. She didn't share my love of boats, so even in our spare hours we were seldom together, and she was unhappy. While I didn't want to hurt her I was becoming more and more aware that I didn't love her. I had a deep dark hole inside, and I had thought that somehow she would fill it. She couldn't, of course – no one could have. And as long as that hole was there, I was never going to be able to have a real relationship, because while I felt that empty I had very little to give, no matter how hard I tried.

Not only that, but Julie wanted children and I didn't. After my own childhood experiences I was terrified of getting it wrong, so that a child of mine might suffer in some way or even end up in care, and I couldn't face that responsibility. I felt that so many adults got it wrong as parents and carers – how was I to know if I could get it right?

After five years of marriage, we agreed to part. She stayed in the flat, so I needed somewhere else to live. I went to visit a friend, hoping to stay, and found he was working abroad and had rented his house to a woman called Margaret. She told me she was looking for someone to share it with her. It seemed like a good idea, so I moved in.

That was in 1985, when I was thirty-two. For the next few years I went to college to improve my education. I became an adult trainer – a teacher for adults – and, to my surprise, I found I was very good at it. I also joined a training course in quality assurance for business. I was soon offered an exciting and challenging job, working with unemployed managers and as a management consultant. It was a world away from my past, and I was amazed to discover abilities that I never knew I had. I worked extremely hard and after a few years I left my job to have another go at running my own business, offering employee training to local businesses. It did very well, and within a couple of years I had twelve associates who worked with me.

By the time I turned forty I felt I had come a long way. I had qualifications and experience and had created a business I loved, doing something worthwhile.

A year later my father died, after a series of heart attacks. I was very sad to lose him, and wished that we had been able to talk more about the past before he went. There was so much I would have liked to know. I didn't stay long at his funeral. I felt, as I had felt many times before, that he had a new family who loved him very much, and I was part of his past.

Although my working life was moving forward in leaps and bounds, my personal life was at stalemate. After the marriage ended I didn't want to get involved with anyone again because I didn't want to cause any more hurt. But eventually I more or less sleep-walked into a relationship with Margaret. We were both lonely and we were sharing the same house, so perhaps it was inevitable. For the next few years we rubbed along together comfortably enough, but once again, in my heart I knew our relationship had more to do with convenience than with real love, and Margaret knew it too. I had always hoped to find a deep, fulfilling love, but by this time I had come to accept that I probably never would. I sometimes wondered whether it might have happened with Irene, if we had found one another again. All those years after our parting I still thought of her with a pang of longing, but in all that time I hadn't heard anything about her, so I told myself I was probably being foolish, and resigned myself to settling for what I had.

24

Alan and Irene

Irene

By the time I was forty-seven I felt I had made a life for myself. I loved my job, I loved seeing my grandchildren, and I had some good friends. I still lived alone, because although I'd had one or two relationships, I had never met anyone I wanted to settle down with. That was a real sadness, and there were times when I felt lonely. Despite my lovely family and friends, at the end of the day I would go home and it was just me and the four walls. I had never moved from the little house in Silksworth – I never had a reason to, and all my memories of my children were there. So I would potter round my little garden, or cook myself a meal for one, and wonder if this was it – would I always be alone? It certainly seemed that way.

I still taught fitness classes at the gym several days a week, and was proud that, despite my back problems, I had kept working. I got on well with the rest of the staff and often had a good laugh with the women in my classes.

One day I got chatting to one of the customers, Margaret, who'd been coming for quite a while. She told me she worked as a manager in a local residential home. She mentioned her partner and said he worked away from home a lot. Then she mentioned casually that he had been in a children's home.

I told her I had been in a children's home too, one called Rennie Road.

'I wonder if Alan knows it,' she said.

I felt my heart skip a beat and my face flush. 'Did you say Alan?'

'Yes,' she said, looking at me curiously. 'My partner's name is Alan.'

Despite the thudding of my heart, I tried to sound casual as I said, 'I knew an Alan there. I wonder if it's the same one.'

'He comes in to pick me up sometimes,' she said. 'I'll introduce you next time.'

'Fine,' I said, but inside I was in turmoil. I told myself I was being ridiculous. Just because she knew an Alan who'd been in care didn't mean it was my Alan. There must have been thousands of Alans in the care system at that time. But I had a feeling, deep down, that it was him. I tried not to hope too much, but it was impossible not to be excited. For the next few days I barely slept. It felt both strange and wonderful that I might really be about to see Alan again, after more than thirty-nine years. Would we recognise one another? The anticipation was almost unbearable.

When Margaret arrived for her next exercise class I wondered whether she'd spoken to him. But there wasn't time to ask her before the class started. After we finished, I left the class members to get their things together. As I walked through the door from the gym, a well-dressed man in a suit and tie walked in through the front door across the other side of the reception area.

It was Alan.

His blond hair had darkened but his blue eyes were just the same, and for a few seconds we stood looking at one another, both of us unable to say a word.

In those moments I saw the little boy he had been, his fair hair parted, wearing short corduroy trousers, a grey tank-top and stout black shoes. And as the memories came flooding back I felt as if my heart would burst. I wanted to take his hand and run out of the gym, just as we used to run off to the woods.

'Irene?' he said.

Then I became aware that the rest of the class, including his partner, were coming out behind me. 'This is the boy I used to play with when I was a young girl,' I told them. Everyone laughed, and Margaret said, 'So you do know each other. Isn't that amazing?'

The next few minutes were both painful and wonderful. I longed to ask Alan so many questions – what had happened to him after he left Rennie Road, where he'd been since then and whether he'd missed me the way I'd missed him. Instead he, Margaret and I chatted politely and she asked us how long it was since we'd last met and what the homes were like.

I did my best to answer. But it wasn't easy, and I could see Alan was struggling too.

After a few minutes, Margaret said, 'We'd better be off.'

'Hope to see you again and catch up a little more,' Alan said. He looked at me with such warmth and tenderness that I longed to hug him. But I smiled and nodded and watched as he turned and walked out of the door with Margaret.

Alan

As I pushed open the door of the gym and saw Irene walking out of the exercise studio, it seemed as if time was suspended. We just looked at each other. For a second I wasn't sure it was her, but then it was as if the mist cleared and I could flash back almost forty years, to a day in May 1960 when the sun was bright and I felt truly happy. Underneath the spring trees, I was hand in hand with my long-lost love in the magical bluebell woods. And in that instant I realised that, despite all that I had lived through over the years, my feelings, untouched and untarnished, were still as they had been that day. In one startling moment I was seven again and desperate to see her. And although she had changed with time, I could see the hint of red in her hair, and the freckles were still there.

I wanted to take hold of her there and then and hold her tight. But a minute later Margaret came out of the gym behind Irene and was standing next to me, and the staff gathered around us as Irene told them that we had known one another as children.

I stood and smiled and chatted while all the time I was in agony. I had found Irene, and I was going to have to turn around and walk away from her.

The pain I felt as I looked at her and said goodbye was indescribable. How could life be this cruel? I knew, from the second I saw her, that I wanted to be with Irene, as I had always wanted to be with her. But I couldn't: I was in a relationship with another woman.

For a long time I agonised. Should I end things with Margaret and then go back to find Irene? I couldn't bring myself to do it. I wasn't the sort of man to just dump someone I had been with for over a decade. And despite my longing for Irene, I felt afraid too. Did she feel the same way? Would she want me too? Or was I just clinging to an old hope?

I thought of her all the time, and not long after that first meeting I offered to pick Margaret up from the gym so that I could see Irene again. She was in reception when I walked in, and I felt such a rush of love when I saw her. I had a couple of minutes with her before Margaret came out – just enough to tell her that I hoped we'd be able to talk more soon.

After that I knew that to go back and see her at the gym would be worse than not seeing her at all. I couldn't face talking to her with people around, unable to say the things I longed to say.

As these thoughts and feelings battled inside me, my relationship with Margaret became increasingly strained. Even though I tried to carry on as normal, she sensed that something had changed and she became very distant. She barely looked at me or spoke to me, and I wondered how we could go on. I was tempted to walk out and look for Irene then, but I knew that if I was ever to do that, things had to be resolved in the rest of my life.

Events took a new turn when I was unexpectedly made redundant. I had sold my business a few years earlier and taken a well-paid management job, so losing it came as a shock. Shortly afterwards I was offered contract work in Scotland. Margaret wasn't happy, and said that if I went she wouldn't be coming too, even though without this job I would be on the dole. In the end I decided to go. It offered me a way out – of my deteriorating relationship with Margaret and of my turmoil over Irene. It would give me an income, which I needed, and some space.

While I was relieved to be in Scotland and away from the constant tension with Margaret, the period that followed was a very bleak one for me. I was afraid that my one chance of being with Irene had gone, and in many ways I felt that I had lost everything. For the first time in my life I felt a depression come over me.

For the next few months I concentrated on work, and during this time Margaret and I agreed to end our relationship. It was over anyway; we simply hadn't said it. In the following months we lost touch. So I was shocked and deeply upset to hear, almost two years later, that she had died of complications from late-onset diabetes. She had been ill for some months before her death, and I felt very sad – had I known, I would have gone to see her.

Margaret's death and my increasingly painful neck and back problems only added to my low state of mind. I was diagnosed with spondylosis and osteoarthritis and a problem was found with the discs in my lower spine – I had a trapped nerve and another partially trapped nerve, the result, I felt sure, of the beatings I had suffered as a child, and in particular that one catastrophic beating by the Stanhope headmaster when I was twelve and he broke his walking stick across my lower back.

When my back pain became so bad that I had to give up work, I knew it was time to go back to Sunderland and to find Irene again. It had been over three years since we met at the gym and in that time it seemed I had lost heart with life. What a fool I had been. I hadn't followed the path I knew was right, I had thrown away the chance of happiness with Irene, and since then nothing had worked out.

Irene was the one for me – I had always known it. And I would find her again. I had no idea whether she would still be at the gym, but somehow I would find her. And this time, I wouldn't let her go.

Irene

It broke my heart when Alan didn't come back to the gym again. Day after day I watched the door, hoping he would walk through it, and I hung around after Margaret's fitness class, hoping he might collect her. But he never did.

He had been back just once since that first meeting, and when I saw him I felt so happy that I wanted time to stop still, right then. He asked me how I was, and when he leaned over the reception desk our hands brushed, for a fleeting second. But after that he disappeared.

I told myself I only wanted to see him for a cup of tea, to catch up on old times. No harm in that. But I knew I was kidding myself. The moment I saw him I knew that this was the man I wanted to be with and that I would never want anyone else in the same way.

I couldn't contact him. He was with someone else. I had no right to expect him to break up with Margaret and be with me. But that didn't stop me wishing and hoping that somehow, without anyone being hurt, it would be possible. It got to the point where thinking about him and missing him was making me ill. Having found him and lost him again was desperately hard. And it seemed I had lost him. The months passed and he never reappeared, and then Margaret stopped coming to the gym and sometime afterwards I heard Alan had gone to work in Scotland. I was puzzled, and desperate for answers. Had he broken up with her? If so, why had he gone to Scotland?

With a huge effort, I resolved to get on with my life and put my energy into my work and spending time with my daughter and grandchildren. When my spirits felt very low, I reminded myself of how lucky I was to have them.

I had been having worsening problems with my back, and a couple of years later I finally had to leave my job. I missed the gym and my friends there an awful lot. Soon after this I received a telephone call from the residential home where Dad was living. They told me he was very ill, and by the time I arrived there he had died. I was devastated, because I felt that in many ways we were just starting to really get to know each other and there was still so much unsaid.

When my sister Greta died of breast cancer not long afterwards, I fell apart and I couldn't stop crying. It was as though a great well of grief opened up inside me, for all the people I had lost and all the loneliness I had endured. I had a severe breakdown and had to seek professional help from a clinical psychologist. With his help, I began to understand that my problems first began when I lost my mother. In the years that followed, as I was passed from one person to another and then put into care, I locked away all my fear, grief and loss. This had left me in a constant state of stress and tension, rather like a clenched fist that never relaxed, and it was inevitable that one day it would all become too much. Losing Alan for a second time, and then my job, my dad and my sister, was more than I could bear, and out it all came. I went through a very deep depression, but with the help I was given and the love and support of Joanne and Pat, I came through.

Once I was feeling better I felt I needed a fresh start. I even went out with someone new. But in my heart I knew that I was only going through the motions of a relationship because, despite all my good intentions, I couldn't forget Alan.

Alan

It was another year before I managed to save enough money to come back to Sunderland and move into a flat near the city centre. The building contained two other flats, and luckily for me my neighbours were great. I often chatted to Jan, who lived upstairs, and it felt like an extraordinary coincidence when she told me that her sister had been in the Cottage

Homes and in Rennie Road, though not at the same time as me. It seemed there were many of us still around.

I had seen my brothers from time to time, but I hadn't seen the rest of my family for some years. So it felt like another big coincidence when I bumped into Sonia, the oldest of my half-sisters, and discovered that she lived in the very next street.

It was good to see her again and I decided I must get in touch with other family members. But first I wanted to find Irene. I knew she'd be shocked to see me after so long. And I knew that she might have found someone else, but I had to find out if there was a chance for us. I hoped she would still be at the gym, because I had no other way to find her. But when I went there and asked, I was told that she had left some time ago. The girl there didn't know Irene's address, and my heart sank. How was I to find her now?

I realised I was going to have to rely on fate to bring us together again. But I could give it a helping hand. She had to go shopping in the city centre, I reasoned, so I spent my free time walking around the city streets, hoping that when she did come, I would be there looking for her.

Some days later I was in a store in town with Sonia when I spotted Irene. The place was crowded, so I dodged down an aisle and worked my way around to where she was. By the time I got close to her, I was tingling with anticipation. I reached out to put my hand on her shoulder, but when she turned around it wasn't her. Red-faced, I apologised and explained that I'd mistaken her for someone else.

My sister asked me who I'd thought it was, so when we got back to the flat I told her, and Jan from upstairs, the story of me and Irene. It was the first time I'd ever told anyone about her and I was surprised how good it felt to talk about it. They seemed to be genuinely moved by my story and they wanted to know a lot more, but I was still cautious about revealing my feelings, as it made me feel very vulnerable.

Not long after this I went to visit my brother George. It was good to see him, and after leaving his house I decided to walk a different route back to my flat as I needed to collect something from a shop in town. As I reached St Michael's roundabout I glanced up and saw a car coming around it – with Irene sitting in the passenger seat! I began to wave and she spotted me and began to wave back. I could see her saying something to the man driving, but the car didn't stop and within moments she had disappeared. I stood looking after her, wondering why she hadn't stopped. Was she with someone else? Was it me who had to wait for her now?

Well, I would. I would wait for however long it took. And if I could spot her once, I could do it again. I just prayed that it would be soon, and that I wouldn't be missing her like this for another five years.

I talked over what had happened that day with Jan and Sonia, and told them I would never have another relationship unless it was with Irene. I would wait, and make sure that when we met again I was free for her. I was no longer happy to settle for someone who happened to come along, grateful that anyone would want to be with me, and heading for disaster. Irene was the woman I would go to the ends of the earth for, the woman I had always loved and would always love. Somehow, I would find her again and tell her just how I felt.

Irene

When I saw Alan walking near the roundabout I was stunned. He had a bag on his back and was waving to me, and I waved back frantically and shouted, 'Sound the horn! Pull up!' The man I was seeing, who was driving, said, 'Why, what is it?' Within moments we'd left Alan behind, and because I felt unable to explain we didn't go back. But my thoughts were racing. He's back! Where does he live? I've got to find him! Suddenly everything had changed. Alan wasn't in Scotland, he was back in Sunderland. I just had to find him.

As soon as we got home, I plucked up the courage to end my relationship. My heart hadn't been in it. And now that I'd actually seen Alan, I knew for certain why that was.

I decided, right then, that I would never go out with anyone else again. It had to be Alan or no one. If I didn't find him – well, at least I had my family. But if I was meant to be with someone, then I knew it was Alan.

25

At last

Irene

For the next few days I drove back over the same route, past St Michael's roundabout, hoping that Alan might live close by and that I might spot him again, but there was no sign of him. I decided I would look out for him every time I went out anywhere, in the hope that we'd be lucky enough to bump into one another again. It was comic that, in the event, three months later I was busy chatting to a friend as we walked through town and only by chance turned my head to see Alan across the street.

My heart lurched, and before I could even think about it I shouted out his name.

I didn't notice that heads had turned towards us when I cried out, or that people had stopped to watch. All I saw was Alan spinning around and running across the street to me. We flung our arms around each other. I was laughing and close to tears, telling him, 'I've been looking for you. I'm not with anyone.' As he told me the same things I felt all the broken pieces of my heart rush back together. I knew that we could be together at last.

He kept tight hold of me as he turned to my friend and said, 'I've loved this lady all my life,' and I thought at that moment it was the most wonderful thing I had ever heard. My friend just stared open-mouthed. That's when I noticed the small crowd that had gathered round us, all staring and smiling. Blushing, I realised that I must have shouted very loudly.

Alan wrote my number on his hand and told me where he was living, but it just wasn't sinking in; I felt I was in some kind of wonderful dream. He was saying over and over, 'I'm not losing you again.' Would I come over for a meal that evening, he asked. He would call me at seven to confirm.

Reluctantly we let go of one another and said our goodbyes. 'Where did he say he lived?' I asked my friend on the way home. I hadn't taken it in, I was just so overwhelmed to find him. My friend pointed to his house. I couldn't believe that I drove past his front door almost every day, often having to wait almost at the bottom of his garden for the traffic lights to change.

My head had been in such a whirl and all I could think of was seeing him again that evening. Then suddenly I remembered that I'd arranged to baby-sit for Joanne that evening, and I had to be there at six thirty. I hadn't taken Alan's number and I couldn't bear to think that he would call me at seven and I wouldn't be there.

I closed my eyes and said a little prayer that Alan would ring early. 'Call me at six,' I whispered.

Alan

I'd walked into town, no matter what the weather, every day for the three months since I'd seen Irene at the roundabout. I was always looking out for her. So it took me totally by surprise when it was Irene who spotted me.

The moment she called my name I knew it was her, and in that moment my whole life changed. It was as if I had been in a tunnel and suddenly emerged into the sunshine.

All I remember is holding her and telling her over and over again that I was free, then telling her friend I loved her, then writing her number on my hand and checking to make sure I'd got it right.

When we parted I headed back to the shops to buy some wine. I wanted our first hours together to be so special. I could hardly believe that we would be able to talk properly for the first time in forty-five years. I went back home, and then had to go and tell Jan and Sonia about meeting Irene again because I couldn't wait to tell someone. They were both delighted and wished us well.

I'd said I would ring at seven, but in the end I couldn't wait. By six o'clock I was desperate to know that she was really coming, so I rang her, an hour earlier than we'd arranged. Irene said she'd been willing me to ring early, because she had to go and baby-sit for her daughter. She'd be with me in a couple of hours.

Now I knew she was definitely coming I felt happiness wash over me. I made pasta with a simple Bolognese sauce and salad and lit candles on the table. By the time the bell went I had checked everything a dozen times.

When I opened the door, Irene looked so lovely that I felt the breath catch in my throat. Without a word, I put my arms around her. Standing there together, feeling her so close, her heart next to mine, her arms around me, I knew I had never been happier.

Later we sat over the meal and talked and I took her hand across the table and couldn't stop smiling. Looking at her in the candlelight I was sure of one thing – I could never let her go again. So when Irene told me, softly, that she didn't want to leave, I told her I had no intention of letting her go, now or ever. We had waited too long to be parted again.

Irene

It's hard to describe the intensity of that first night together. All that I had wished for, for so long, was mine. I felt so full, and happy, and complete. And yet it was just the beginning. The next day we talked and talked. There was so much to find out, so many questions to answer.

I was shocked to learn that Alan had never been adopted in Whitby. We had both been told so many lies. Learning about that hurt me deeply. Had the authorities really thought the friendship of two small children so dangerous?

But worse was to come. I felt indescribably sad when I heard how Alan had struggled to reach me through those years. I felt tears well up when I realised he was barely two hundred yards away on that winter morning in 1960 when I thought he was lost to me.

Alan comforted me and, with his arm around me, said that it was best we tell each other everything, so that we could put it behind us and look forward to all the good things ahead.

So we carried on talking and sharing all the experiences we'd both been through. Alan didn't know that I'd spent the rest of my time in care at Rennie Road, while he was being moved from place to place.

As we talked we were fascinated to discover some of the coincidences and near-misses we'd had. I could hardly believe that Anita in the second-hand shop was Alan's stepmother, and that he might even have been upstairs, having a cup of tea with his dad, while I was chatting to her. Or that Alan had moved into a house just a few hundred yards from where I lived. For a couple of years we had walked down the same streets and used the same shops, gone to the same cinema and the same market and visited the same night clubs. How close we must have come to bumping into one another, yet our paths never crossed. We may even have brushed past each other without realising it, on a busy street or in the darkness of the night clubs.

That wasn't the only time we came close. We realised that the figure I'd felt was so familiar on Seaburn beach could well have been Alan, in his red t-shirt and shorts.

We had come so close to finding one another, but it had never been meant to be – until now.

Alan

We knew that one extraordinarily passionate night could not make up for a lost forty-five years, but it helped! And the next day was our first together as adults, free to be with each other and to love at last.

It was then that all of the years between our parting and then finding one another again began to run through my mind. They say you see your whole life when you die, but I was seeing it now and it was like being reborn. That hole inside me, there for so long, began to fill when I realised that at last we could be together.

We talked and talked and were constantly surprised as we found out more and more about the things that had happened to us over the years. There was a look of shock and horror on Irene's face when she realised I'd never gone to Whitby. She had been deceived for so long.

I was shocked myself when she told me how she had searched for me in Whitby over and over again, and I realised we had been to the same beach, looking for one another, for all those summers.

We realised that morning that it would take years of talking to discover all the things that had happened over the years. But we were both very moved to learn that we had each been searching for the other, and had never given up hope of meeting again. Now we knew, for sure, that we were meant for each other and nothing would keep us apart again.

In between the serious talking we still felt like the children we had been and we found ourselves in fits of laughter at the silliest of things. A nod or a glance would be enough to take us back in time, each understanding exactly what it was like for the other. We had both been through so much, but being together would be our therapy and heal us.

Irene

My family were amazed when I told them the story for the first time. At last, after holding it inside for so long, I wanted the world to know about us. Joanne and her children and my sister Pat were so glad that I'd found my real love at last and welcomed Alan with open arms.

The days I spent with Alan now were the happiest I had ever known. For the first time in my life I was filled with a great sense of belonging. And despite all the sad tales we had to tell of the past, we laughed together so much. I hadn't giggled that way since I was nine years old.

Soon after we got together we decided that we had to go back to Whitby and visit the special places where we used to play together. So we set off in the car for a day trip. Being there brought so many mixed emotions to us both. I had to hold back tears when I thought of the many times I was there on my own looking for Alan. And he felt sad thinking that he'd been there with the other boys from Stanhope and that we might have coincided.

We went into a fish restaurant and sat talking over lunch. Alan told me how much he loved boats and I told him about my fear of water, ever since the boat trip I'd been on in Whitby when the boat began to sink. I could still remember all the children screaming, and how terrified I was.

Alan looked uncomfortable and then admitted that he had been the one to flood the boat. He'd been in a different part of the same boat, with some of the other boys, when he'd noticed a cork-like object sticking out of the deck. He wondered what it was for and began to tug at it. Eventually it just popped out and water rushed in. Apparently it was a drainage plug to get water out of the boat when it was on shore. I practically choked on my fish when I heard that!

He remembered everyone screaming and the mad rush to get the boat to shore before it sank, and how on our safe return he had to hide underneath the camp huts while the search was on for the guilty person. He never did get caught. We ended up laughing about it. And to make up for giving me a lifelong fear of water, Alan offered to give me swimming lessons.

Our day out in Whitby was wonderful, and we decided we would go back there as often as we could.

Alan

After our trip to Whitby I decided I wanted to take Irene away somewhere just to be together and discover the world. Alas, I had no money, but I did have a tent! And Irene had a car, so we headed for the highlands of Scotland.

It rained and rained and the midges were wild, so the romantic moments I had in mind were just a little dampened. But despite a few hardships, our spirits were still buoyant.

And we did manage one day on the beautiful island of Iona. It was magical, with clear blue skies, warm sun and white sand beaches.

After we returned home we began planning the next steps in our lives. We wanted to be together all the time, so that meant deciding where we should live. At first we felt that we should find somewhere new, a home that would be both of ours from the start. We spent weeks searching for somewhere suitable, but without success. So we thought again about the homes we already had. My one-bedroom flat was too small, so that left the house where Irene had lived for the past thirty years.

Irene said she had something important to show me, so she took me to her house and we went into the garden. There among the flowers were some beautiful bluebells. She had planted them a long time ago to remind her of those days in our bluebell wood. We hugged for a long time after that and then agreed that Irene's house was the right place for us to make our future together. I gave notice on my flat, packed up my things and moved in. And from the first day it felt so right – the house was ours. We decided to redecorate it from top to bottom, to celebrate.

Over the next year we carried on visiting Whitby. We relived the moment when we had been spotted rolling around together, and separated. We even stood on the very spot where Auntie Nan stepped out of the door and caught us. But now we were laughing.

We went to other places in our past, too. I showed Irene the old East End of Sunderland where I'd been born, and she took me to Burdon Hall, where she'd been sent as a toddler. But it was our visit to Rennie Road that gave me the biggest surprise. It was the first time I had been there since the day I was taken away. I hadn't realised until then what an effect it would have on me. My feelings had lain, unchanged, somewhere deep in the core of me, and now they came to the surface, as raw as that day in 1960. I felt seven years old again and defenceless, and was so overwhelmed that I had to leave the street. It came as a shock to find that my childhood pain was as great as ever. It felt as if I had another person living in me, and until that moment I had never noticed.

We walked to the top of Bunny Hill and gazed out at the view. The bluebell woods had gone, and so had the aerodrome and the parachutists floating from the sky. A Nissan car factory stood there now. But the old castle was still there, and in the distance Penshaw Monument still stood proudly on the hill.

So many of the places we visited had changed. Even the shipyards that cluttered the riverbanks had all gone. There were no mines, no railways and no dray horses to draw the carts full of beer barrels around the town. The area where I was born is now a pleasant residential area. But our memories of innocence and summer days, parachutists and bluebells will stay for ever.

We went to the other children's homes where we had been, houses where we had lived, schools we had been to and places we had worked. We even headed out across the dales to the castle at Stanhope, where I showed Irene my bedroom window. And I took her to the wild grouse moors I crossed on my last unsuccessful attempt to see her again.

It was a journey of discovery, piecing together the lives we'd led after we'd been parted. Who knows how things might have been if that separation hadn't happened? Would we have been as strong together as we had to be apart? We would never know. All we knew for certain was that we were together at last, and nothing else mattered.

26

Will you ...?

Alan

Walking past a travel shop one day we spotted an affordable holiday in Tunisia for seven days. With the money we had saved by deciding to live at Irene's, we booked it.

It was perfect. The hotel was lovely, and so was our room, which had patio doors that opened into a garden of orange trees and palms. The path through the garden led past the pool, down through the dunes and on to the beach of silvery sand. We had a lovely week, sightseeing and soaking in the warmth and the friendly atmosphere.

Meanwhile, I was making plans. I knew exactly what I wanted to do, and I made sure all our new friends at the hotel knew too. Only Irene was in the dark.

Our last day dawned and I knew it had to be now or never. I asked Irene to come for one last stroll along the beach, and we headed through the sand dunes down to the sparkling sea, the sun glinting off its surface so brightly that it dazzled us. We'd walked this beach every day, collecting pieces of bright blue pottery washed up with the tide; we planned to bring them home, along with white periwinkle shells, for Irene to stick on what would become our Tunisian Pot.

Irene decided to go in for a paddle. She went in up to her knees, splashing around and laughing, and urging me to join her. But I had other things on my mind. I was pacing the shore, waiting for her to come out of the water, and I was a little nervous. This was it: my moment had come.

We both knew that we wanted to be together, and yet I still felt so nervous proposing. Perhaps would-be bridegrooms always do!

She ran out of the water and up the beach and we walked on, hand in hand. When we'd got a little way from the water's edge I turned to her and then went down on one knee and said, 'Irene, I love you. Will you marry me?'

She looked so surprised that for a moment she couldn't speak. Then she said, 'Yes, oh, yes, of course I will.'

I stood up and slipped a simple gold engagement ring I had chosen on her finger, and we hugged and kissed, both of us laughing and close to tears. Then, right on cue, a friendly waiter from the hotel – I'd briefed him earlier – appeared across the sand, snapping away with a camera to catch the moment.

We headed back to the hotel, and as we reached the pool a big crowd of fellow guests were waiting for us. Word had spread, and everyone knew about it and wanted to join in the party.

'Did she say yes?' one of them called.

I was going to tease them and pretend she'd said no, but I couldn't do it because I couldn't wipe the great big smile off my face. Irene laughed and called back, 'She said yes!' and champagne corks popped, flowers appeared and everyone toasted us.

I felt so relieved and happy. Everything went just as I'd hoped it would. It had taken a bit of planning – but it was a touching, funny and utterly memorable end to a wonderful holiday. We flew home the next day, engaged and blissfully happy.

Irene

When my friend Dawn entered me into a competition with a local radio station to find their Bride of the Year, I told her she was mad. But she said she thought our story was the most romantic one she'd ever heard, and she thought other people would think so too. I laughed and said she could go ahead, but I never expected to win.

So I was amazed when, a week or two later, the radio station called to say I had won. The prize included a wedding dress, the flowers, the cake, the car and the bridesmaids' dresses, as well as an exotic honeymoon. It was the first time I'd ever won anything! Alan and I were thrilled, and I sent flowers and chocolates round to Dawn to thank her.

Winning the competition meant we could afford a bigger wedding than we had originally planned. I asked Joanne to be my chief bridesmaid and to give me away, and my granddaughter Faye, along with Dawn, to be my bridesmaid. I chose a beautiful strapless white dress with a full skirt. And when it came to the colour of the bridesmaids' dresses I knew exactly what I wanted: it had to be a special shade of blue – the colour of bluebells.

Sadly, I was not in contact with my son, Michael, so we couldn't ask him to be involved. Alan asked Joanne's husband Dean to be his best man and my grandson Liam to be his pageboy. It made me so proud that all of my close family had accepted Alan as one of their own and that he felt the same way about them.

Alan

By the time our wedding day came around, Irene and I had been together for three blissfully happy years. We were both so glad to be together that we enjoyed every moment. We hardly ever disagreed about anything, and if we had different opinions on something we'd usually end up laughing about it. After all we'd been through, we both knew that we never wanted to spend another day feeling sad. And with so much to be grateful for, every day seemed like a day to celebrate.

Winning the competition was – almost literally – the icing on the cake! It meant we could ask more people, and in the end our guest list reached almost a hundred.

We had found one another again on 10 May, and we hoped to marry on the same date. We tried a whole host of possible venues, but none of the places we liked had 10 May free, so in the end we settled for 12 May 2007, in the Mobray Suite at the Sunderland Civic Centre.

Our wedding day set the seal on the love we had always had for one another and was the most special day of all. And it seemed our happiness was infectious. Since Irene had won the competition, all the local press had taken an interest and our story was spreading. So when Irene arrived at the wedding in a beautiful white vintage car, quite a crowd had gathered.

Meanwhile I was waiting nervously, with a roomful of our guests. Irene came in to the song we had both chosen, 'At Last' by Norah Jones. No other song could have expressed it all so well for us. She looked so beautiful. I held my breath, and in that moment the world stopped still and I could see my red-haired girl saying, 'Yes,' on Bunny Hill, forty-seven years earlier.

Irene

It felt fitting arriving with Joanne, the lovely daughter who had always been my rock and kept me strong when times were hard. When I saw Alan my eyes filled with tears, so that

I could hardly make out anyone, just rows of shapes in the room. He looked so handsome.

After we had taken our vows Alan's brother-in-law, Keith, read out a passage that Alan had written. It was called 'Love':

Today, we are here to celebrate love.
Love comes in many forms, love of family, love of our
 children, love of our friends.
Even a love of beauty and music are expressions of our
 love.
True love is like fire, it burns with a passion for what is
 good.
True love is like light, the darker the night the brighter
 its light becomes.
True love grows stronger when faced with adversity and
 is not weakened by it.
The passing of years can never dim its brightness.
However, in the daily rush of life our minds may wander
 from it.
Moments like this act as reminders that our loves are
 just as strong.
It only takes a moment to remember that our loves never
 go away.
It's only our attention on it that wandered for a while.
Therefore, today, we family and friends celebrate a true
 love that a lifetime kept apart.
And today, here, with their love still strong, these two
 best of friends at last become one!

That seemed to say it all for us. And for the rest of the day we had a wonderful time with our family and friends – the perfect wedding. Every now and then Alan and I would catch one another's eye and grin like kids. We knew what we were both thinking: 'We did it! In the end they couldn't keep us apart. We found one another, and nothing and no one will ever part us again.'

The day after our wedding we got into the car and headed to the one place that felt right as our honeymoon location: Whitby. We had booked a little fisherman's cottage overlooking the harbour and our special beach. We had decided long before that our honeymoon would also be a new beginning. We would go to Whitby in happiness and wash away, for ever, the dark times in our pasts. And from that time on we would be so busy creating happy memories to share that the past would no longer matter.

That evening we sat on our little patio, watching the boats passing back and forth across the harbour. It felt so peaceful, especially after the hectic days of preparation for the wedding, just soaking in the beauty of the moment. Below us gardens were terraced into the cliff and a path worked its way down between them to a little door in the wall that opened right on to the sand where we had played. And, in what seemed like a perfect touch, we saw that all around the edges of the little gardens, vibrant with colour, grew dozens of bluebells.